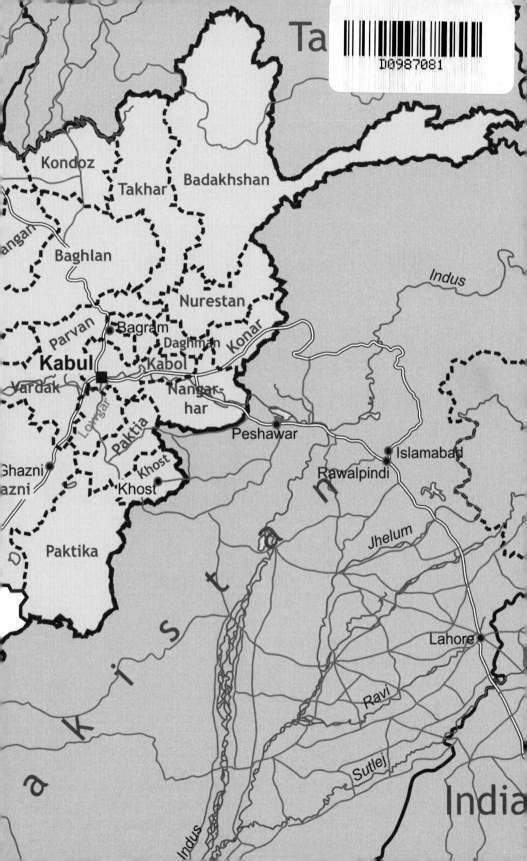

"*In the Warlords' Shadow* is a rare insider's account into the Special Operations program Village Stability Operations, which was so devastatingly effective against the Taliban insurgency in Afghanistan. Dan Green's on-the-ground perspective as both a civilian and a member of the military provides an insightful look into how Special Forces and SEALs eventually adapted their strategy to the unique demands of Afghan stability—in a sea of Special Operations memoirs, this one stands alone." **—Dick Couch, author of *Always Faithful, Always Forward* and *The Warrior Elite***

"At a time when the Islamic State and other violent extremist terror groups are fomenting instability around the world and at home, Dan Green has an answer to defeating them. *In the Warlords' Shadow* is an honest and hard-hitting account of how Village Stability Operations changed the game in some of the most violently contested places of rural Afghanistan. Dan's lessons come first hand from a warrior-diplomat who immersed himself in the local environment on an unprecedented scale. If we are serious about ending the longest war in U.S. history, our politicians, policy makers, and senior military leaders would do well to take numerous margin notes inside the pages of this book." **—Lt. Col. Scott Mann, USA (Ret.), author of *Game Changers: Going Local to Defeat Violent Extremists***

"Why is counterinsurgency doctrine more effective in some settings than others? And what are the universal keys to successfully battling an insurgency, despite the unique challenges of each conflict? These are among the questions that Dan Green answers in *In the Warlord's Shadow*, a highly detailed and illuminating look at COIN efforts in Uruzgan Province, Afghanistan. This well-researched, first-person account gives both historians and small-wars practitioners an invaluable resource to examine the war in Afghanistan—and future conflicts that will demand the dedicated strategies, tactics, and skillsets of counterinsurgency." **—Bill Ardolino, author of *Fallujah Awakens: Marines, Sheikhs, and the Battle against al Qaeda*, recipient of the 2014 General Wallace M. Greene, Jr. Award for distinguished nonfiction**

"This book accurately describes why the fifteen-year effort of American nation building in Afghanistan failed. Narrated in detail by an expert, this account will be studied by a generation of officers. For the civilians in our government, especially in the White House, it should be required reading." **—Bing West, author of *The Village* and *No True Glory***

"Dan Green delivers a vivid firsthand account of the liberation of the southern Afghan province of Uruzgan from Taliban rule. *In the Warlords' Shadow* is a unique combination of a personal memoir, scholarly study, and narrative history of the innovative Village Stability Operations program he helped realize. Always engaging and often compelling, Green's work earns a place alongside counterinsurgency classics like Bing West's *The Village* and Stuart Herrington's *Silence Was a Weapon*. No detached academic or armchair strategist, Dan Green offers the striking proposition that success in Afghanistan is actually possible, one valley and one village at a time." **—Dr. Kalev I. Sepp, former Green Beret and coauthor of *Weapon of Choice: U.S. Army Special Operations Forces in Afghanistan***

IN THE

Special Operations Forces,

WARLORDS'

the Afghans, and Their

SHADOW

Fight Against the Taliban

———◆◆◆———

DANIEL R. GREEN

NAVAL INSTITUTE PRESS

ANNAPOLIS, MARYLAND

This book was made possible through the dedication of the U.S. Naval Academy Class of 1945.

Naval Institute Press
291 Wood Road
Annapolis, MD 21402

Library of Congress Cataloging-in-Publication Data is available.
ISBN: 978-1-61251-815-2 (hardcover)
ISBN: 978-1-61251-816-9 (ebook)

♾ Print editions meet the requirements of ANSI/NISO z39.48-1992 (Permanence of Paper).
Printed in the United States of America.

25 24 23 22 21 20 19 18 17   9 8 7 6 5 4 3 2 1

First printing

The views expressed in this work are solely those of the author and do not necessarily represent the U.S. Department of Defense or the U.S. Department of State.

The conversations and speeches recounted here are based on the author's notes taken at the time, and some dialogue has been paraphrased. Any errors or unintentional omissions are the author's alone.

Although this is a nonfiction work, the names and key details of currently serving and former U.S. Navy SEALs and U.S. Army Special Forces have been changed to protect their identities.

A bibliography is not provided given the limited number of citations in the text. Full citations, however, are provided where appropriate.

Maps were created by Jay Karamales.

CONTENTS

FOREWORD

W
ith the United States' participation in the war in Afghanistan significantly diminished as a result of the Obama administration's drawdown, many journalists, historians, and academics are providing their perspectives on what has gone well and not so well in our nation's longest war. These perspectives are important, but they are often a snapshot in time or limited to the combat experiences of a particular military unit. What distinguishes *In the Warlords' Shadow* from the rest is author Daniel Green's rare and unique personal perspective that spans from strategic to operational to tactical. Green has "touched" this war like no other, in uniform and out. He was in the Pentagon on 9/11 and saw the war on terror at its very inception. But unlike most in Washington he was determined to get on the ground and do something about it. He went on to serve in Uruzgan Province, Afghanistan, with a Provincial Reconstruction Team (PRT) as a State Department civilian, in a policy advisory role in the Office of the Secretary of Defense, as a naval officer in the coalition headquarters in Kabul, in Iraq during the Anbar Awakening, and back to Uruzgan as a tribal advisor with Navy SEALs and U.S. Army Green Berets. Green provides an extraordinary view on the war from every level that is rare for those seeking to understand it and a future treasure for historians who will one day rely on first-person accounts.

I first met Green in the spring of 2006 days after I embedded with a United Arab Emirates Special Operations Task Force in Uruzgan Province. Green strode up to me with his characteristic smile and immediately peppered me with insightful and curious questions about working with Arab coalition members in the heartland of Taliban tribal support. He was the first person I had encountered in that tour of duty that was focused on understanding Afghanistan's tribes, how they were interwoven into local political dynamics, and how the Taliban was taking advantage of the collective ignorance of the Western coalition. Green and I met as southern Afghanistan transitioned from U.S. to NATO responsibility for stabilization efforts in the region. Specifically, security responsibility for Uruzgan had been transferred to the Dutch along with Australian special forces. I'll never forget strolling through the Dutch headquarters for the first time, hearing the static humming of radios and glancing across the half-dozen or so operational maps tacked to the wall. I noticed a glaring deficiency. None of their maps of the province and surrounding area had any information on the local tribes. I curiously asked a staff officer if he had any tribal data or maps depicting their boundaries. He shrugged and said it was something they were very keen to eventually figure out. The neighboring Australian headquarters staff officers, by contrast, were very clear that they had no desire to understand the complex tribal-political dynamics at play. In their words, they were in Afghanistan to kill as many "baddies" (slang for Taliban fighters) as possible.

Green, on the other hand, along with the officers in the PRT he advised, had come to learn that in Afghanistan, understanding the tribes meant *everything*. Not to say we were perfect on the American side. I watched as my fellow special operators, along with their partnered Afghan police forces, cleared Taliban fighters out of village after village only to find out later that their partnered police force was essentially a tribal militia. These local security forces were aligned with the Uruzgan Province strongman governor Jan Mohammad Khan, and the "Taliban fighters" we were helping him clear were young men of rival tribes that were sick and tired of getting the shakedown from Khan's thugs.

Aside from seeing the war from multiple levels, Green is one of the very few individuals with multiple tours in the same province. This meant that even on a tactical level, one officer empowered to apply lessons learned could make a tremendous difference. It also meant he had a unique perspective on the dramatic changes of how we engaged the Afghans and the enemy from 2005 to 2012. From his positions in Washington and in the field, Green outlines the history of American efforts to institutionalize local security efforts in Afghanistan. He walks the reader through the American military's realization that its "clear, hold, build" methodology wasn't working because of the chronic lack of Afghan army and police forces to hold terrain after it was cleared of Taliban influence. Green aptly guides the reader through how that realization led to a series of experiments in utilizing localized militias and auxiliary forces, and why they failed.

By 2012 the American military, particularly its special operations command, had come to fully embrace tribal outreach, so much so that they were authorized to raise and train local defense forces to oppose the insurgency. They also learned that it was absolutely critical to live in the villages with the Afghans to truly understand what was going on. In a survivalist society, many unscrupulous characters will use well-meaning but ignorant Western officers to get their way, from power and support to settling feuds. As Green points out, we could no longer commute to the fight for a few hours on a patrol and then go back behind fortified bases to sleep, shower, and play video games. Green, SEAL Team Two, and their partnered Green Berets were truly in the midst of a rural counterinsurgency at its most basic level: the village. Only then could they even begin to unravel the centuries old, complicated tribal and subtribal dynamics and ever-shifting allegiances to understand who was friend, foe, or somewhere in between.

Green walks us through a day in the life of the special operators running the Village Stability Platform, a small but potent mix of special operators, government liaisons, and support personnel that worked closely like never before with local Afghans to secure clusters of villages and even entire valleys in the midst of traditional Taliban strongholds. He describes the day-to-day challenges of SEALs and Green Berets living among the Afghans in their villages as they vetted, trained, and mentored the Afghan Local Police forces. Green shares the successes of the program as Afghan villagers took back control of their roads, reopened local shopping bazaars, and regained control of their tribes. Green visits bases that were under siege by the Taliban during his first tour in 2006, where soldiers were immediately attacked upon leaving their base and never left in anything less than a heavily armed armored vehicle. Yet by 2012, and years of Village Stability Operations (VSO), the special operators left their bases in pickup trucks armed with only pistols to meet with local Afghan officials. He also describes Taliban efforts to strike back and undermine the VSO program because they saw it as a direct threat to their control of the Afghan countryside. Yet the VSO program not only enhanced security in rural Afghanistan, it also rehabilitated a tribal governing structure that had been decimated by forty years of invasion, civil war, Taliban rule, and strongman politics. Its crowning achievement was connecting that tribal structure to a democratically elected central government and connecting the Afghan people to their government from the bottom up.

Through his multiple tours, Green has drawn some consistent and important conclusions. Though *In the Warlords' Shadow* is set primarily in one province, the events there are a microcosm of not only the broader war effort across Afghanistan but other unstable hot spots around the world. For example, the American-led coalition's dilemma of siding with heavy-handed Afghan leaders that aggressively opposed the Taliban versus weak but well-meaning technocrats who sought better governance was a dilemma they faced across Afghanistan. Green saw that dilemma and many other shortfalls play out firsthand, such as the lack of an overarching strategy, ever-changing goals, the constant turnover in personnel leading to little continuity of knowledge, and the absence of metrics in understanding whether we were winning or losing. Most of all Green presses home that in a land where every valley, every village, and region differ widely, local knowledge and relationships are the critical ingredient to success.

The reasons behind the deficiencies in the American war effort are important to comprehend not only for understanding the evolution of the war in Afghanistan but also for understanding key elements to defeat a determined insurgency. They are lessons the U.S. national security establishment must embrace because, like it or not, groups like the Taliban, al-Qaeda, the Islamic State, and Boko Haram will continue to take advantage of impoverished rural tribal societies to further their twisted ideology of radical Islam. The West must learn how to meet these groups where they are—among the villages of the developing world—and the lessons found in *In the Warlords' Shadow* are a shining example of how that can be done.

LT. COL. MICHAEL G. WALTZ, USAR
Author, *Warrior Diplomat: A Green Beret's Battles from Washington to Afghanistan*

ACRONYMS

ALP	Afghan Local Police
AMF	Afghan Militia Force
ANA	Afghan National Army
ANAP	Afghan National Auxiliary Police
ANP	Afghan National Police
ANSF	Afghan National Security Forces
AOB	Advanced Operations Base
AOIC	assistant officer in charge
AP3	Afghan Public Protection Program
AUS	Australia
BAF	Bagram Airfield
BFC	Battlefield Circulation
BMP	Blow in Place
CDC	Community Development Council
CDI	Community Defense Initiative
CDS	containerized delivery system
CENTCOM	Central Command
CJSOTF-A	Combined Joint Special Operations Task Force-Afghanistan
CMRG	Civil Mine Reduction Group
CO	Commanding officer

COIN	counterinsurgency
COMKAF	Commander, Kandahar Air Field
CTU	Combined Team Uruzgan
DAT	District Augmentation Team
DCOP	district chief of police
DDR	disarmament, demobilization, and reintegration
DFAC	dining facility
DRW	Deh Rawud
EOD	Explosive Ordnance Disposal
FOB	Forward Operating Base
GIRoA	government of the Islamic Republic of Afghanistan
IDF	indirect fire
IED	improvised explosive device
IJC	ISAF Joint Command
ISAF	International Security Assistance Force
JORSOF	Jordan Special Operations Forces
KAF	Kandahar Air Field
KIA	killed in action
km	kilometer
KMH	kilometers per hour
LDI	Local Defense Initiative
MATV	MRAP all-terrain vehicle
MISO	Military Information Support Operations
MNBTK	Multi-National Base Tarin Kowt
MRAP	mine-resistant ambush-protected
NATO	Northern Atlantic Treaty Organization
NDS	National Directorate for Security
ODA	Operational Detachment Alpha
OEF	Operation Enduring Freedom

PAT	Provincial Augmentation Team
PCOP	provincial chief of police
PRT	Provincial Reconstruction Team
PT	physical training
RCIED	remote-controlled improvised explosive device
RPG	rocket-propelled grenade
SEAL	sea, air, and land
SF	Special Forces
SOCS	Special Warfare Operator senior chief petty officer
SOF	Special Operations Forces
SOTF	Special Operations Task Force
ST2	SEAL Team Two
ST4	SEAL Team Four
TIC	troops in contact
TK	Tarin Kowt
U.S.	United States
USAID	United States Agency for International Development
VBIED	vehicle-borne improvised explosive device
VSCC	Village Stability Coordination Center
VSO	Village Stability Operations
VSP	Village Stability Platform
VSSA	Village Stability Support Area
VSTT	Village Stability Transition Team
XO	executive officer

TIMELINE OF KEY EVENTS IN
URUZGAN PROVINCE, AFGHANISTAN

September 11, 2001   United States is attacked by al-Qaeda

November 2001   U.S. Army Special Forces arrive in Uruzgan Province

January 21, 2002   Jan Mohammed Khan appointed governor of Uruzgan Province

Spring 2002   Provincial capital shifted from Khas Uruzgan District to Tarin Kowt District

July 1, 2002   Wedding bombing in Deh Rawud District

Summer 2002   Forward Operating Base (FOB) Tycz is established in Deh Rawud District

March 28, 2004   Uruzgan Province is divided in two, creating a predominantly Hazaran Dai Kundi Province in the north

April 2004   22nd Marine Expeditionary Unit arrives

Summer 2004   FOB Ripley is established in Tarin Kowt

Summer 2004   Tarin Kowt Provincial Reconstruction Team is established

Summer 2004   25th Infantry Division arrives

Fall 2004   FOBs Anaconda and Cobra are respectively established in districts Khas Uruzgan and Char Chena

October 9, 2004   Afghan presidential election

December 22, 2004   Permanent Provincial Reconstruction Team site is opened

March 2005   Uruzgan Provincial Shura re-established

September 18, 2005	Provincial Council and Wolesi Jirga elections
Summer 2005	Australian forces arrive in Uruzgan
January 5, 2006	First suicide vest attack in the province
March 2006	Jan Mohammed Khan removed as governor of Uruzgan
March 18, 2006	Abdul Hakim Monib appointed governor of Uruzgan
May 2006	Dai Kundi Province district of Gizab given to Uruzgan
May 1, 2006	First suicide car bomb attack
June 2006	Taliban overrun Chora District Center
June 3, 2006	Coalition and Afghan forces repel Taliban from Chora District Center
June 2006	Achikzai tribal leader Haji Abdul Maleem Khaliq Khan's wife is shot and blinded by Coalition Forces troops
August 2006	Dutch forces assume control of Uruzgan
August 2006–2010	Series of patrol bases are established throughout Tarin Kowt and Chora Districts
December 19, 2006	Mullah Aktar Mohammed Osmani is killed by Coalition Forces air strike
June 15–19, 2007	Taliban attempt to overrun the District Center of Chora. Dutch, Australian, and U.S. troops repulse the attack with assistance from Rozi Khan's Barakzai tribesmen. This event would eventually be called the Battle of Chora.
September 2007	Abdul Hakim Monib removed as governor of Uruzgan
September 2007	Asadullah Hamdam is appointed governor of Uruzgan
May 2008	Governor Hamdam holds election for district chief of Chora. Former provincial police chief Rozi Khan is elected.
September 2008	District Chief of Chora Rozi Khan is accidentally killed by Australian Special Forces
November 2008	Chairman Mullah Mawlawi Hamdullah resigns from the Provincial Council
August 20, 2009	Presidential, Provincial Council, and Wolesi Jirga elections held
February 2010	Taliban leader Mullah Abdul Ghani Berader is arrested in Pakistan

March 21, 2010	Asadullah Hamdam removed as governor of Uruzgan
June 2010	Villagers in Gizab District, Uruzgan, rise against the Taliban
August 2010	Dutch forces depart Uruzgan
August 2010	Rozi Khan's son, Mohammed Daoud Khan, is fired as district chief of Chora by the government of the Islamic Republic of Afghanistan
September 18, 2010	Wolesi Jirga elections held
November 13, 2010	Rozi Khan mosque is dedicated
December 13, 2010	New Uruzgan Province governor Mohammed Omar Shirzad is appointed
May 2, 2011	Al-Qaeda leader Osama bin Laden is killed by U.S. forces in Abbottabad, Pakistan
July 17, 2011	Former Uruzgan Province governor Jan Mohammed Khan is assassinated in Kabul
July 28, 2011	Complex attack on Uruzgan governor's compound with car bombs and several suicide attackers
August 2011	Matullah Khan is appointed provincial chief of police for Uruzgan Province
October 30, 2011	Rozi Khan's son Mohammed Daoud Khan is assassinated in Kabul
February 7, 2012	Taliban commander Abdul Samad and his men reintegrate with the government of the Islamic Republic of Afghanistan
February 28, 2012	Protesters march in Tarin Kowt against Koran burnings
March 2, 2012	Uruzgan National Directorate for Security assassinated at his home
March 24, 2012	Former Uruzgan member of Parliament Haji Khairo Jan is assassinated
March 26, 2012	Suicide vest attack in Chora injures four Coalition Forces members
April 2, 2012	New governor of Uruzgan announced
April 14, 2012	New Uruzgan governor Amir Mohammed Akunzada sworn in

May 13, 2012	President Hamid Karzai announces transition of Uruzgan to Afghan control
May 20, 2012	Suicide vest attack near Uruzgan Provincial Police Headquarters, two U.S. personnel killed
June 20, 2012	Transition ceremony of Village Stability Transition Team Gizab to Afghan control
July 17, 2012	Uruzgan transitions to Afghan control
July 30, 2012	Uruzgan Judge Taj Mohammed assassinated by Taliban at mosque
August 30, 2012	Five Australian soldiers are killed in Uruzgan Province
September 30, 2012	Last U.S. surge troops leave Afghanistan
November 2012	Village Stability Platform (VSP) Khod closes
November 2012	VSP Tagaw is closed
November 2012	VSP Saraw is transitioned to the Afghan National Army
November 2012	VSP Sayagez is closed
December 2012	VSP Nawbahar is transitioned to the Afghan National Army
January 2013	Village Stability Support Area (VSSA) Tinsley/FOB Cobra is transitioned to the Afghan Auxiliary Police
February 2013	VSSA Anaconda is transitioned to the Afghan Auxiliary Police
February 2013	VSSA Tycz is transitioned to the Afghan Auxiliary Police
April 2013	VSP Chora is transitioned to the Afghan Auxiliary Police
April 23, 2013	Taliban leader Mullah Omar dies in Pakistan
October 28, 2013	Uruzgan Provincial Reconstruction Team permanently closes
March 5, 2014	President Karzai announces appointment of Amanullah Temuri as governor of Uruzgan Province
March 10, 2014	Uruzgan governor Amir Mohammed Akunzada removed from office
March 26, 2015	Uruzgan residents stage a protest demanding the arrest of killers of the Uruzgan Police Chief General Matullah Khan

April 5, 2014	Afghan presidential elections are held
March 18, 2015	Uruzgan provincial chief of police General Matullah Khan is assassinated by a suicide vest attacker in Kabul
April 26, 2015	Acting Uruzgan provincial chief of police Gulab Khan is assassinated in Tarin Kowt
April 28, 2015	New Uruzgan provincial chief of police General Toryalai Abadyani is appointed
September 21, 2015	Afghan President Ashraf Ghani appoints Mohammad Nazir Kharoti governor of Uruzgan province.
January 31, 2016	Sixty police abandon seven posts in Uruzgan's Dehrawud District
May 29, 2016	Taliban Shadow Governor and Military Chief are killed by Afghan Army Forces
May 31, 2016	Taliban overrun 11 police check-posts in Uruzgan's Gizab district
June 15, 2016	Uruzgan District Char Chena reportedly falls to Taliban forces.
June 27, 2016	Former High Peace Council head and tribal elder Abdul Baqi was assassinated by unidentified gunmen in Tarin Kowt.
September 8, 2016	Taliban military forces enter Tarin Kowt District
October 27, 2016	Taliban forces overrun Afghan National Army forces in Chora District
November 6, 2016	Uruzgan Provincial Governor Mohammad Nazir Kharoti says the Taliban are one or two kilometers away from the provincial capital and dozens of Afghan Army soldiers have defected to the Taliban.
February 11, 2017	Twenty insurgents killed by airstrikes outside Uruzgan provincial capital of Tarin Kowt

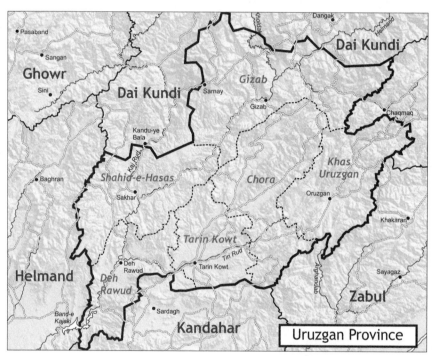

Map 1. Uruzgan Province

Map 2. Special Operations Task Force-South East

1. SOTF-SE HQ—Tarin Kowt
2. AOB 1220—VSSA Tycz
3. VSP Tagaw
4. VSTT Saraw
5. VSSA Tinsley/Cobra
6. VSP Khod
7. VSP Kajran
8. VSTT Chora
9. VSSA Anaconda
10. AOB Trident 2210—
    Camp Mogensen
11. VSP Bagh
12. VSP Sayagez
13. VSP Walan Rabat
14. VSP Shobar
15. VSTT Nawbahar
16. VSP Shar-e-Safa
17. VSSA—Operational
    Detachment Alpha 2210D
18. VSTT Gizab

SOTF-SE
Village Stability
Operations/Locations
2012

IN THE

WARLORDS'

SHADOW

ONE

Uruzgan Redux

Unlike the others, Wentworth was unable to consider his
tour in Vietnam as "just another assignment" in his career
development. And because of this, there was no doubt that
he would be coming back.

—John L. Cook, *The Advisor*

The mottled terrain of Afghanistan's desert with its sea of brown
and khaki colors interspersed with brief flashes of snow whipped
by my window as the C-130 cargo plane I was traveling in trudged
north from Kandahar Air Field en route to Uruzgan Province. Unlike my
first trip to the province along the same route in 2005 when I had arrived as
the U.S. Department of State political advisor to the province's Provincial
Reconstruction Team, I was returning with the U.S. military, this time as
a mobilized lieutenant in the U.S. Navy Reserves. Although my status had
changed, going from civilian advisor to a member of the military, my job
had largely stayed the same; I would still be working as a tribal and political
engagement officer, but this time for Special Operations Task Force-South
East. As I sat along the inside of the cargo plane, cradling my M-4 rifle
as it leaned against my legs, I was deep in thought about my return to a
province I hadn't seen in six years. Alone with my memories, cocooned in
my winter jacket with the great roar of the cargo plane's engines muffled
by earplugs, I contemplated second chances in life and wondered how I
would react to unearthing memories long settled about a province and its
people I had set behind me. I wondered how things had changed and how

I would react to being back at the base I had once known intimately but was now somewhat soulless since the people who had given life to it were gone, some of them now dead. As the plane banked to the left, my gear for the eight-month deployment shifted with it and a sharp blast of wintry February air shook me from my reverie as the plane prepared to land at Multi-National Base Tarin Kowt (MNBTK), or Forward Operating Base Ripley, which some of us old hands still referred to it by.

Returning to Afghanistan in early 2012 had been the last thing on my mind after my last tour there three years prior. It had been a heady time to be in country as attention returned to Afghanistan after significant security gains in Iraq and after the war started to get the resources it had long needed as well as the attention it deserved. At that time, I had mobilized and deployed to Kabul, where I had worked as a liaison officer for International Security Assistance Force Joint Command (IJC), a three-star command focused on the operational aspects of the war, and to the U.S. Embassy's Office of Interagency Provincial Affairs, which was charged with coordinating the efforts of our diplomats, development experts, and other members of the civilian surge in the provinces throughout Afghanistan.

The IJC had been established in October 2009, a couple of months before my arrival, to coordinate the various regional commands in Afghanistan and to get them to work together. It had also been created to help implement the campaign plan ISAF commanding general Stanley McChrystal had devised called Operation Omid (Hope), which sought to apply a counterinsurgency approach to the war in Afghanistan for the first time. It was an unusual period to be in Afghanistan. As much as the U.S. war effort was starting to get better-resourced and better-led, the broader mission of "defeating" the Taliban had morphed to simply "degrading" them in preparation for some sort of peace negotiation. To that end, President Barack Obama had announced a withdrawal date for our forces, regardless of conditions on the ground, which seemed to undercut the same determination to succeed that the additional resources conveyed. As difficult as it was to reconcile these two notions, it was even more difficult for the Afghans to understand. They had always feared we would abandon them, much as we had after the Soviets had withdrawn in 1989 and the

Afghan communist government had collapsed in 1992, and because of this they were starting to hedge their bets.

As these great issues swirled around me I focused on my job as a liaison officer trying to get the State Department and IJC to work together better. We were trying to coordinate the classic "shape, clear, hold, build, transition" approach to removing the Taliban from an area and then providing a hold force as well as a viable local government to prevent them from returning in over eighty key terrain districts. We would have covered more districts, if not the whole country, were we not forced to prioritize our selections. Even with the renewed attention paid to the conflict, the war did not receive the resources it required, especially when the president hadn't supported the higher troop requests of our military leaders. My time in Kabul had been a frustrating experience to say the least, as the culture clashes between the U.S. military and the U.S. Department of State were exacerbated by leadership clashes between U.S. ambassador Karl Eikenberry and General McChrystal. Instead of building a "team of rivals," as the president had hoped to do by including former rival Sen. Hillary Clinton and President George W. Bush's secretary of defense Robert Gates in his cabinet, among other officials, he ended up creating rival teams that frequently fought, especially as the mission changed in Afghanistan. Since we were no longer focused on "winning" and the unifying focus of prevailing against the Taliban was in dispute, even our most senior U.S. officials began to hedge their bets just like the Afghans. Additionally, being a Navy O-3 (a lieutenant), and a staff officer at that, in a command bristling with general officers, Army colonels, and a whole assortment of NATO officialdom wasn't the most rewarding experience. I missed being out in the provinces, where the clarity of purpose was much sharper since we were closer to the fight and there were no large concentrations of high-ranking officers. Things were going to be different this time, or so I hoped.

After my 2009–10 Afghan tour, I had largely decided that the best days of my deploying life were behind me. I had served in Uruzgan Province with the State Department for a year (2005–6), which had been incredibly rewarding, and had had the privilege of deploying to Fallujah, Iraq, in

2007 attached to a Navy SEAL team for six months and participating in turning that city and the province of Anbar against al-Qaeda. While I was still in the Navy Reserves, I had made peace with the fact that I needed to concentrate on affairs at home, and I started working at a think tank as a research fellow. I started to write a book about my first tour in Afghanistan with the State Department and wrote countless articles about how to wage the war more effectively. Although I still contributed to the war through my writings, my attention had now turned to Yemen, the one place in the world at that time with a viable al-Qaeda affiliate that was determined to attack us. It was a breath of fresh air to study a part of the world uncluttered by all the focus of Washington, D.C.'s policy makers, and Yemen was beguiling, with its rugged mountains, open deserts, powerful tribes, weak state, and determined foe that lurked within its borders. My focus was to be short-lived.

A few months into 2011, I casually sent an e-mail to the former deputy commander of Special Operations Task Force-West (which had been in charge of Anbar Province when I had deployed there in 2007), a Navy SEAL named Michael Hayes who had been promoted to full commander since our service together. Mike had recently completed two years as the director for defense policy and strategy at the National Security Council, where he had the unusual distinction of being a White House fellow asked to stay on board in a substantively senior and influential position. Upon returning to the teams, he was ready to get back into the fight. He was unique as SEALs went but, from another perspective, quite common as well. He had completed a bachelor's degree in mathematics and then went on to finish a master's in public policy at Harvard University, and he also spoke Spanish and German fluently. In these respects he was different from many of the SEAL officers I had previously deployed with, but due to his unusual attributes and seen from another perspective, he was fairly common in the Special Operations community, which frequently attracted high-quality people with eclectic backgrounds. His response set me back on my path to Afghanistan: "Dan! I had misplaced your number and was trying to find a way to reach you! I'm in charge of SEAL Team Two now and am preparing to go to Afghanistan. Would you be interested in going

over there? You can have any job you want, I just want you to go with us."
I quickly determined that he would be going to Uruzgan Province, the
site of my first tour in Afghanistan, and would be working on what was
termed the Village Stability Operations program. Mike would be in charge
of Special Operations Task Force-South East which was responsible for
Uruzgan, Dai Kundi, and Zabul Provinces in southern Afghanistan, and
he would have a mix of both SEALs and Green Berets working with him.
Quite honestly, as amazing as the opportunity sounded, I was reluctant
to go again. It was not that I lacked any motivation to help a friend and
serve my country. I was simply tired. I had deployed three times, worked
at Central Command (CENTCOM) in 2010 on a review of the war for
three months for Marine general Jim Mattis, and wanted to return to a
more sedate life. But the opportunity to serve again in Uruzgan Province,
to see the place I had poured so much of my life into, was a unique opportunity, and to do that with a good friend and alongside a SEAL team was
too much to pass up.

Over the next several months, Mike had me travel to Virginia Beach,
Virginia, to participate in various training programs with the team. On
a couple of occasions, he had me speak to the senior leaders of the team
including the officers and senior noncommissioned officers about the
province of Uruzgan and about Afghanistan more broadly. I put together
some maps of the area and walked the SEAL lieutenant commanders,
lieutenants, senior chiefs, and chiefs through the crazy world of southern
Afghanistan. Mike sat next to me during the conversations to underscore
the importance of the talks, and these subtle signs of support from the
commander paid dividends and really encouraged the men to ask questions. It was clear that this mission was going to be different from my
previous tour alongside Mike's SEAL team in Fallujah in 2007. We would
not be focused on conducting unrelenting direct-action missions against
the enemy, much as the teams had done in Iraq during most of the war,
but would instead be focused on a different strategy, one more effective
in the long term. Our mission was to fight the Taliban using a holistic
strategy that confronted their military arm as much as their political strategy and that mobilized the population to resist insurgent intimidation

by enlisting them in local defense forces. The program was called Village
Stability Operations/Afghan Local Police and would require small teams
of Navy SEAL and U.S. Army Special Forces to live in remote villages
and valleys, partner with local villagers, and work alongside Afghan police
and the army to fight the Taliban in a comprehensive manner. The teams
would assess the local tribal, political, and factional friction points—which
frequently prompted villagers to partner with the Taliban to seek redress
or seize power—and then simultaneously work to address these issues as
well as raise a local police force that would protect these communities
from Taliban intimidation. It was a tall order to say the least, and even
taller for a SEAL team conditioned to conducting purely direct-action
raids and not trained to work as closely with locals such as in the Green
Beret community.

Largely for these reasons, Commander Hayes had endeavored to
shape his SEAL team into the force it needed to become instead of the
force it had always been. I had assumed that most of the team had served
in western Iraq during the Anbar Awakening and were at least familiar
with the role of tribes and the benefits of raising local forces. But Mike
told me that at least 60 percent of SEAL Team Two had been on either
one deployment or none at all and those who had been deployed had
largely been involved in direct-action missions in Baghdad and had not
worked with the local tribes in Anbar to fight al-Qaeda. Additionally,
almost none of the team had been to Afghanistan. Mike was a dedicated
student of history and required the SEALs to read *The Village* by Bing
West (1972), which was about a Marine unit working in Vietnam as part
of the Combined Action Platoon program. That effort consisted of small
Marine detachments embedding in villages and raising local forces to fight
the Viet Cong insurgency. He also sent his men to a desert training facility
out west to go through a simulated training program of living at a Village
Stability Platform site, which were the small bases where Village Stability
Operations were conducted. There were dozens of role players there acting
as Afghan villagers, and the men had to physically construct their site,
conduct meetings with the "locals," and plan and conduct both training
operations for these villagers as well as missions against a simulated enemy.

Hayes also made sure to work with his SEAL leadership team to talk through the mission, to think about how they would conduct themselves, and what success looked like. He always made sure to emphasize that this mission was not exclusively about combat and that one yardstick of success was getting the Afghans to step up to be part of the solution.

As part of that effort, Mike wanted me to help the team by getting them up to speed on Afghanistan, act as his eyes and ears to improve the mission and inform decision making, assist with mission planning, and act as a mentor for his men when required. He also wanted me to serve as his strategic advisor on the political and tribal dynamics of Uruzgan, to help him think through the operations of the task force, and to help the other sections of the command with their work. To these various ends, Mike asked me to wear the rank of a lieutenant commander, even though I was still a lieutenant, in order to carry some weight not just with his men but with other U.S. units "inside the wire" as the deployment progressed. Additionally, Afghans are as rank-conscious as we are so he wanted to make sure my rank reflected, at least in part, my experience. In November 2011, my book about my first tour in Uruzgan, titled *The Valley's Edge: A Year with the Pashtuns in the Heartland of the Taliban*, came out, and in early February 2012 I finally defended my dissertation for a PhD in political science from George Washington University. Two days after I defended it in the conference room of the Political Science Department I was on a plane to Afghanistan ready for the mission to start. As I dusted off distant memories of Uruzgan, trying to remember once again the various tribal and village names and key figures of the area as well as the politics, I began to shift my mind back into the world that is Afghanistan and the insurgency it faced.

TWO

The Village War

Special Operations Forces had an enemy-focused approach to how we conducted operations. . . . As a battalion commander for two rotations, did we do population-centric operations? We sure did. But I was focused on the enemy. The enemy was a viable threat that operated in the rural areas very effectively and we went after them. My theory at the time was *pressure, pursue, punish.* My three Ps now: *presence, patience,* and *persistence* [emphasis added].

—BRIG. GEN. DONALD C. BOLDUC, USA

A s I stepped off the ramp of the C-130 onto the new concrete runway of Multi-National Base Tarin Kowt, I stretched my legs and took in the giant behemoth that had become the base. The small isolated outpost on the edge of the frontier that had once been my home was gone. It had been replaced with a sprawling forward operating base jam-packed with soldiers, vehicles, concrete, and, quite simply, clutter. Whereas before I could smell fresh straw from nearby villages, hear the gentle bleating of sheep, and watch the simple life of the villagers from the confines of our small base, we were now hidden behind rows of concrete walls, secluded from the population, with the constant smell of jet fuel and sewage burning my nose. I instantly became nostalgic for my old life at the base. My last tour in the province had been during the summer of 2006, after I had served there in 2005 for ten months, when the fighting season was at its worst and the insurgency had returned with

8

a fierceness and scale that had been unprecedented since the initial U.S. invasion just five years previously. At that time, I was serving as the political officer to the Tarin Kowt Provincial Reconstruction Team, named after the capital of Uruzgan Province, and had been asked to come back to the province to fill a gap between the rotations of two political officers, to report on local events, and to preside over the transition of then Forward Operating Base Ripley to the government of the Netherlands. The theory at the time was that since we had "defeated" the Taliban, peace keeping, reconstruction, development, and good governance efforts would take over. The Dutch were well-suited to the task and I was excited that they were bringing additional resources to the Provincial Reconstruction Team and seemed determined to prevail. They were quite proud of introducing what they called "the Dutch approach," which was a balanced program of development initiatives, tribal outreach, and a less kinetic strategy. As the saying goes, however, the enemy also has a vote.

Even as the national anthems of the United States, the Netherlands, and Afghanistan were played at the Uruzgan Province transition ceremony in August 2006 and the American flag was lowered, the war had already fundamentally changed. Security conditions throughout Afghanistan significantly worsened in 2006 as a resurgent Taliban movement seized control of large swaths of the country, calling into question the effectiveness of the "warlord" strategy as well as Coalition and Special Operations Forces (SOF) counterterrorism approaches.[1] Throughout southern Afghanistan, the Taliban insurgency returned with a size, intensity, and lethality unprecedented since the U.S. invasion in 2001.[2] The insurgency was larger, more disciplined, and increasingly operating as a conventional military force. The Taliban were now overrunning district centers, directly attacking Coalition forward operating bases, and using more advanced tactics such as sniping, suicide attacks, and combined operations, many of which would have been extremely rare to encounter in previous years. The level of skill required to undertake these types of attacks and the experience level of the insurgency's leadership indicated that the Taliban were not a spent force but had gained new strength. They also mobilized

local Pashtun tribes and villagers, which had been marginalized by the
Karzai government, so many Taliban operations assumed more of the
character of a popular insurrection than military forces preying upon
the population. The Taliban's renewed strength had a lot to do with
a U.S. focus on constant clearing operations against Taliban fighting
forces instead of dealing with the insurgency's political strategy to
harness the population to its advantage. Similarly, due to a lack of local
security forces, communities opposed to the Taliban were often unable
to defend themselves and frequently fell prey to intimidation. As the
insurgency worsened, lessons were starting to be learned by U.S. forces
both about Afghan culture and about the requirements for stability
utilizing a counterinsurgency approach. The relatively peaceful years
from 2001 to 2005 in Afghanistan had been shown to be a false peace
as the Taliban insurgency geared up to reassert control of the country
and push the Afghan government and Coalition Forces out of the area.

The United States was beginning to realize that however effective its
clearing and direct-action missions were against the Taliban insurgency,
absent a viable local partner that could hold a cleared area, it would have
to repeatedly "reclear" villages.[3] Additionally, Afghan villagers were motivated by a variety of reasons to join the Taliban insurgency, many of which
had nothing to do with the Islamist movement's religious ideology. Some
villagers joined due to tribal and village frictions, others because they were
disappointed by the Karzai government, while many were intimidated
into doing so or were seeking a steady paycheck. What was becoming clear
was that the United States and the Afghan government had to confront
the Taliban insurgency holistically, addressing its political, tribal, and economic aspects as well as its military wing. In a sense, the United States had
to use the Taliban's structure and strategy against it. Some of this process
of learning benefited from the U.S. experience in Iraq, where U.S. forces
actively enlisted the Arab tribes against al-Qaeda in the western Iraqi province of Al-Anbar, which led to significant security gains. A revised U.S.
approach would need to blend military and political strategies relatively
seamlessly and be based in the villages and districts where the people lived.
It would have to be nested in a "shape, clear, hold, build, and transition"

strategy enlisting local Afghans in their own defense in a partnered manner alongside Afghan police and military forces. Instead of constantly clearing villages, U.S. forces would now have a "persistent presence," instead of engaging in direct combat the United States would support Afghans doing so, and instead of using a top-down approach to building stability the United States would need to adopt a simultaneous bottom-up or grassroots strategy as well. The strength of the Taliban movement at this stage in the war was its ability to mobilize the population through intimidation as well as by capitalizing on their grievances and using them to bolster its organizational strength: a people's war.

Even though the Taliban's strategic goals of uniting the Pashtuns, ejecting foreign military occupation, and imposing sharia law were well-known, their tactical political program was less well-understood and its popularity among many Pashtuns even more so.[4] The key reason the Taliban were able to come back with such force in 2006 was their ability to wage an insurgency campaign using a political strategy aimed at winning the support of the population. The Taliban carefully crafted a political program that tapped into Pashtunwali traditions, took advantage of U.S., Coalition, and Afghan government mistakes, and capitalized on the weaknesses of the Afghan state in the villages.[5] Though substantial efforts had been expended by the United States to promote good governance in the provinces, the efforts had been unequal to the task, cumbersome, bureaucratic, and sometimes even counterproductive. The Taliban's positive political program had at least five aspects to it, all of which tapped into Afghan cultural mores: justice, micropolitics, reconciliation, laissez-faire, and village empowerment. While the Taliban would impose their will on villagers if they had to, and they often did so violently, they also had a positive agenda that sought to entice supporters to their banner. In the face of corrupt and/or murderous government officials, a nonfunctioning judiciary, and the perversion or suspension of Pashtunwali traditions, the typical villager had a limited ability to seek justice for the things that bothered him most: murders, theft, assault, rape, and land and water disputes.[6] For the Taliban political agent, this vein of discontent was rich and could be mined by appealing to the structures of justice created by sharia law. While the villager may not have been inclined to support sharia law in its totality, he was likely to do so in the absence of a viable alternative. Because the Taliban agent was sitting in the villager's home, soliciting his grievances, and moving quickly to remedy them, the villager was hard-pressed to support a government that was often distant and abused its authority. Along these same lines, the Taliban practiced micropolitics to a remarkably high degree of sophistication.

The Taliban political agent would find any problem that a village or individual had and make it his own. If a village was hoarding water from a stream, causing a downstream village's crops to fail, the Taliban worked for the aggrieved party. If a tribe had been abused by the Afghan govern-ment, the Taliban joined with its members to seek justice. This political granularity stood in marked contrast to the frequently inept and ineffec-tive efforts of the Afghan state and the sometimes counterproductive work of the Coalition. The Taliban's political program was also furthered by their "do-no-harm" approach to the central drivers of local politics and economies. If a farmer wanted to cultivate poppies, the Taliban allowed it. If he once worked for or supported the Afghan government, he was allowed to reconcile with them. If a tribal leader wanted his authority respected, they did so if it furthered their agenda. Additionally, if villag-ers felt that "their" government did not represent them or had unfairly attacked their interests, then the Taliban preached inclusion, grievance, and justice. Against this well-crafted, flexible, dynamic, and pervasive pro-gram, U.S., Coalition, and Afghan efforts lagged significantly. It was clear that Coalition, SOF, and Afghan government efforts needed to be revised, although the specific requirements of a new strategy were not yet known. In light of the successes of the newly resurgent Taliban, how could SOF simultaneously confront the Taliban's military arm and its political strat-egy in a way that was supported by Afghan communities? How could they build a structure that protected them from intimidation, was vertically integrated yet horizontally dispersed, and leveraged influence in a way that accounted for the weaknesses of the Afghan state?

✧

With a renewed Taliban insurgency able to marshal the people to their banner by capitalizing on local grievances and lack of local security, SOF had to place greater emphasis on understanding how villages worked, why some were stable while others weren't, and how SOF might be able to leverage the population in support of the Afghan government.[7] One of the first areas SOF focused on was gaining a better understanding of Afghan tribes, especially in light of the successes from the Anbar Awakening in western Iraq, which had begun in 2005–6.[8] Much of the newfound interest in understanding tribes stemmed from the successful turnaround of Anbar Province, Iraq, where Arab tribes played a key part in changing the province from a hotbed of the Sunni Arab insurgency to a place where security had improved to the point that U.S. troops were beginning to be withdrawn.[9] The tribes also received new attention because the United States did not then have enough troops in Afghanistan to undertake a proper counterinsurgency campaign due to existing Iraq requirements and required dwell time between deployments. But as tribes assumed a more central role in SOF strategy, it was essential that the U.S. strategy going forward be informed by U.S. military experiences in Iraq, not dominated by them, and that a pragmatic approach based upon Afghan societal dynamics achieve enduring security effects for the local population. Additionally, it was crucial that the enlistment of the population through tribal protective forces be able to actively confront the insurgency without being overwhelmed by it. The effort also had to maintain the active support of the population and reduce the tendency of the tribes to fight among themselves. All this had to be done while the United States simultaneously built the capabilities of the Afghan state without creating a parallel tribal or militia system. Any tribal engagement strategy in Afghanistan that sought to utilize the tribes against the insurgency had to begin with an understanding of how they were different from Iraqi tribes; here SOF's repeated rotations and greater understanding of both Afghan and Iraqi culture began to bear fruit.

Initial efforts to partner with local forces against the Taliban began by working with warlords and their militias that supported the government of Afghanistan. These forces were unaccountable to the people, abusive of the population, and not representative of community groups. Many of the actions of these forces prompted Afghan villagers to join the Taliban in 2006 out of a sense of justice to confront the abuses of "warlord" forces and because they were unable to defend themselves from Taliban intimidation.[10] Early efforts to build the Afghan National Police (ANP) mirrored this initial warlord strategy in that initial recruits often came from one particular tribe or faction, but with a low limit set on the number of ANP in the country, these forces were never sufficient to secure local communities and were not mentored effectively. The next step in the evolution of providing local security was the creation of Afghan National Auxiliary Police (ANAP) in 2006. Its creation was a reaction, in part, to the decision by the then overall U.S. commander, Lt. Gen. Karl Eikenberry, to demobilize the approximately 11,000 Afghan Militia Force (AMF) members that had protected bases, thickened out patrols, and provided logistical assistance to SOF since the beginning of the war.[11] Most of these forces came from the areas in which they worked, so their demobilization created a security vacuum. Eikenberry instructed SOF leaders to tell the AMF members "to go into the army."[12]

The significant deterioration of security throughout southern Afghanistan that came about in part from this decision and from the removal from power of several warlords in the region, which also increased violence as their men refused to do their jobs, prompted the temporary creation of the ANAP program, a Ministry of Interior–led program that included ten days of training focused on basic policing and military skills as well as instruction on ethics and morality.[13] Upon completion of the training the recruits received an AK-47, a police uniform with an ANAP patch, and the equivalent of $70 per month in salary, which was the same as Afghan National Police recruits.[14] The ANAP's missions included guarding checkpoints and providing community policing, and their approximately 9,000 members were assigned areas at locations in six southern Afghan provinces (Farah, Helmand, Kandahar, Uruzgan, Zabul, and Ghazni).[15] The ANAP program suffered from a number of problems, including poor oversight, a weak and ineffective recruitment and vetting process, and predatory behavior against the local population.[16] It also suffered from the lack of local character in its forces (it was a national program), an absence of community and Ministry of Interior vetting, infiltration by insurgents, the presence of petty criminals and drug addicts, monopolization by local powerbrokers, and friction between ANAP members and Afghan National Police members over areas of responsibility.[17] The program was eventually dismantled in 2007, but a number of valuable lessons had been learned from the experience.

The next version of local police, called the Afghan Public Protection Program (AP3), began in Wardak Province in January 2009 and was overseen by a Special Forces company commander.[18] Recruits came from the communities they would protect, were vetted by local shuras and the National Directorate of Security, received three weeks of training from SOF forces, and earned half the salary of a regular police officer.[19] They received AK-47s from the Ministry of Interior as well as uniforms and other support from the Afghan government.[20] The security forces would then protect mosques, schools, bazaars, and other local sites. The initial program had a ceiling of 1,200 recruits and, if it was successful, was projected to grow to about 10,000 members.[21] While the initial results of the program were successful, several factors contributed to its demise. The program's recruiting, vetting, training, and oversight role was transferred from SOF to a conventional forces unit in the province, and the unit did not properly mentor the AP3 members.[22] The force was then used improperly and transitioned from a self-defense effort to a highway police force defending Highway One.[23] Additionally, recruits from other provinces began to join the program, diluting its local character, and its members began to engage in "bribe-taking shakedown" behavior.[24] The program eventually fell under the control of a local Wardak strongman named Ghulam Mohammad Hotak, a former Taliban commander, which further undermined the program after he was allowed to lead a lightly administered AP3 program.[25] Eventually, Special Operations Forces were no longer involved in the program, and the commander of the force largely disregarded local sentiment and never emphasized governance and development, which further doomed the initiative.[26]

The next step in the evolution of local defense efforts was the creation of the Community Defense Initiative (CDI), later renamed the Local Defense Initiative (LDI). Approved in July 2009, the CDI/LDI program emphasized the defensively oriented nature of the local protective force, sought to reduce the influence of powerbrokers through community engagement, and nested its forces with the government of Afghanistan by making them answerable to the Ministry of Interior, while the program was administered by the Independent Directorate of Local Governance.[27] The LDI program attempted to identify communities that had actually sought out Afghan government and Coalition support against insurgent intimidation or had resisted insurgents on their own.[28] The villagers would have to provide their own weapons and in lieu of salaries they would receive development projects and other assistance as a collective benefit. If the LDI site required additional assistance against the Taliban, it could rely upon a nearby SOF unit for support as well as members of the Afghan National Police.[29] While the LDI program was implemented in a number of sites throughout Afghanistan and initially proved effective, it also suffered from a lack of comprehensive oversight, limited Ministry of Interior resourcing, corruption, and a perception that it was not as effective as it needed to be against the Taliban.[30] While success was elusive, many lessons had been learned that proved vital to the later success of the Village Stability Operations/Afghan Local Police program.

As civilian and military leaders shifted their attention back to Afghanistan in 2009–10 following security successes in Iraq, SOF leaders sought to incorporate the lessons that had been learned not just from various community security initiatives across the country but from Afghan culture as well, with the goal of creating enduring local stability. It had become clear that no matter how effective direct action and clearing operations by SOF were at destabilizing the Taliban insurgency, without a viable local partner to maintain security the effects of SOF efforts were short-lived. Additionally, if the sources of instability (e.g., tribal feuds, poor governance, lack of development) were not simultaneously addressed as well, security effects would be temporary. As one SOF commander put it, "It seems like every time I come back here [to Afghanistan], the security situation is worse. . . . Maybe we need to do something different."[31] In March 2010, a new commander took over Special Operations Forces in Afghanistan, but unlike his predecessors who had come from the U.S. Army's Special Forces community, this commander had an extensive background and a great deal of experience with direct-action raids, among other associated tasks. Instead of continuing with a narrowly focused counterterrorism strategy, however, he embraced a holistic approach that sought to address the drivers of instability in Afghanistan's villages as well as the insurgency's political and military strategy. Following a comprehensive review of past security efforts, he proposed a new local security initiative that represented the accumulated wisdom, learned from both mistakes and successes, from the challenge of raising local security forces that were accountable to the people, answerable to the government, and effective at fighting the insurgency.[32] Initially named the Afghan Local Police (ALP) program, it was approved by Afghan president Hamid Karzai by official decree on August 16, 2010, with an initial authorized strength of 10,000.[33] This number was increased to 20,000 to properly protect the number of sites the government of Afghanistan's National Security Council had prioritized.[34] The final ALP numbers were eventually increased to 30,000, with the initial three-year program extended to five years.[35]

The program would be administered by the Afghan government's Ministry of Interior in close partnership with Special Operations Forces and would concentrate on recruiting, vetting, training, and logistically supporting locally raised security forces. Subsequently renamed the Village Stability Operations/Afghan Local Police (VSO/ALP) initiative, the overall approach was a synchronized delivery of population security, local governance, and microdevelopment to rural populations through active community engagement.[36] Special Operations Forces would embed directly in Afghan villages that met four basic criteria: (1) villagers had to want SOF help, (2) villagers had to demonstrate a willingness to resist Taliban intimidation, (3) the location had to be logistically sustainable, and (4) the location had to be "consequential to the overall fight."[37] The SOF teams would focus their efforts on "improving informal governance through village shuras, establishing or co-opting village defense forces, and improving development."[38] By adopting a bottom-up approach to establishing stability, the VSO program fought the Taliban where they were, with an approach based upon their structure, and it organized the population to resist insurgent intimidation and the appeal of their political program.[39] The VSO approach achieved several effects simultaneously. It was partly a (1) local protective force, (2) tribal rehabilitation program, (3) tactical governance initiative, (4) economic program (through salaries and greater economic activity), (5) reintegration program for local part-time Taliban, (6) synchronized delivery of population security, governance, and development, and (7) link for villages to the government.[40] By fighting the Taliban on their own terms with a village-based, long-term, decentralized approach that seamlessly blended civil and military approaches and enlisted the population in its own defense, the program kept the Taliban from accessing the population physically, from appealing to their grievances against the government, and from using economic incentives to entice them to fight.[41] It took many years to craft this strategy, but its subsequent success was due to the ability of SOF to adapt to Afghan cultural norms and use a strategy informed by them to defeat the Taliban insurgency.

Before a single villager joined the VSO/ALP program, a process of community engagement took place, as well as an assessment of the area by SOF in partnership with the government of Afghanistan and Afghan National Security Forces.[42] The point of this endeavor was to determine as accurately as possible the sources of community instability the insurgency fed off of to buttress its efforts and to identify a sustainable basis upon which local security could be created. These engagement efforts were helped by additional enablers given to SOF teams to enhance their outreach efforts. Most teams were given civil affairs elements (soldiers trained in community engagement and development work), military information units, and cultural support teams (e.g., women's outreach) in order to holistically analyze and influence local villagers. Afghan Local Police recruits were nominated by village elders versus just by tribal leaders, vetted by the district and provincial chiefs of police and the SOF team, and then forwarded to the Ministry of Interior for a final check. Each recruit's character was vouched for by a village elder and each recruit agreed to abstain from taking drugs and to undergo a training regimen administered by Special Operations Forces. The recruit's photo was taken, the particulars of his family were chronicled, and he was biometrically enrolled by having his iris scanned. He would then begin a several-week term of training involving weapons familiarization and safety, physical endurance, small-unit tactics, ethics, checkpoint construction, and the duties that came from being a member of a local protective force. Once trained, the new ALP member reported to the ALP commander for the district, who answered to the district chief of police.[43] He was then assigned to a checkpoint in his community, where he used his government-issued and recorded weapon to prevent insurgent intimidation of the community. In addition to uniforms, the ALP also received trucks and motorcycles for mobility, and checkpoints sometimes received PKM machine guns for areas more likely to receive Taliban contact. Each checkpoint had a dedicated commander who also reported to the ALP commander and the district chief of police, and they used Coalition-provided radios to maintain contact. Each ALP member received his regular salary, a smaller portion of a regular ANP paycheck, and logistical and security support from the district chief of police to ensure a basic level of government control of these forces.

As I made my way to the section of the base that housed Special Operations Task Force-South East (SOTF-SE), which was the old compound of the Provincial Reconstruction Team where I had originally worked, I tried to figure out what my role would be and how I could make a difference to the team. The role of tribal and political engagement officer was nebulous, but I was used to having these kinds of jobs with little definition, unclear chains of command, and ambiguous responsibilities. I would figure it out as I went along and try to find opportunities to make a difference. I was determined to make my knowledge of the province and its tribes and people, as well as my experience with counterinsurgency, useful. I arrived at the main offices of SOTF-SE, a one-story concrete brick building surrounded by gravel, and decamped from the commuter shuttle that had transported me and my gear from the flight line. The bitter cold of February kept me sharp as I stacked my things against a wall and made my way into the headquarters. The building for the SOTF was right in the center of a roughly ten-acre complex that had originally been the site of the Provincial Reconstruction Team (PRT) where I had worked seven years previously. At that time, the general plan was to transition the province to the Afghan government and then the PRT would continue on to help establish stronger governance and development. To that end, our goal was to be self-sufficient, so we had our own guard towers, water supply, fuel depot, dining facility, and even helicopter pad all organized into a large rectangle and surrounded by a seven-foot-high concrete wall. Since my previous service here, the original name of the base, Forward Operating Base Ripley, of which the PRT had been a part, was now the SOTF's name. The original base had been named in May 2004 by the 22nd Marine Expeditionary Unit after Capt. John Ripley, the famous Marine who had received the Navy Cross for destroying a crucial bridge in 1972 that prevented a North Vietnamese offensive. While the original concept of transitioning the province to Afghan control seemed reasonable in 2005, the renewed Taliban offensive in 2006 and the general increase in fighting across the country demonstrated that the war would be a long slog. I was eventually shown to my room, which was along the central corridor of the building, and after I dropped my bags off, I made my way to Mike's office.

As soon as I entered the room, Mike sprang from his desk, shook my hand, and said, "Dan, so glad to finally have you here, man! When did you get in?"

"Oh, a few minutes ago," I responded.

"Well, it's awesome to have you here, brother, and let's sit down and talk about things once you get settled."

"Sounds great."

As the commanding officer (CO) of Special Operations Task Force-South East, Cdr. Michael Hayes was in charge of more than 1,500 men operating from twenty-one different forward operating bases and Village

Stability Platform sites spread out over three provinces. He was taller than most SEALs at six feet four, athletic in build, with brown hair and a friendly demeanor. He had been a Big Brother volunteer for years and enjoyed mentoring others. He had completed tours in South America, Bosnia, Kosovo, Iraq, and Afghanistan among other regions and was on his second tour in central Asia. His leadership style was positive and determined, which I had witnessed firsthand in Iraq, and he set the tone for the command with an overarching strategic vision and a willingness to focus on details in support of his personnel. He often used humor to make a point and always exhorted his staff to stay focused on the people in the field. He was also a notorious prankster. Since he knew the mission for this tour in Afghanistan was more than just killing insurgents but enlisting the Afghans in their own defense, he had hand-selected his team to focus on these goals and undertook a determined campaign to shape his SEAL team into a force focused on the well-being of the Afghans. He was a unique mix of tactical experience, national policy making expertise, and positive leadership. I was grateful to serve with him.

The executive officer (XO) of SOTF-SE was a SEAL lieutenant commander named Robert Wright, and we also knew each other from Iraq when his team replaced the one I had been assigned to in Fallujah. Wright had played football at Yale University and was still a solidly built special operator. He would later go on to get a master's degree from another Ivy League university. He had black hair and a mustache, stood about six feet one, and had a quiet and thoughtful demeanor. He was a proud father, and his wife was the daughter of a former SEAL officer. I can only imagine what it was like when he first met her family. He was an administrative workhorse and did all the necessary paperwork and other tasks to free Mike to focus on the mission of the SOTF. Wright and I had again crossed paths in Afghanistan in late 2010 when I had been part of the Mattis review, and we had infrequently kept in touch over the years. His room was right across from mine and it was great to work alongside yet another familiar and friendly face. The other key player was the team's command master chief, Sam Woods, who had long experience in the teams, including having an older brother who was a SEAL.

The Special Operations Task Force was trying to accomplish several things at once across three provinces. The SOTF (so-tiff, as it was called) was the central hub for special operations from Zabul Province on the border with Pakistan, through to Uruzgan at the northern edge of southern Afghanistan, to Dai Kundi Province in the center of the country. Our mandates were to fight the Taliban across these areas, principally by increasing the numbers of Afghan Local Police, liaising with and working alongside the Afghan government to grow governance, transitioning sites to Afghan control where feasible, and working with our Afghan security partners. Because our operations were so far-flung across a dozen or so districts and our teams were operating in such austere locations with small numbers of men, we were a transit hub for fuel, ammunition, water, food, equipment, men, and material with helicopters, planes, and convoys constantly churning out missions to resupply our bases. Additionally, because the SEALs and Special Forces soldiers were in such small numbers at their Village Stability Platform (VSP) sites (most numbered around thirty-five to forty men), we were also a necessary lifeline for air cover, unmanned aerial vehicles, and medical support. The VSPs came in different shapes and sizes depending upon how well-developed the Afghan Local Police were in an area.

The typical VSP's life span began from the initial insertion of the team to the fulfillment of their *tashkeil* (billets) of three hundred or so Afghan Local Police. Once the ALP had been recruited, the Special Operations team would then either transition the site to the Afghan government or to a U.S. conventional forces unit with a small number of SOF advisors and its name would then change to a Village Stability Transition Team (VSTT). The final type of VSP was the Village Stability Support Area (VSSA), which not only served as a stand-alone Village Stability Platform but also supported other VSPs in the district. The VSSA served as a central hub for the area and would push out water, ammunition, fuel, and other supplies to the VSPs in its district. While the SOTF was in charge of the whole area, it worked through two subordinate commands. The provinces of Uruzgan and Dai Kundi were led by an Army Special Forces major from 1st Special Forces Group at Forward Operating Base Tycz in a district in western Uruzgan called Deh Rawud. It was the headquarters for the Special Forces Advanced Operations Base (AOB) for Uruzgan Province. The province of Zabul was led by a SEAL lieutenant commander from Team Two and was called AOB Trident, located in the province's capital of Qalat. Each of these commands had day-to-day responsibilities for leading and supporting the Village Stability Platforms.

The vast majority of the Afghans within the SOTF were from the Pashtun ethnic group, which was a plurality of Afghanistan's population, but in Dai Kundi Province a different ethnic group, the Hazarans, were in the majority. The Taliban were overwhelmingly from the Pashtun population and were Sunni Muslims, while the Hazarans were Shia Muslims and, as they were quick to remind us, historically descended from Genghis Khan's Mongolian raiders. Both groups were similar in appearance, short in stature with black hair and lean figures, but the Hazarans were Asiatic in appearance and were the historic and implacable foes of the Taliban. The Pashtuns were generally against the Taliban too, but due to tribal and other rivalries they would sometimes align with them. In addition to these main ethnic differences were tribal histories, the residue of past conflicts with various Afghans having once been communists, mujahedeen, with the Taliban, against them all, or, at some point, members of all three. Additionally, the society was wracked by years of conflict, and a survivor's mentality had set in as well as a thirst for justice or revenge for past wrongs. Politics was a zero-sum game, groups constantly sought power, and Afghans practiced a form of politics that had the complexity of four-dimensional chess. It was a wilderness of mirrors and as much as we thought we were in charge of things, our actions were seemingly always ignorant of the real game that was going on among the Afghans. Largely for these reasons, Mike had asked me to be his advisor on the Byzantine world of Afghan politics and the complexities of the insurgency.

THREE

The Warlord's Shadow

Nobody really enjoys a blood-feud; it is a legacy of hatred
that exterminates some families and makes even the strongest
suffer. Yet undying shame would come upon the family that
did not take its turn in the feud.

—LOWELL THOMAS, *Beyond Khyber Pass:
Into Forbidden Afghanistan*

It is quite astonishing, in retrospect, to realize these many years later just
how little we knew about the Afghans when our forces first invaded
the country in 2001. I can only imagine how little the Afghans knew
of us. The province of Uruzgan was ground zero for initial U.S. efforts to
topple the Taliban in southern Afghanistan. The desolate patch of land
that constituted the province, which sat on the edge of the Hindu Kush
Mountains to the north and the sprawling wasteland of the Margow and
Khash deserts that dominated the south, was an excellent place to launch
an insurgency against the Taliban. When a Special Forces team inserted
into the province to help a little-known tribal leader named Hamid Karzai
start a rebellion, it was impossible to know just how important these initial
moves of the new global War on Terror would reverberate over the following years. Karzai activated a network of former mujahedeen fighters and
leaders, tribal members from his Populzai tribe, and other Afghans simply
ready for a new beginning who had grown tired of the Taliban's harsh
rule. A harrowing account of the Special Forces team's actions, Karzai,
and the challenges they faced are in Eric Blehm's 2011 book *The Only*

Thing Worth Dying For: How Eleven Green Berets Fought for a New Afghanistan. As the Special Forces team and Karzai pushed south from Uruzgan to take Kandahar Province, the center of power in southern Afghanistan, Taliban leaders and various tribes affiliated with them began to offer their support and pledges of allegiance to him. Karzai had only one request of the Taliban. He called on them to release two prisoners: Jan Mohammed Khan and Mohammed Nabi Khan Torkhi. Both of these figures would eventually play central roles in Uruzgan's politics, but in tragic and opposite manners.

Jan Mohammed Khan, or JMO, would eventually become Uruzgan's longest-serving governor in the province, leading the local government from early 2002 to spring 2006. He was straight out of central casting when it came to Afghanistan's strongmen or warlords: he was in his late fifties, around five feet six, bald, and blind in one eye, and his beaming smile was framed by a full black-and-gray beard. He had all sorts of ailments and aches, some from having fought the Soviets, others from beatings he had gotten at the hands of the Taliban, and others from simply being well past the life expectancy of the normal Afghan. When the Soviets invaded Afghanistan in the late 1970s he was a night watchman at the local high school and did odd jobs around the campus. By the end of the Soviet invasion he was a preeminent leader of the mujahedeen in Uruzgan but by no means the dominant power in the area. Through a mixture of bravery, ruthlessness, savvy, leadership, and outside patronage, he had fashioned for himself a fighting force that made him a power with which to be reckoned. When the Taliban moved north into Uruzgan in the early 1990s, JMO and other local mujahedeen leaders agreed to create a united front to prevent them from taking the province. At the last minute, Jan Mohammed Khan switched sides and allowed the Taliban to enter through his tribal area in the southern part of the province and vanquish his foes. The Taliban, in return, demobilized JMO's militia and allowed him to retain one personal bodyguard, and he quietly returned to his farm to cultivate his fields (including poppies) and family (which would eventually grow to thirty-two children from five wives). He was left alone by the Taliban just as long as he followed their rules, but he had other plans. He started to make secret trips to Pakistan to consult with Hamid Karzai and Karzai's father, who was then head of the Populzai tribe, after they had both fled there following their break with the Taliban. Jan Mohammed Khan was reportedly visiting the family when Pakistani intelligence assassinated the senior Karzai in 1999 as he returned home from praying at the local mosque. The fact that JMO was with Hamid Karzai at this crucial time further cemented their relationship.

When I first met him in early 2005, he was at the height of his power. Even though he was illiterate and had no formal training in the administrative side of governing, he had a certain roguish charm he used to great effect and was incredibly savvy politically. As the local representative of the Afghan government, that is to say President Hamid Karzai, who had appointed him, he always got the support he needed for his various projects, but he also used his power to settle a multitude of blood feuds with his rivals as well as to strengthen the position of his tribe and supporters vis-à-vis his competitors. He had two central tools he used to simultaneously "secure" the province and to implement the nefarious plans he had against his opponents. The first was his newly reconstituted militia, which had been laundered, so to speak, into official security forces and were called the Afghan Highway Police. They numbered around three hundred in 2005 and were led by JMO's cousin, Matullah, a central figure I will return to later. This force protected the main road between Uruzgan's capital of Tarin Kowt down to Kandahar City in the south. It was a dusty patch of road meandering through the desert, skirting several villages, and winding its way through the mountains to the city. It was a lifeline for the province as well as a source of corruption, and the thirteen-hour drive down it was a harrowing adventure, with the ever-present threat of ambushes as well as car crashes due to thick dust clouds. The second tool he used to project power locally was the U.S. military, including both conventional and Special Forces, which unwittingly helped him consolidate his position.

The overriding focus of U.S. efforts in Afghanistan at the beginning of the war was to defeat the Taliban by killing them under the rubric of "counterterrorism." If you were a member of the Taliban you were a target, and if you weren't, such as if you were Jan Mohammed Khan, who had been imprisoned by them, you were a stalwart U.S. ally in need of constant, almost unquestioned support. Our initial Special Forces teams partnered with Jan Mohammed Khan and his militia in pursuit of the Taliban, and in return for our support, the Afghans provided the United States with intelligence on the enemy, fighters to pursue them, and logistical assistance such as buildings our forces could use and protection for our bases. At this time in the war, we knew very little about the tribes, their histories, leaders other than those who worked with the government, and everything else beyond the main villages. We were blind to the real concerns of the people and were unknowingly facilitating tribal imperialism. By this time, Jan Mohammed Khan was the Populzai tribal leader in Uruzgan, and with his tribal leader Hamid Karzai president of the country he had almost unfettered power.

What we didn't know and would only grasp much later in the conflict was that no single tribe really dominated the province. Many were relatively equal to if not stronger than the Populzai in strength and numbers, and others were quite small, but they all agreed that one tribe could not dominate the area without repercussions. Largely for these reasons, as U.S. forces accompanied the Afghan Highway Police on missions against the Taliban, we became associated with one tribe and one faction and were sometimes seen as oppressors of the people. We had become associated with one side of a tribal feud of which we knew nothing, but our actions convinced other tribes that we were either duplicitous in our protestations of building a new, inclusive Afghanistan or dangerously naïve about the tribal power game. It was not uncommon, for example, for the governor's militia to dump the bodies of dead Taliban in the main traffic square of the province as a warning to others. We somewhat innocently believed that all these dead men had been members of the Taliban, but little did we think that this same gesture, viewed from a different perspective, was an attempt to intimidate the governor's tribal rivals. We once asked the governor in 2005 whether all the dead men in the traffic circle were Taliban, and he responded, "They're dead, aren't they?" We got the message.

The tribes of Uruzgan were organized into two large confederations. The dominant faction was called the Durrani, who had historically come from the more settled tribes that farmed along the rivers and streams. Largely for this reason, they were much wealthier than their tribal rivals in the Ghilzai confederation and tended to own the best land, have regular access to water, control the best trade routes, and end up in positions of leadership in the government. The Ghilzai had historically been nomadic people taking their families back and forth via camels and mules between Afghanistan and Pakistan as the seasons changed. The various governments of Afghanistan had tried a number of schemes to settle the tribes on arable land, the most famous being the Marjah area in Helmand Province with its planned communities, but some members of this tribe continued their ancient wanderings. The tribes that chose to settle down often did so in areas that were less arable, where wells had to be dug deeper, and where trade routes were far away. These tribes were poorer and often had worse leadership since their tribes were weaker, not as well-educated, and far less powerful. When the Taliban were in power, many members of the Ghilzai tribe had been given powerful positions; Taliban leader Mullah Omar was famously a member of the Ghilzai subtribe of the Hotak. Similarly, many members of the Durrani tribes were excluded from power, although many did join the Taliban as well, and formed the nucleus of support for Karzai and his allies in the south. In the tribal hierarchies of Afghanistan, Karzai's tribe, the Populzai, were at the top of the heap of the Durrani confederation with the Barakzai, Achikzai, Mohammedzai, and Alkozai, among others, at varying levels of importance and power. The Ghilzai tribal confederation, in contrast, was less well-defined but included the Hotak, Noorzai, and the Torkhi. Each province in southern Afghanistan had these and other tribes, and their power relations fluctuated massively. Much of the conflict throughout the region was due to these tribal feuds.

One of the great rivalries of Uruzgan Province had been the decades-long feud between members of the Populzai and Barakzai tribes and their respective leaders, Jan Mohammed Khan and Rozi Khan. Like the governor, Rozi Khan was a well-respected mujahedeen leader who also led his tribal faction, and when Karzai arrived in Afghanistan in 2001, he appointed him the provincial chief of police (PCOP). Thus the politics of balancing different power groups against one another so no single group was too strong continued, with JMO as governor balancing against Rozi Khan. The police chief was also illiterate and stood at around five feet seven, but he had received some education and was not nearly as rich or perhaps as ruthless as the good governor. It was unclear what started the difficulties between both men; rumors had swirled around the province for years as to what specific event precipitated a deep hostility between them. There had been several assassination attempts on both sides, although Rozi Khan seemed to suffer the most from them, which eventually led to the suspicious deaths of both men and one of their sons. Rozi Khan was accidentally killed in 2008 by Australian forces in Uruzgan, and Jan Mohammed Khan was killed on July 17, 2011, by the "Taliban" in Kabul. Rozi Khan's family blamed the Populzai tribe for using the Australians to kill their leader, and Jan Mohammed Khan's family blamed Rozi Khan's supporters for the shooting death of the then former governor. Not too long after the former governor had been killed, Rozi Khan's oldest son, Daoud Khan, was assassinated in Kabul on October 30, 2011. By 2012, Rozi Khan's next oldest son, Khoshal, whom I remembered as a young boy in 2005, was now leader of his family, and Haji Mohammed Qasim Khan, the oldest son of Jan Mohammed Khan, was head of his family. But even though the fathers of both men were well respected and even feared, their tribes did not automatically follow the leadership of the sons, and ambitious members of both factions vied for power. A wary standoff between their respective supporters continues to this day, and rumors of future assassination plots are prevalent. Of the various tales of how the feud started that swirled around town, a few seemed to persist the most. One tale had it that Rozi Khan had killed the brother of Jan Mohammed Khan in the 1980s, while another had it that Jan Mohammed Khan had repeatedly used his militia to try to kill Rozi Khan with a series of impro- vised explosive devices, which would invariably be blamed on the Taliban, when the Barakzai leader was provincial chief of police. Some blamed the feud on the mad scramble for Taliban property soon after the U.S. inva- sion, as unoccupied compounds, cars, money, and furniture were scooped up by both men, and each felt he had been cheated out of his due. It was a sordid backstory to U.S. efforts to pacify the province and so much of it predated the U.S. presence that it was difficult to see what sort of solution could be reached.

The second person Karzai requested the Taliban release was Mohammed Nabi Khan Torkhi, a key leader of the Ghilzai tribal confederation in Uruzgan Province. He was also a famous mujahedeen leader but in the mad scramble for government and security positions after the U.S. invasion in 2001, he mostly missed out, longing for a sinecure in Kabul. But even though he and Jan Mohammed Khan had both been detained by the Taliban and clearly enjoyed the support of Hamid Karzai, this did nothing to mitigate the governor's thirst for power. He quickly sought to exclude Torkhi from power, branding him, as well as the Ghilzai more broadly, as Taliban and trying to have his militia kill him or have the United States do it under the pretense of fighting the Taliban.

When Karzai first arrived in the province and sought support among the tribes, he balanced the tribal power centers, giving the governorship to the Populzai, the provincial chief of police position to the Barakzai, and the Chora District chief position to the leader of the Achikzai tribe. The Ghilzai were excluded since so many of their members had supported the Taliban. Mohammed Nabi Khan Torkhi, who was also a Ghilzai, eventually went into exile to escape these plots, but strangely was still loyal to Hamid Karzai, who likely saw him as a counterbalance to Jan Mohammed Khan and Matullah. Later events would validate these concerns.

The assassination of former governor Jan Mohammed Khan on July 17, 2011, in Kabul and the ascension of Matullah to provincial chief of police soon thereafter underscored a generational shift in local politics. The old mujahedeen commanders, including former provincial police chief and later Chora District governor Rozi Khan, had died or been killed, while others simply retired from public life in favor of more vigorous and youthful men. Unlike the older generation, however, this one had grown up under the U.S. presence in Afghanistan. They knew our ways, used our acronyms, exploited the usual problems that came with the frequent rotations of military units, and had seen their rise often tied to U.S. largesse. Perhaps because many of them hadn't been mujahedeen commanders, they had found politics a more fruitful way forward in life than military service. They were also a bit slicker than the old warhorses, more savvy in the ways of politics, comfortable with technology, and also more progressive about where they wanted to take the country. They still practiced a bit of the old Afghan politics of divide and conquer and trying to leverage unknowing U.S. units against their opponents. Unlike in the past, however, they had institutions to exercise influence by, with, and through, were less dependent on us, and exercised authority in a more mature manner. I was looking forward to seeing how local politics had evolved since I had been away. In many respects, the struggle for power was starting to leave the realm of the warlords and enter the world of politicians.

After a few of days of adjusting to the time zone change and figuring out the rhythm of camp, I was ready to get to work. Wright found a small section of a table I could use as a desk in what we called our "nonkinetic" cell. This part of the SOTF was the engine room for tribal engagement, civil affairs, information operations, and political outreach for the headquarters. Wright kindly moved a huge communal printer that sat on the table I would be using, shunting it under the desk, and procured a computer for my use. My table-mate was an Air Force major named Scott Bradley, who was the Provincial Augmentation Team (PAT) leader for the province. Scott was an atypical Air Force officer, which probably explained why he was so effective in this type of work. He originally hailed from Texas, graduating from Texas A&M, and was a proud member of the Corps of Cadets. He had had a fairly predictable Air Force career, but he had an independent streak and was drawn to eclectic experiences. Scott had been head of an ROTC program at a historically black college, an experience he cherished, and then volunteered to be part of an innovative program called Afghan Hands. The program was set up in 2009 and allowed select members of the military to receive additional language training in the two dominant languages of Afghanistan, Dari and Pashto, complete a series of tours in Afghanistan over a number of years, and have follow-on stateside positions that also worked the Afghan portfolio. It was an effort to mitigate the incredibly disruptive effects of having units and military personnel constantly rotating in and out of country, losing the wisdom they had accumulated from firsthand experience. Scott was about five feet nine, rail thin from constantly running, and extremely diligent about his position.

As the PAT leader for the province, Scott was in charge of working with provincial Afghan officials to help them develop good governance practices and to attempt to solve the myriad political and programmatic problems our units faced in the field. Scott had a partner in Zabul Province, who undertook similar work there. He also had a network of District Augmentation Team (DAT) members in several of Uruzgan's districts who reported to him and, in turn, he reported to a regional Village Stability Coordination Center in Kandahar, which then reported, finally, to a Village Stability National Coordination Center. The whole goal of this effort was to better connect local stability efforts with district, province, and national initiatives through a tightly organized network of U.S. officials to maximize the government of Afghanistan's performance. This was especially important in defeating the Taliban's local political program as well as in leveraging Afghan informal networks, which also shaped government behavior.[1] In a sense, it was its own tribal network and shadow government. It had to be able to reach as many villages as possible, continually liaise and embed with government officials, conduct political action, and exercise persistent presence and performance. The program complemented the efforts of the Village Stability Operations program by providing a basic structure with which to undertake the essential nonkinetic tasks (e.g., improving governance, connecting villages to the central government, facilitating development programs) that provided stability to rural Afghanistan.[2] In many respects, he was doing the exact work I had done with the State Department seven years before. His position was as much a commentary on the lack of U.S. diplomats in Afghanistan's countryside as it was on the need for the military to understand and use local politics to achieve its ends.

Two other colleagues I would get to know quite well were an Army captain named Ed Ho'omalu, who was in charge of Military Information Support Operations (MISO), and Army Captain Alberto Hernandez, who was in charge of civil affairs. Ed was a former enlisted soldier who had done a tour in Iraq and had previously deployed to Uruzgan as well. He was a solidly built and proud native Hawaiian and an experienced Army diver, about five feet ten, and he was also in charge of a network of MISO officers and soldiers who conducted psychological operations against the Taliban. These activities encompassed different activities, from advising the command on how to react to something the Taliban had said to crafting radio announcements and leaflet drops to shape local opinion. He also conducted opinion polls of the Afghans, had loudspeakers and sound trucks available to conduct public engagement, and worked to understand how the Taliban used propaganda to achieve their goals.

Alberto was a proud Puerto Rican, a former enlisted soldier with a wiry frame that belied his great strength and endurance. He was in charge of all civil affairs efforts in the SOTF and had small teams at most of our bases. The soldiers who were members of the civil affairs community were trained to work closely with local communities on small-scale development projects such as drilling wells, constructing small footbridges, and building schools and providing humanitarian assistance from flooding and other catastrophes.

However much Ed and Alberto were trained to study, understand, and shape the actions of local Afghans, they were also professional soldiers and were just as able to fight the Taliban when called upon. It was quite common, for example, for Ed to go out with the SEAL teams when they conducted clearing operations since he was not only solid physically and knew the terrain and enemy well from his previous tour, but also provided great value with his ability to assess and shape Afghan attitudes. It was not uncommon for Ed to conduct shuras (community meetings) with tribal elders after a clearing (or kinetic) operation.

That we were all in one room and in relative proximity to each other underscored how much thinking about the war had changed. As important as fighting the Taliban was to our efforts, it was equally if not more important to fight the Taliban's local political strategy and their ability to sway opinion against our operations and against the Afghan government. The nonkinetic cell also contained our Afghan Local Police logistics staff and our press operations, and we were right next door to Hayes' office as well as operations. Over the next eight months, Scott, Ed, Alberto, and I would forge a strong team to fight the Taliban's strategy while also maneuvering within our own chain of command and the Afghan government to make sure a holistic strategy was pursued.

Our marching orders were pretty straightforward, as the mission statement for Special Operations Task Force-South East made clear: "SOTF-SE conducts Special Operations activities, executes population-centric/COIN [counterinsurgency] operations, and builds competent and reliable Afghan Security Force capabilities in order to enable the Government of the Islamic Republic of Afghanistan to protect the Afghan people and provide sustained security through governance and development within Uruzgan, Zabul, and Dai Kundi Provinces."

What this meant in practice is that our tasks were to (1) secure and expand Village Stability Platforms, (2) expand the government of Afghanistan's influence, especially to outlying districts and villages, (3) recruit and train Afghan Local Police, (4) execute operations in direct support of Regional Command-South's strategic objectives, and (5) support an Afghan-led process of reintegrating insurgent fighters back into the government of Afghanistan. Only a few years earlier this mission statement and our tasks would have been dramatically different, more focused on "finding, fixing, and finishing" the enemy rather than on creating resilient Afghan governance and security networks that reinforced each other. The centrality of building relationships with the Afghans, recognizing the importance of local politics, and building Afghan institutions were now key tasks for us. What the Afghans did and were capable of doing were more important than what we could do on our own. As we undertook this work we were also focused on building up the Afghan government's capacity to assume greater responsibility for the war. Thus, a number of our tasks also focused on (1) training a capable and sustainable Afghan National Security Forces (ANSF), (2) assisting the ANSF/Afghan populace to restrict the insurgency and malign actors in under-governed spaces (seams), (3) linking networks of influence to develop government of Afghanistan influence on village and district governance, and

(4) transitioning responsibility for independent security, governance, and development throughout Special Operations Task Force-South East.

An element of the SEAL team was also embedded with the Afghan commandos, mentoring and training them while also conducting combat operations with them. Thus, when we wanted to embed a new Village Stability Platform into a district, the commandos and SEALs would clear out the area, conduct initial community engagement meetings, and then prepare the village for the insertion of one of our teams. Additionally, when a particularly large concentration of Taliban were discovered or a VSP needed more firepower for a mission, this element would deploy again to help. It was a complex set of sometimes competing tasks, and the trick was striking the right balance between kinetic operations and nonkinetic and figuring out the best way to get community members involved in their own defense, while connecting with the government. It was a lot to accomplish, and it was made more difficult because all our efforts were conducted against a political timeline of withdrawal that prompted many Afghans to hedge their bets and for the Taliban to wait us out. It was an unusual time to be in the war when we finally knew what was required to prevail but our political leaders no longer had much of an appetite to win.

After a week or so, I stopped by Hayes' office to talk more about the mission, my initial observations, and how I could contribute most effectively. Mike was as gracious as ever and closed his plywood office door so we could commiserate. Mike started off by saying, "I want your help in helping me think through how we measure success on this tour."

"What do you mean?" I asked.

"Well, it's always easy to measure the kinds of things we typically do like number of firefights with the enemy, amount of money spent, how many meetings, etc. . . . but I want to focus more on the effects of what we do rather than just on what we do."

"Hmm . . ." I thought for a moment about how to do what he asked.

Mike continued, "We're always good at counting how many bad guys we kill, how many improvised explosive devices we find, and even today,

how many Afghan Local Police we recruit, as if that number alone represented the sum total of our actions."

He could tell I was intrigued. "You don't have to have an answer just
yet and I want you to think about it over the next few weeks."

"Got it," I said, my mind beginning to crunch on the problem.

"What are your impressions of things thus far?" he asked.

"Well, quite honestly, I'm amazed at how much our thinking about
the problem of the Taliban insurgency as much as our resourcing of the
solution has improved since I was last here in 2006. It is just remarkable.
However, I think we need to get our nonkinetic guys out and about and
working more closely with the provincial government and the Provincial
Reconstruction Team."

"I completely agree," Mike quickly stated, "and I want you to make
that happen."

I added, "I also think it would be useful for me to go with you on
some trips as you make your way around the SOTF in order to refresh
my experiences with the area and to learn more about the VSO program."

"I couldn't agree more and, in fact, we're heading out to some bases
pretty soon and I want you with me. As I see it, I want you on every trip
not only to see what's going on, but to also help me write up the trip notes."

I immediately laughed at the suggestion that once again I would be
helping the SEALs write up their meeting notes. "Sounds good!" I said as
I got up to leave and grab chow.

After receiving my marching orders from Mike, I focused on learning as
much as I could about the changes in key personalities and politics of
Uruzgan since I had last served there. I had kept up with things from
afar and wrote what I could in my book, but I really wanted to hear what
Scott and Ed had to say; Alberto would eventually join us a month or two
later once he rotated in country. The killing of Osama bin Laden by U.S.
forces in Pakistan on May 2, 2011, reverberated throughout Afghanistan
as much as it did in Pakistan and the United States. Unsurprisingly, the
Pakistanis would not allow this intrusion into their country, as they saw
it, without repercussions for the United States and our Afghan allies, in

particular President Karzai and his closest supporters. As part of their plan they launched an assassination plot against former governor Jan Mohammed Khan in Kabul, and he was gunned down on July 17, 2011, by two young men from Uruzgan asking for charity from the governor. His death struck President Karzai particularly hard, and when the former governor was buried the president jumped into the burial pit, cradling the coffin as it was lowered, tears streaming from his eyes. Ten days later, the Taliban, supported by Pakistan, launched a complex attack in the heart of Tarin Kowt, a clear political signal of disapproval in this stronghold of Karzai's Populzai tribe. Simultaneous suicide car bombs went off in front of the governor's compound, and several Taliban ran into the courtyard, eventually occupying a squat two-story building that had served both as the bank for the local government and as a radio station. It had also served as the headquarters of the initial U.S. Special Forces team that had partnered with Karzai in 2001. Once these Taliban fighters were holed up in the building, all the security forces in the immediate area unloaded their AK-47s, machine guns, and rocket-propelled grenades at the building. All the attackers were eventually killed.

While the attack was thwarted and a handful of people were killed, the reputations of local security officials were tarnished, and the provincial chief of police was sacked. The next month, the Afghan government announced the appointment of Matullah as provincial chief of police for Uruzgan. His title was now General Matullah Khan and he was in charge of much more than the police forces in the area. The killing of his uncle Jan Mohammed Khan by Pakistani intelligence left the local Populzai without a leader. A delegation of prominent Populzai elders made their way from Kandahar Province to Uruzgan to appoint Haji Mohammed Qasim Khan, the former governor's oldest son, as the new leader of the tribe. As they held aloft a new turban to place upon his head, a symbolic gesture of his assumption of power, he declined the right and insisted that Matullah be named the leader of their tribe. It was a significant and dramatic gesture and marked an amazing rise in power for Matullah. He had gone from being an illiterate thug of his uncle, enforcing his writ across the province through their militia, to the head of all police forces in the province and head of his tribe. Two months after his ascendency, Mohammed Daoud Khan, the oldest son of the former Barakzai tribal leader Rozi Khan, was gunned down in Kabul, thus ensuring that during this time of weakness for the Populzai, their rivals, the Barakzai, would not use it as an invitation to seize power.

On the political front, a succession of governors from outside the province had been appointed to head the local government since the removal of Jan Mohammed Khan in 2006. Each had been well educated, diligent, and focused on improving the life circumstances of local residents, but they all suffered from various forms of local opposition. It was not that they lacked ability, but since their only forms of power and patronage came from a local government that was invariably too weak to govern and too undermined by powerbrokers, they inevitably had to rely upon the Tarin Kowt Provincial Reconstruction Team for money, resources, logistical support, political assistance, and development programs. However well-intentioned our efforts were, they were always a bit slower than we wanted them to be, not robust enough, and limited in their scope.

The newest governor for the province was a man named Mohammed Omar Shirzad, who hailed from northern Afghanistan and had been appointed on December 13, 2010. He was almost six feet tall, neatly dressed in local garb (although preferring not to wear a turban) and was quick with a smile. He was committed to his job, but Matullah didn't like him, and all sorts of problems seemed to plague his administration: government programs became delayed, political support in Kabul was anemic, and local powerbrokers abstained from serving in government. He was in a difficult spot, and the petty politics of power divided the local government against itself, which inevitably helped the Taliban. I was looking forward to seeing what other changes had taken place in the province as the deployment went on, but I first needed to see some of our Village Stability Platforms and learn more about how they were changing the province.

—◆◆◆—

FOUR

The New Frontier

Guerilla warfare depends chiefly for its success on the support of the people of the country. Guerillas cannot have regular lines of communication, and are obliged to resort to the villagers for food and shelter and for their intelligence as to the movements of Government forces.

—JOHN BAGOT GLUBB, *The Story of the Arab Legion*

When U.S. forces first invaded Afghanistan and began operations in Uruzgan, the government seat was in the eastern portion of the province in a district called Khas Uruzgan, which was also the name of the main village there. At that time, Uruzgan was a gigantic province that included the future province of Dai Kundi to its north and stretched from the center of the country to the northernmost portion of southern Afghanistan. Politically, the Khas Uruzgan area was a mix of Pashtuns, who were Sunni Muslims largely led by the Barakzai and Achikzai tribes, and the Hazarans, who were different ethnically than the Pashtuns and followed Shia Islam. Once Jan Mohammed Khan became governor of Uruzgan in 2002, the province was split in two and the provincial capital was moved to Tarin Kowt, a small village that politically favored the Populzai, who resided nearby. The province of Dai Kundi would eventually have its own capital in a village called Nili and its own Hazaran governor. Administratively, Uruzgan Province was split into five districts: Tarin Kowt in the center, Deh Rawud to the west, Chora to the east, Khas Uruzgan to the far east, and Shahid-e-Hasas in the northwest. A sixth district of Gizab was added in 2006 that bordered Dai Kundi Province to the north. All the districts were Pashtun except Gizab, which was roughly half Hazaran, and Khas Uruzgan, which had a substantial Hazaran minority.

The province was a mix of deserts and barren mountain ranges, and locals lived along the few creeks and rivers, which were fed by natural springs and snow runoff from the mountains. These cultivated areas were rich in vegetation and were often referred to by our soldiers as the green zone. You could sense and even smell the moisture in the air when you crossed into them from the desert. Overall, though, the province was incredibly arid and no vegetation really lived outside the areas cultivated by humans. Securing a reliable water source and owning arable land were central to the existence of Uruzgan's locals. The Afghans were always looking for ways to get one more foot of cultivated land from the river beds, which were naturally watered as well as rich in nutrients, and more water by digging new wells or channeling existing water flows onto their holdings. Water was such a scarce resource that many villages had a dedicated person called a *miraw* charged with distributing the precious commodity and resolving the inevitable disputes that arose over its use. The most common complaints in the province involved disputes over access to and ownership of water and land. These disagreements would often escalate into actual fighting and the outcome could impact the politics of power between the various tribes. Most villagers had no property records and couldn't read them if they did. Because formal judicial processes were largely nonexistent, arguments were frequent.

While most of the province was locked in a struggle for basic resources, the district of Shahid-e-Hasas, so named by the Taliban since "Shahid" meant martyr, was blessed by the terrain to have plenty of water. Two large rivers coursed through its narrow, mountainous valleys, eventually merging into one that traveled through Deh Rawud District to its south and eventually to the Helmand River. The district was blessed by geography for its abundance of water, but its terrain also facilitated the Taliban since it bordered the volatile province of Helmand to its west and its infamous Bagran Valley, a key ratline insurgents used to move from Pakistan to

Uruzgan, where the valley ended near Shahid-e-Hasas. The area's numerous valleys and mountains, standing at the foot of the Hindu Kush, made the area almost impossible to pacify, and the lonely outpost there, Forward Operating Base Cobra, had struggled mightily to secure the area. The base had been at risk of being overrun when I had last served in the province in 2006 when the insurgency had reached new heights. Foreign fighters such as Chechens, Saudis, Yemenis, Pakistanis, and others were quite common by 2006. They brought their advanced tactics of sniping, improvised explosive devices (IEDs), financial resources, and organization to a newly emboldened Taliban. The Special Forces team that had served there in 2006 had lost seven of its forty men and had twenty-two casualties. The Taliban had such a lock on the local population that a Pashtun villager who had visited the base, ostensibly to share information about the Taliban, had been gunned down in sight of its walls and his father had had his throat slit but somehow managed to stumble to the gates of Cobra where he received medical assistance. I met this unfortunate man in 2006 as he continued to heal from his wounds. I once saw him closely watch several Taliban prisoners as they were led to the detention facility and witnessed him slowly draw his finger across his neck, signaling his hope they would soon be dead. Every single road out of the base had been seeded with IEDs and, due to our long presence there, the Taliban knew all the best ambush and choke points to launch attacks and bury explosives. It was a sordid place. We never had enough troops to secure the area and the population was unlikely to turn against the insurgency since they were largely unprotected.

Prior to my 2012 deployment I had read and learned a great deal about the Village Stability Operations concept but had never seen it in action or visited one of our teams at a Village Stability Platform site trying to implement it. My first opportunity to visit one of these outstations presented itself on February 20, as Commander Hayes continued his trips around Uruzgan and Zabul Provinces to familiarize himself with the terrain, the enemy situation, and the dynamics of each team. This kind of hands-on leadership style was quite common among the more successful commanders I had witnessed on my various deployments, and I was fortunate to have a chance to go along. We were leaving that morning and taking the provincial chief of police, General Matullah Khan, with us to meet with the elders of the district and to get to know the men at the base who were members of the U.S. Army's Special Forces. It was also important to have Matullah see his police officers and for the district commander to have a chance to talk to him about his challenges. We had apparently had a great deal of success with the VSO program there, and FOB Cobra, sometimes called FOB Tinsley, was now the central hub for three other VSPs in the area called Saraw, Khod, and Kajran. Each site was positioned along a key valley intersection or population center to raise local forces, with Kajran actually being in the neighboring province of Dai Kundi to serve as a plug of sorts for insurgents coming up the Bagran Valley.

We staged near the flight line just outside FOB Ripley and waited for our Blackhawk helicopters to arrive. The brisk winter air was rejuvenating, and I thanked my lucky stars I was wearing long underwear for the trip since the mountainous air would be bracing. Not too long after we arrived, Matullah and his entourage drove up and met us near the concrete slab. I hadn't seen him in seven years and there he was, at the height of his power and with a trail of blood behind him. He exchanged pleasantries with Mike as well as with Colonel Archer, the commander of Combined Team Uruzgan (the overarching command for all of Uruzgan's military units) and me. Mike explained that I had served in the province before and would be acting as his adviser. Matullah welcomed me graciously and shook my hand in a soft manner. He was such a study in contrasts, well known as a cold-blooded killer but gentle in his own way. It was the way of the Afghan. Soon thereafter our helicopters arrived and we boarded, en route to the remote section of Uruzgan called Shahid-e-Hasas.

As we lifted off, I glanced out the window to see how Tarin Kowt, the capital of Uruzgan, had changed since I had last served there in 2006. Our once modest base perched on the edge of town was now surrounded by the sprawl of a provincial capital on the make. The newly paved road of 2005 that ran from the town center past our base on the way to Kandahar had brought local development along with it. All sorts of adobe houses, neighborhoods, and shops lined the route, and whole new sections of town had sprung up. As we gained altitude, I also noticed a new concrete bridge just north of town that crossed a raging river we used to have to drive through in our Humvees, and a newly paved road snaked its way north into the district of Chora. A new traffic circle had also been erected in the middle of town and several new buildings had been built on the governor's compound. A small building at the governor's headquarters also bore the scars of the complex attack that had taken place in July 2011.

As we made our way to the northwest portion of Uruzgan, the majestic terrain of the province revealed itself. Countless rivulets meandered along the countryside, with small outcroppings of villages perched along particular curves of the river or along small plateaus as their fields radiated out in a fan-like pattern. As we pushed north toward the mountains, small wisps of snow revealed themselves as the rich, natural colors of the landscape and the rural life of the Afghans flew past us. We finally approached FOB Cobra, which sat next to the main village in the district. We then circled around before landing on the makeshift landing pad filled with gravel and plates of metal to keep the dust down.

After departing the helicopters, we made our way past the outer Hesco wall (wire and mesh baskets filled with dirt and rocks to form protective barriers) of the base, and I quickly noticed a collection of damaged and broken-down vehicles to our right, silent reminders of the destructive power of improvised explosive devices. Some of the trucks the local police used were blasted apart, and various Humvees were in different states of disrepair. So many units had served at the base since its founding in 2004 that many of the vehicles had sat in this particular metal boneyard for nearly a decade; security had been so precarious no mission could be mounted to remove them. Additionally, prepackaged pallets of water, fuel, firewood, and food were arranged all over the base, waiting to be pushed out to the three other stability sites in the district. We finally grounded our gear at the tactical operations center and took a quick tour of the base while Matullah and his men got settled. The base had originally been built by the 25th Infantry in 2004 and had been named Cobra because Company C was there. Their sister unit, Company A, had been in eastern Uruzgan at another base named Anaconda. The base commander of Cobra was jokingly referred to as Cobra Commander after the famous G.I. Joe figure. Since 2005, the base had been exclusively run by Special Forces teams, and their mix of informality and professionalism permeated the place. Most of the men lived in shipping containers, encased in concrete with sandbags on their roofs, arrayed around a central fire pit. Guard towers ringed the base and a makeshift shelter protected several ribbed boats used by the Green Berets for operations along the river. A gym had once been covered from floor to ceiling with photos of women from *Maxim* magazine, among other titles, and the chow hall was run by local Afghans. Several memorials to soldiers killed in action in the district were arrayed along the base's walls, and their concrete edifices counted off the years of the U.S. presence in the area. I kept my eyes open to see if a memorial existed for my friend Sgt. Clint Newman, who had been based at Cobra in 2006 and had been killed along with three other soldiers by five antitank mines. I was never able to find a memorial for him. It was a surreal feeling to be back at the base.

We eventually gathered near the motor pool and I was frankly surprised to hear the base commander, Capt. Sam McNulty, tell us we would be taking a handful of unarmored trucks to the district center, which was within sight of the base, and would not be wearing body armor or helmets. We were going to attend a shura with area tribal elders, and Matullah was going to meet with them and the district chief of police, a man named Wali Dad. The mere thought of leaving the base without any protection other than some pistols in unarmored vehicles would have been unheard of the last time I had served in Uruzgan. Since I had last visited the district seven years before, more than 380 Afghan Local Police had been recruited, vetted, trained, and deployed, and Afghan National Police numbers had increased as well. Could this new security be the result of the Village Stability Operations program? I had little time to process the thought as we were soon ambling along the bumpy road to the district center, passing by a checkpoint within sight of the base and entering the gate of the district center. The district center also served as the district chief of police's headquarters and, as we pulled in, several Afghan police officers in their standard dark blue uniforms stood in different guard positions or watched curiously from the side as our convoy approached. The center was surrounded by a white wall reinforced, in places, with Hescos, and a number of police trucks were parked along its edge, some bearing clear signs of combat. The usual piles of various parts and pieces of old trucks were there, as well as a giant pile of firewood. A small half-circle of plush chairs had been brought outside and they were arranged around a wooden podium in preparation for Matullah's meeting with the village elders. Two parallel rows of plastic chairs had also been brought out, and a series of brightly colored plastic mats had been arranged for the guests to keep their feet off the ground. Matullah exchanged pleasantries with the police who were there and a small group of them surrounded him, happy to see their boss from the provincial capital. It was as if a minor celebrity had arrived. We eventually entered the district center and met with the police chief and district chief in the main meeting room. Pictures of Matullah, President Karzai, and a past Cobra commander were on the wall above the desk, and we shoehorned ourselves into the green velvet chairs as the meeting began.

Matullah began the meeting by stressing the importance of shuras and community support. "We must have the respect of the people, their trust; when there is trust between the people and their government things are much easier. It used to be that we would have police with no training but now they must learn how to be professional and to develop the skills and abilities to do their jobs. Cooperation is critical. The Special Forces are strong and have the toughest jobs and we must learn from them so they can return to their families. We must be with the people. If we are, everything is easier." I was struck by his sincerity and, quite frankly, his wisdom about the need to have the support of the people. This seemed to be a changed Matullah, but I would reserve judgment.

The district governor, a young Afghan named Haji Mohammed, requested that the district receive more Afghan Local Police billets and said they needed Matullah's help in opening up a road to the province of Dai Kundi to the north. Matullah responded, "I have requested more from the Ministry of Interior. You should have no problems reaching Kajran. Where are your local police?"

A quick discussion ensued about where the checkpoints were located. The police chief then said, "We need more weapons."

Matullah said, "You have weapons."

"Yes, but we have 208 people and only 150 weapons. Some are damaged."

They then discussed moving around checkpoints. "What is the state of your vehicles?" Matullah asked.

"We need more vehicles."

"We need more time to fix the vehicles but we have had no luck."

The police chief went on, "We are fortunate that we have no improvised explosive devices. The people are supportive. Some insurgents are intimidated by the local police. Everything has changed. The Coalition Forces used to conduct random searches but no more. The people are supportive and very happy. It was very bad before but no more, the people are happy. Trust with respect."

"That is the way to do it," Matullah said. "A message should go out to all your people that you are the protector of the community."

The police chief added, "It is good to have you speak to the people at the shura. . . . [R]elations are good in Char Chena [another name for the district] and people are very respectful, they share information, and have all agreed to the security plan. We play the role of bringing the villagers and the tribes together. I spoke with the local police about the need to respect the people."

It was a productive meeting and demonstrated to me how the concept of bolstering the local police by channeling resources through the province had empowered the district chiefs of police. They now had authority, resources, and the support of the province to do their jobs. It was an amazing thing to witness after previously seeing local police act more like predators against the population than their guardians. We got word that the elders had arrived, and we departed the room and convened outside.

Matullah greeted each elder. There were about forty altogether and they had traveled from far and wide. They huddled around him bringing their concerns to him. Their wizened faces and gray beards indicated their social standing in the community. To a man, their clothes were immaculate and their personal dignity paramount, and each had a large shawl wrapped around his shoulders to ward off the chill. Almost all their turbans were pitch black and their *salwar kameez* (traditional Afghan clothing) were all earth tones, a mix of dark brown, gray, black, green, and tan; the only spot of color (sometimes white, red, or some intricate design) came from the small skull cap each man wore to anchor his head covering.

The first speaker was a local elder I had known for many years, a man named Mohammed Ishmael. He stood at the podium and stated, "The people have suffered for too long. We hope our leaders pay attention to our communities and we must have more projects and assistance for the people."

At this, another elder spoke up: "We welcome Matullah and are happy to have him and the district chief here to hear our problems." As the meeting progressed, one elder at a time spoke and they collectively praised the work of the local police and Matullah as well as the district chief of police. They were happy that their communities were peaceful and they argued for more police, greater pay, and more support from the province to continue the good work.

Once the elders concluded, Matullah walked to the podium. "I am very happy to have the elders here and it is good to hear that things are good here. We must continue to do better. We must have a proper police organization. We must get rid of drug-addicted people and have people with clean records. We must continue to properly train our police in the rule of law and they need your help." Many of the elders nodded in support. "We will have more police next year in Khas Uruzgan and Char Chena [Shahid-e-Hasas]. If you hear of anyone stealing money, contact me. The Coalition Forces support the people and with the support of the community, we will be successful. We have had fighting for thirty years and tribal issues have not been resolved. We must work for the people and their interests."

The commander of the Afghan Local Police, who reported to the district chief of police Wali Dad, spoke up, "We need more weapons. I have one checkpoint with nine men and only three weapons. We need bullets to clear more of the areas."

An elder chimed in, "The roads are bad, you are our leaders, take the problems to the provincial government."

With these concluding words the call to prayer echoed out from the local mosques and the men prepared to leave. They each approached Matullah, pressing into his hand small pieces of paper noting their concerns to him, many sharing a laugh, and quickly departed. Matullah spoke with several of the police as we prepared to depart.

We finally left the district center and returned to FOB Cobra, grabbing lunch in the dining facility. It was a remarkable thing to see Matullah act as both a compassionate leader as well as a competent police official. He was more concerned about making sure his police did their job and maintaining the support of the community than saddling up to go after the Taliban in the kinds of raids he used to lead in 2005–6. The focused attention that the Village Stability Operations program gave to the police empowered district chiefs of police with resources, and the mentorship our guys provided gave them the confidence to do their jobs. Additionally, our men acted as trusted agents, helping to bridge the gulf between the tribes and local officials at the district level and between the provincial government and local government. Furthermore, because tribal elders played a central role in selecting their local police recruits, they were naturally supportive of the program since they gained a form of patronage they could use to build support. Local elders also became central players in security decision making, further bolstering the program. As security increasingly became the norm, other forms of governance increased as well. It was a remarkable thing to witness, but I would need to see other stability sites before I would be convinced of the general soundness of the Village Stability Operations approach.

FIVE

General Khan

> The great Durrani tribe, which has traditionally supplied the royal family of Afghanistan, are the most important histori- cally. The live in the middle and lower reaches of the Helmand River Valley and Kandahar has long been their capital. . . . The other group which could, if it cared about such things, claim Afghan nationality, is the Ghilzai. The Ghilzai are the only true nomads among the Pathans.
>
> —JAMES W. SPAIN, *The Way of the Pathans*

Having last served in Uruzgan six years before, it was oddly comforting to return to the area to witness the apogee of Matullah's power. After starting as an illiterate militia leader, he was now head of the province's police forces. Matullah was a late-thirties Populzai tribesman from Uruzgan's capital of Tarin Kowt and a survivor. Tall and lanky, his narrow features were hidden behind a wispy black beard, and his balding pate suggested an older man. He was constantly being targeted by the Taliban, so he had already aged well beyond his years and suffered from a variety of stomach and other ailments due to hypertension. Too young to participate in the mujahedeen in the 1980s, he lacked the fighting prestige and respect that came from having fought the Soviets. Outside of a brief stint as a driver for a Taliban leader in the 1990s, he resolutely opposed the Islamist movement in large measure because of his affiliation with Hamid Karzai's tribe, but also due to the nature of his rise to power. Matullah's life changed dramatically after 9/11.

When U.S. Special Forces units arrived in Uruzgan Province in 2001 and began their long association with the area, Matullah and his uncle, Jan Mohammed Khan, became their steadfast allies in the struggle against the Taliban insurgency. While his uncle JMO, as he was referred to by the United States, was the brains and political leadership of the province, it was Matullah who was the brawn. He led his uncle's militia, and what had begun as a couple of hundred men eventually ballooned into a force of several thousand. While he ably fought the Taliban alongside U.S. forces, he also chastened and punished his uncle's political and tribal opponents, which fostered a series of blood feuds and created enemies from the families of those he had killed. Following his uncle's assassination in 2011, he finally rose to the height of his power when he was appointed provincial chief of police by President Karzai and added the honorific "Khan" to his name to denote his newfound status. It was thought that Matullah would best be able to protect the interests of Karzai and the Populzai in the province. Perhaps due to his age, the consolidation of his power, and the marginalization of his opponents, he had effectively adopted the mien of a wise tribal elder, less dominated by the thirst for power and more sanguine about his opponents.

On February 22, I joined Hayes and Maj. Ben Jacobs, the commanding officer of the Special Forces Advanced Operations Base, on their trip to Matullah's house, which was just in sight of FOB Ripley. Jacobs was a U.S. Army Special Forces major who was responsible for Uruzgan and Dai Kundi Provinces, and he answered directly to Special Operations Task Force–South East as his higher command. He was with the 1st Special Forces Group and his AOB was in Deh Rawud District to the west of Tarin Kowt at FOB Tycz. Jacobs was a thoughtful and solidly built Special Forces officer from Idaho who had married his high school sweetheart and had been with the Army since he had graduated college. He had grown up in a predominantly Mormon area but was not a Mormon himself, which likely sensitized him to seeing things from a different perspective. Although plain-spoken, he was a deeply reflective leader and had a rich understanding of the dynamics of insurgency. He was quite adept at leveraging the Afghans to meet his goals of building Afghan Local Police forces and confronting the Taliban's political and propaganda efforts. I thought it would be interesting to accompany him and Hayes to Matullah's house and to witness their interactions.

We departed in the early afternoon and piled into the mine-resistant ambush-protected (MRAP) all-terrain vehicles (MATVs) that had replaced the ubiquitous Humvees I had principally traveled in during past deployments. The MATV was a much larger vehicle than the Humvee and stood several feet higher in the air. Its V shaped bottom allowed IED explosions to course around the vehicle, and its turret gunner sat inside the truck using a set of television monitors to guide the crew-served machine guns that accompanied each vehicle. It was thought that moving the gunner inside the vehicle would reduce casualties, but along with safety came less situational awareness. We had to put on five-point harnesses, which would prevent us from crashing around inside the vehicle if we hit a mine, and combat-lock our doors to maintain the structural integrity of the vehicle during a blast. The key luxury, however, was the air conditioning, but it almost didn't feel right to have it. My last time in the province consisted of traveling in Humvees and struggling mightily to stay awake from the oppressive heat, all the while seeing salt crystals gather along the edges of my clothing from dried sweat.

We took a sharp left from the front of our gate and meandered along the desert road to Matullah's house, quickly passing by the outer guard post of his compound and into his courtyard. Our vehicles squeezed through his front gate after a guard lifted a small barricade and circled around as the drivers maneuvered their unwieldy charges into a line ready to depart. We disembarked from our metal cocoons and quickly met with Matullah, who was standing near his personal mosque with his ever-present security guards hovering close by.

We took off our helmets and sunglasses, exchanged pleasantries, and followed him as he escorted us to a building he used solely for entertaining. After we entered the structure I noticed a large assembly hall to my right, which was covered in thick green carpet and had elaborate lighting fixtures hanging from the ceiling. We quickly ascended the stairs of the building en route to the second floor. Once there we grounded our gear, readjusting our camouflage after taking off our armor, and walked on to the terrace of the building, which had several small rooms alongside it. The terrace overlooked a copse of small trees that had been cultivated into neat rows, and we had a clear view of the town of Tarin Kowt as well as our base. The placement of Matullah's house provided him with a number of advantages. He clearly benefited from the security bubble our base provided, but the house also allowed him to monitor our convoys and personnel. It was now customary for us to intercept radio traffic from someone in Tarin Kowt reporting on our convoy movements, and while I would like to say I thought it was the Taliban, I often wondered who else it might have been. Matullah also had ready access to our base as well as its flight line so that he could get helicopter support for his trips as well as greet important Afghan visitors who flew into town. Back in 2005, the United States paid Matullah for the external security his men provided our base, but one often wondered how much they protected us or kept us in check. One noticeable side effect of the placement of his house, however, was that Matullah and his family frequently suffered from the sweet, sickly smell of sewage wafting over their compound from the two very large sewage lakes that now graced our base. As Afghanistan's summer heated up, the drying sewage became even more potent. Perhaps it was a little cosmic justice for him not to have everything to his liking.

As the leader of the Populzai tribe's militia forces for his uncle back in 2005–6, Matullah controlled the only legitimate security force in the province other than the nascent police forces of his uncle's erstwhile rival Rozi Khan. When I formally interviewed Matullah in 2005, his force numbered around three hundred men, and they controlled the main checkpoint into Tarin Kowt from Kandahar and had ambitions to build checkpoints all along the road to that major city of southern Afghanistan. His militia was then called the Afghan Highway Police, after being laundered into official security forces. Any other rival militias were deemed illegal, with the United States and the United Nations disarming these groups under a program called Disarmament, Demobilization, and Reintegration (DDR).

All sorts of weapons were turned in by the Afghans (although many were deliberately useless as the Afghans always hedged their bets), and these men would then receive some money and access to training programs to start a business or learn a trade. The program had lofty goals but essentially forced all the rivals of the governor to disarm while the governor remained armed. As the governor preyed upon his rivals, the Taliban found ready-made allies among the disgruntled tribes and factions. After effectively gaining control of the main road into town, Matullah's highway police earned money from special "taxes" on vehicles and fees for "protection," and they now had a reliable route to move poppies/heroin and other goods to make money. It was a classic shakedown scheme, but Matullah's avarice was limited since his own tribe and allies also used the roads. It was not beyond him and his men, however, to steal property from rival tribes.

All the tribal rivalries in the province created a messy situation. I once stumbled upon Matullah in a nearby village called Chora in 2005, where he and his men were in the process of stealing about a dozen cars and trucks from a rival tribal leader who had seized them from fleeing Taliban members. These vehicles were later sold by then governor Jan Mohammed Khan for thousands of dollars. This same tribal leader had also been pushed out by the Taliban in the early 1990s when Matullah's uncle colluded with the Islamist movement to defeat his opponents. Matullah's personal wealth was rumored to be in the millions, and he had recently acquired a third wife, a nineteen-year-old for whom he had reportedly paid $100,000 to the family. He had also acquired three up-armored Humvees for his use, which he always had with him as he went around town. Each had been painted dark green and had four or five police officers and their own crew-served weapons.

Times were good. With Matullah's ascendency to the position of Uruzgan's provincial chief of police in 2011, he had complete control of all the police forces in the area and was uncontested. Additionally, our use of the Village Stability Operations program, which worked through his office to build local police forces, further extended his power and influence. Based upon my initial observations, it seemed as though Matullah had grown magnanimous with his rivals, since most were either gone, dead, co-opted, or checked by his power. Our meeting with him was going to be interesting.

Ever the gracious host, Matullah led us to one of his meeting rooms, and we settled into his plush chairs while he sat behind a simple wooden desk. A collection of wildly colored plastic flowers sat on his desk as well as photos of past American commanders who had worked with him. As soon as we sat down, a young Hazaran boy wearing a skull cap, simple sky blue vest, and traditional Afghan garb entered carrying two small trays with snacks. It was an odd assortment of dried grapes, small nuts, and sugar treats. After placing these on the two glass tables in the center of the room, he quickly left and came back with another tray with small glasses and a pot full of hot chai tea, the glasses clinking as he made his way into the room. As drinks were poured, Hayes and Jacobs got to work. This was the first meeting with Matullah for Jacobs, but Hayes had already met with him on four other occasions. My recent trip to FOB Cobra with Hayes and Matullah had already demonstrated that security was possible in Uruzgan, and we were determined to continue to spread the Village Stability Operations program more widely in the province. Discussion initially began concerning the northernmost district in Uruzgan called Gizab, where a local revolt against the Taliban had taken place in June 2010. After tiring of the Taliban's barbarous behavior, local villagers had risen up and killed several dozen of the Islamists. Their actions took U.S. leaders completely by surprise, and the Special Forces command quickly sent in a team to partner with the villagers and to raise a local police force. Because the area was partly Hazaran, implacable foes of the Taliban, and very mountainous, local villagers had been able to hold off the Taliban fairly easily even though the Islamists were always looking for opportunities. There was now talk of transitioning the district to the Afghans and moving our team there to a new district to continue the process of raising local forces.

Much of the discussion about the district concerned the district chief of police, a man named Lala, who ruled the area with a remarkable mix of ferocity against the Taliban and concern for his people. He had famously burned down a whole bazaar the Taliban had been using as a headquarters in the area to send a message that local cooperation with the Taliban would not be tolerated. While his actions wouldn't meet our standards of acceptable behavior, it was considered "Afghan good enough" since it seemed to have the desired effect. The central issue for the district revolved around pay for the Afghan Local Police. Paying them on time was a constant struggle. The Ministry of Interior was ostensibly in charge of the ALP program, but, like many Afghan institutions dealing with corruption, the lack of trained civil servants and, frankly, ethnic politics, it always had problems delivering pay on time. Our U.S. forces played a key role in making sure the money flowed, and the fact that our men were present in each of Uruzgan's districts ensured that the logistical system worked as well as it did.

Hayes began the meeting: "It's very important that the ALP get paid in Gizab. The MOI [Ministry of Interior] will eventually catch up but we need to make sure the men are paid on time."

Matullah responded, "Lala has 400 men working for him in Gizab but he pays them by splitting the pay he receives for his 200 ALP in half. He recently collected three months of pay instead of two last week."

Each district chief of police (DCOP) had to travel to Tarin Kowt to collect not only pay for their men but also weapons, vehicles, Hescos, barbed wire, and other materials and support from Matullah since he was the provincial chief of police. He controlled the distribution of all these goods, which greatly expanded his power but also knit the province together in a logistical and security network.

Jacobs said, "I have men in each of Uruzgan's districts and they meet regularly with the DCOPs. I collect our reports and send them to the provincial level for your use. I want to work with you at all levels and develop relationships between the districts and the provincial government." Jacobs was doing the classic Green Beret pitch: "Let me help you by working side-by-side with you as a brother in arms."

Matullah nodded his assent. Hayes then obliquely referenced the fraught working relationship between the police chief and the governor.

"It's difficult for career military men to work with politicians," Hayes said. "They come and go but military and police professionals like you and me stay forever. Although it can be difficult to work with politicians and hard to build a system that will last, that's how we're gonna save Uruzgan. It's what's best for the people. I know you believe that."

Matullah didn't respond and grabbed a handful of grapes to eat. Matullah then switched subjects to our recent trip to FOB Cobra. "The people were not happy in Shahid-e-Hasas in the past," he said, "not getting along well with the government. Special Forces and the ALP have improved things with new teams."

Hayes said, "That's a useful insight; we would like to do more with you. You were like a rock star at Cobra. We can take you to other sites to see your men and visit with the people."

Matullah said, "I've worked with Special Forces for eight years and they have always been my friends." Things seemed to be going well.

The discussion then turned to a former Taliban commander named Abdul Samad, whom Hayes and his men had helped join the side of the government in the far eastern Uruzgan district of Khas Uruzgan. Hayes said, "I have lost friends to the Taliban and have killed the Taliban but am very happy with Samad and would like to have more like him. Do you trust him?"

"Yes," Matullah answered.

"We must get more *tashkeils* [paid positions] and could use your help," Jacobs said. Hayes added, "Must have jobs or no more re-integration [a term used when insurgents joined the government]. We can change that area and Uruzgan."

Matullah said, "Other Taliban will be encouraged if Samad gets a job."

With more of our efforts focused on confronting both the military as well as the local political strategy of the Taliban and actively enlisting Afghan locals in their own defense, we were starting to see various Taliban either coming over to the government side or contemplating it. Hayes and Jacobs seemed pleased by Matullah's response.

Hayes said, "Will you go to the provincial security meeting with me? Easier if you go, not just the governor." This security meeting was held by the governor. A separate meeting called the Operations Coordination Center–Province, which had representatives of all the security organizations, met once a week.

Matullah seemed unenthusiastic about the security meeting since it was led by the governor, a man he did not hold in high regard, but he said he would attend. The meeting reviewed a few other outstanding issues regarding the ALP program, but it had been generally productive. Matullah seemed to have a firm grasp of the logistical issues he was responsible for, was keen to visit more ALP sites around the province, and had expressed at least a willingness to attend the governor's security meeting. He also agreed to host Hayes and Jacobs at his house for lunch, which was yet another clear sign of our positive working relationship with him.

While there would never be a movie made of these kinds of interactions, it was clear that local Afghan leadership backed by U.S. forces with adequate resources made a profound difference. We concluded the meeting in the late afternoon, and as we trundled along the road back to FOB Ripley, I reflected on what I had witnessed.

I was impressed with how much Matullah had changed. He was now in charge of the whole province and seemed to have a strong grasp of the issues and responsibilities he now shouldered, although I would need to see more of him. Over the next week, several incidents took place in Tarin Kowt that gave me further evidence that not only were the Afghan National Police more capable but that Matullah's leadership was instrumental to its success. The next day after our meeting we received reports that a vehicle-borne improvised explosive device (VBIED) had entered the provincial capital. Our intelligence was sketchy, but the vehicle had arrived, and no sooner had it shown up than the police captured and disarmed it. It had been placed in the same location as a prior VBIED attack against the governor's compound in 2011. This was all due to the work of the local police.

On February 28 the local ALP in Shahid-e-Hasas captured a Pakistani placing an IED in the road, further evidence of the secret hand of the Pakistani military in Afghanistan's affairs. That the locals had stopped it was further evidence that the ALP program was working; they had a vested interest in securing their own roads. The final event was more momentous. Several Qur'ans were accidentally burned at Bagram Airfield by a cleaning crew of U.S. soldiers, which caused protests all over the country. Tarin Kowt was not immune. Several hundred locals marched through the provincial capital to protest the desecration of the Muslim holy book, and our operations were put on lock down. Encouragingly, Matullah's Afghan National Police handled the protestors with a firm but just hand and actually had men deployed in riot gear to keep things in order. We played no part in their activities and they did everything on their own. I never thought I would see such a wondrous sight when I first served in the province seven years ago. It was amazing to see the police be so proactive and have the appropriate response to the problem. Things had changed significantly since I had been away. As impressive as these changes were to witness, I was more impressed with how much our own forces had changed; we were no longer just focused on finding the Taliban and killing them. We were now involved in empowering the Afghans to protect themselves, and from what I had seen thus far, we were having a great deal of success.

In many ways it was nice to be back in Uruzgan, which, even though I had spent only a year there, had been my first tour in a combat zone and had left an indelible imprint on my personal and professional life. The place was full of all sorts of firsts for me: first Humvee ride, first helicopter ride, first experiences with death. As I settled into my job and began to venture out to our other bases, I wanted to explore what our modest outpost in 2005 had become. It had gone from a dusty Forward Operating Base in a province no one had heard of to a sprawling Multi-National Base that had, over its lifespan, housed military personnel from the Netherlands, Australia, Jordan, and Singapore as well as countless other U.S. units rotating through the area since its construction in 2004. Although I never knew exactly how many units had rotated through the province since we had first invaded Afghanistan, I suspected it was probably close to forty or so, an astonishing number. The now sprawling minitown had had simple beginnings, starting with the decision by then governor Jan Mohammed

Khan to select this desolate patch of desert just outside the small village of Tarin Kowt as the site of the base. The then commander of the 22nd Marine Expeditionary Unit, Col. Frank McKenzie, had literally laid out the initial base with JMO by placing a map on the hood of a Humvee and plotting out its general design. Colonel McKenzie had selected the name "Ripley" to honor the courage, valor, and example of Col. John Ripley, USCM, who as captain had received the Navy Cross for heroic actions during the Vietnam War. The goals for the base were ambitious even though the layout was initially pretty small.

It was generally thought that once security had improved in Uruzgan the only enduring feature we would leave behind would be a Provincial Reconstruction Team that would partner with the local government, facilitate development, and mentor province, district, village, and tribal leaders. We were so confident in those early days that the Taliban had been defeated and that just a few "dead-enders" were hanging on that focusing solely on "nonkinetic" tasks seemed realistic. I distinctly remember an effort that was made in 2005 to convince the United Nations to open an office in Uruzgan when the then commander of Regional Command-South, a U.S. Army colonel in charge of seven provinces, brought them to Tarin Kowt for a grand tour. He had invited the heads of all the various departments within the United Nations office in Kabul down to our little province, where he proceeded to give them a tour of the area. He even went so far as to have all our soldiers leave their body armor behind as a demonstration of how safe conditions were in the provincial capital. We never thought it was that safe, but the idea that the province seemed secure is now almost laughable. But these were the views of many of us at that time, laboring away in the simple belief that the Taliban could never return to power and that a little bit of development, the bolstering of local government, and a reliance on warlords would fix most problems. Unfortunately, reality had a habit of puncturing the balloons of improbable notions, and the enemy always had a vote as well.

Multi-National Base Tarin Kowt was the hub in the province for conventional forces, Special Operations Forces, the Provincial Reconstruction Team, and our mentors who worked with the Afghan army. It was a sprawling mini-metropolis embodying the strengths and weaknesses of our approach to fighting the war in Afghanistan. We were well-resourced, but with greater support came more regulations. When SEAL Team Two first showed up each member of the team had been given a rape whistle, which was required for all new arrivals in country. As you can imagine, the odds of a Navy SEAL being raped are incredibly remote to say the least, but the mindset that such an inflexible application of a regulation represented gives you an idea of how common sense was now quite uncommon. One of the SEALs stated the obvious quite well: "I pity the woman who tries to rape me" as he looked derisively at the small, orange-colored whistle in his hand. Similarly, everyone had to have ready access to a reflective belt at night and was chastised quite heavily if they were found without one. A new expression in 2012 seemed to also capture the changed times: "Gosh, I went to war and a garrison broke out." These rules largely pertained to personnel at the larger base at Tarin Kowt of which Forward Operating Base Ripley and the Special Operations Task Force were a part; the SOTF's headquarters was a small island of common sense within it.

When I had arrived in Uruzgan in early 2005, the 25th Infantry, which was then in charge of the province, lived in simple tents, and the best structure on Forward Operating Base Ripley was a modest command building and a dining facility assembled from particle board. The Provincial Reconstruction Team had lived in similar circumstances until it built its own facility on the base, which eight years later served as the headquarters of Special Operations Task Force-South East. It had concrete walls and buildings, proper shower facilities, and electricity, and it was built to be self-sufficient and lasting. Fast-forward several years, and the base was a grotesque symbol of comfort and bureaucracy. Paved sidewalks replaced dirt and gravel, and a minivillage of shops, social hangouts, and nighttime activities had supplanted an austere sense of service. Additionally, with greater resources came additional regulations, and the "corporation warrior" had arrived, more interested in advancing his career than in accomplishing missions. During the Vietnam conflict such men were often referred to by the draftees as "lifers" due to their untoward interest in hitting the wickets of promotion versus winning the war they were involved in. Increasingly, innovation was seen as insubordination, and a convoluted command-and-control system prevented a coherent approach from being used to address the province's problems.

A perfect example of this unfortunate tendency was a U.S. Army colonel who was in charge of this sprawling mélange of units, personalities, nationalities, and missions. He had a small command element of which he was directly in charge, and he sought to exert his will over the SOTF and the Provincial Reconstruction Team. He was a most interesting man. His body type was that of a small southern town's football coach, but he had a method of peacocking around with boastful claims that perhaps concealed his profound insecurities. His usual questions to build rapport with a soldier were "Where ya from?" and "What's yer favorite sports team?" He had modified these questions for the Afghans by asking them, "What village ya from?" and "What's your tribe?" and so on. When SEAL Team Two first arrived, Commander Hayes met this colonel at an event at the governor's compound and a most interesting clash of professional cultures ensued. The colonel had been a tanker his whole life and was prone to saying that he had led more brigades than General of the Army Omar Bradley, the great World War II general and the first chairman of the Joint Chiefs of Staff. In addition to the wonderfully preposterous nature of his comparison, the colonel then warned Hayes that he had a lot of "battle scars" from Special Operations Forces and that if he got in his way he would bowl him over. As you can imagine, a hefty, five-foot-nine colonel was simply not that intimidating to Hayes, who stood at six feet four and 230 pounds and was a SEAL team commander. Hayes continued to grasp the colonel's hand and then stepped forward into the colonel's personal space to say, "Sir, that's not a great way to welcome a colleague." I suppose the colonel thought his martial display of verbal bullying would somehow cow Hayes, but he quickly backtracked as Hayes flashed him a determined look. Without missing a beat, he asked his two questions: "Well, uh, where ya from? What's your favorite sports team?" Hayes finished shaking his hand, stared him in the eyes with his jaw firmly set, and said "Virginia Beach, sir" and walked away. The good colonel also affected a faux Texas swagger, although he had grown up in New England, and he often sprinkled his conversations with homespun expressions earned from a stint with the Army Cavalry, such as "I earned my spurs," "That dog won't hunt," and "giddy up" as well as various "tankerisms." He once said at a meeting, "The ALP are like a saddled ass, they go where you lead them." He tried his best, but he seemed a bit mismatched for the demands of the situation.

A more disturbing feature of the war in Afghanistan by 2012 was the "new" insider threat problem, wherein trusted Afghans turned against U.S. soldiers and tried to kill them, often successfully. As we learned more about Afghan culture and took a more hands-on approach to building the security forces and mentoring government leaders through embedded mentoring, we became more exposed to the Afghans and them to us. Such work required mature judgment, tact, diplomacy, and patience as well as a willingness to truly understand the interests of the Afghans. The Special Forces community, the fabled Green Berets, were expressly designed to build indigenous security forces, but due to the size of the Afghan army and the fact that the Special Forces community had many other competing tasks, this crucial job of training and mentoring the Afghan army fell to regular U.S. Army units (frequently National Guard), reservists, and the other services. The challenge of using this approach was that conventional army units are much younger and not expressly designed to work with indigenous militaries as are the Green Berets. This caused all sorts of frictions with the Afghans. An innocent comment from a young soldier or an Afghan being exposed to a Western men's magazine could cause great offense. Additionally, because the Afghan army had grown so quickly and vetting was imperfect at best, a lot of Afghans were let in who had either sympathies for the Taliban or, in some cases, mental difficulties that weren't helped by the pressures of war. The Taliban were also looking for opportunities to sway an Afghan soldier on leave or to question his honor for working with the "infidels," which caused some to turn against us as well. It was a difficult set of problems to manage and it had a corrosive effect on the attitudes of the soldiers toward the Afghans. A certain level of distrust now existed, and with the war lingering for eleven years at that stage and many soldiers showing signs of fatigue due to frequent rotations, the heady days of us working alongside our "brother" Afghans were behind us. As these barriers of mistrust were built, it became harder to develop relationships with the locals. The overall relationship was now fraying even as we embedded with their military units, mentored and liaised with their political leaders, and tried to build the country to an unprecedented degree. In some respects, the relationship was like that of a friend who had overstayed his welcome.

SIX

Rise of the State

If the government performance is going to be effective and keep pace with the aspirations of the people, while at the same time creating an atmosphere of order and stability, the main essential is to establish a sound administrative structure. The best of plans, programmes and policies will remain nothing but good intentions unless the machinery exists to execute them so that they make their impact throughout the country.

—Sir Robert G. K. Thompson, *Defeating Communist Insurgency: Experiences from Malaya and Vietnam*

I t was heartening to witness the immense changes that had taken place within Uruzgan's police, and even though I had my qualms about how Matullah would handle his newfound authority, things seemed to be progressing. The other major pillar of power in the province was the governor, an Uruzgan outsider named Omar Shirzad, who had been appointed to his post on December 13, 2010. Based upon my experiences in the province and from having spoken with my colleagues, it was already apparent that the governor and Matullah were not getting along. This had also occurred when Matullah's uncle, Jan Mohammed Khan (JMO), was around against two other outsiders, Abdul Hakim Monib in 2006 and Asadullah Hamdam in 2007, who had both been appointed governors of Uruzgan once JMO had been removed. The local powerbrokers always seemed to reject competent outsiders, but frankly people like JMO had little to offer the population themselves and often had horrendous public

64

records of their own. There were times I felt that this political microdrama of insider versus outsider was just another broken record playing itself out since most of these problems stemmed from a lack of local democracy and public accountability. Everyone was always appealing to President Karzai, typically with dueling packs of village elders who would travel to the capital to impress upon him how either completely corrupt the governor was (and then not offer a legitimate alternative) or how great his actions were in the province. These problems constantly plagued Afghanistan because the government was incredibly centralized but society was decentralized. Regardless, today was my first mission downtown to attend the now weekly provincial administration meeting presided over by Governor Shirzad. As I assembled my gear I couldn't wait to see how much the area had changed since I had last been there six years before.

On March 5, Major Bradley, Captain Ho'omalu, and I journeyed to the governor's compound to attend the weekly meeting; no such meeting had taken place when I had last served in the province, so things were looking up. My plan of getting our nonkinetic cell out and about was working. We set out first thing that morning and departed in a convoy of three MATVs. It had been challenging work just assembling the vehicles and force protection to go because, once again, a perception existed that these kinds of political engagements were not really the responsibility of Special Operations Forces and that the Provincial Reconstruction Team should take the lead. Since I had worked at the same PRT seven years ago, I knew all too well that however much they were in the lead in good governance, reconstruction, and development, maintaining situational awareness for our command was essential. Additionally, because we were with the Special Operations Command, we had other resources, training, and priorities that often built on the PRT's work, but not always.

Once we left the base we turned left onto the main road into town, a road that had been paved when I was in the province in 2005. A series of small shops, homes, food stalls, and even a car wash now lined the busy thoroughfare. Our cumbersome vehicles tried to maneuver between the numerous cars, trucks, and motorcycles that zoomed along the road without regard to local traffic laws, and I noticed a number of Afghan police along the road, which was a good sign, and busy shoppers all around. I also noticed much more economic activity and development in the provincial capital and more cars versus trucks as paved roads increasingly became the norm in the area. We quickly approached downtown, which was divided into a large X where two roads met in the middle, and swung around the traffic circle in the heart of Tarin Kowt. This particular circle had been notorious when I had last served in the province since it was the site where then-governor Jan Mohammed Khan would dump the bodies of dead "Taliban." While this practice no longer took place, it was jarring to be back in the same area and to think about how much had changed since that time. The circle now had large pictures of Afghan president Hamid Karzai, former governor Jan Mohammed Khan, and General Matullah hanging from its second story, as much signs of local officials as demonstrations of power. We finally approached the governor's compound and our convoy slowed down. The front gate was now a military encampment and had large concrete Texas barriers, several checkpoints, and nervous-looking guards surrounding it. In 2005–6, a flimsy metal gate was the only protection, but with the development of car bombs things had changed appreciably. We slowly maneuvered our way past the serpentine barriers and entered the governor's compound.

The compound was perched on a ledge overlooking the expansive Tarin Kowt river valley, and its location defined the western edge of town. The provincial headquarters was several acres and contained not just the governor's offices but additional government buildings as well. In some respects, it was sort of like a mini–green zone for the province. Our vehicles pulled up to a bullet-riddled, three-story building in the main courtyard that had served as the local treasury and location of the provincial radio station in 2005. The same building had served as the first headquarters for our Special Forces teams in 2001 but was now largely abandoned due to substantial combat damage. The complex attack the Taliban had mounted the previous July, in large part a reaction to the Osama bin Laden raid, had ended in this building as the remaining Taliban fighters retreated to it after initially detonating two car bombs at the entrance to the compound. Once they had fallen back to this position, the governor's guards and Afghan army unloaded on the building and so, in addition to the bullet holes, it also had spiral rings from rocket-propelled grenades and scorch marks from a fire. The building had clearly played a significant role in local history. I also noticed that an old Soviet BMP, a small troop carrier, that had originally been in the courtyard was now gone, likely sold for scrap. Jan Mohammed Khan's guards used to eat lunch or lazily snooze on it in the early afternoon. After we dismounted our vehicles, we proceeded to the compound's inner courtyard, and as our group walked there, I noticed a brand-new modern meeting hall to my left, its yellow edifice striking to my eyes, and then a multistory government building to my right, clear signs that local government capacity had improved. The inner courtyard had its own wall and gate and had been reinforced with Hesco walls. As we entered, an oasis greeted us. This inner courtyard was where the governor held all his meetings and where he met visiting dignitaries. Two large gardens full of roses greeted us as we entered, and two open verandas, where the governor used to hold court with local residents, had now been enclosed with screens and windows. A peacock squawked in the distance, and I would later notice several others that just meandered around the area. The main governor's building was still there, but a small meeting room had also been built to its right where we would be meeting that day.

Over the course of my year in Uruzgan in 2005–6, I spent more time at this compound than anywhere else in the province other than FOB Ripley. Because it was the seat of local government, all the province's officials met here at some point or other, and dozens of local villagers were always present looking to petition the governor for some redress. Other government offices such as the police, education, health, public works, information, and haj and religious affairs directorates, among others, had their offices along the compound's adjoining road, and I had spent countless hours at these locations getting to know the directors and their concerns. At that time, local government was more a hope than a reality. I eventually undertook a survey of the local government trying to figure out what capabilities they had, the backgrounds of the directors, how the various parts of the government worked together or didn't, and simply how it functioned. Almost every significant leader in the province including the governor, police chief, and several of the directors were illiterate, and most had few resources other than what the Provincial Reconstruction Team could provide. Since the Soviets had expended a great deal of resources to train local Afghans in engineering, policing, construction, education, and health, most officials with any training were former communists. These same officials were often our most reliable partners. Most other officials seemed to have been placed due to their tribal affiliations and political influence, which meant they often had little background in the areas for which they were ostensibly responsible. The provincial government did virtually nothing outside the capital, so the Provincial Reconstruction Team I worked on served a valuable role in building local capacity. I was certainly optimistic that things had improved since I had been away in light of the amount of time and energy the governments of the Netherlands and Australia had expended to build local governance.

My colleagues and I entered the meeting room to the right of the inner courtyard and saw a series of plush chairs that lined the room, with an area for the governor and deputy governor to sit at the front. Since the governor was in Kabul, which was frequent these days as he fought to keep his position while advocating for the province, the deputy governor was presiding over the meeting. A number of provincial directors showed up, although the empty seats suggested many were not there, and Scott, Ed, and I sat to the side of the room after we grounded our gear. A ten-foot-high photo of President Karzai hung from the ceiling in the front of the room, and windows lined the walls, letting us see the lush rose bushes outside. The meeting began with a mullah, a local Muslim religious leader, reciting a prayer and all the participants except us raised their hands to the middle of their chest with palms up until the prayer finished.

The men and a few women briefly wiped their faces with their hands while softly uttering "al-hamdullah," or "praise God." The deputy governor was a frail, older man with a white beard and hair and dressed in traditional Afghan garb with a black turban, light-colored *salwar kameez*, and a black vest. He held a sheaf of papers in his hand as he sat in front of the provincial officials and surveyed the room. He was also a senior Populzai tribal elder, which gave him traditional authority as much as his government position gave him governmental authority. He stated they would be discussing the justice system in the province, road construction, and the national Afghan budget for local projects.

The deputy governor began the meeting by stating:

> There is a meeting in Kabul to discuss reconstruction projects for next year. Uruzgan is a backwater province and the government does not pay us much attention. It is our responsibility to develop the province and we must do more to build the roads and highways. The local people are complaining about IEDs and if we can pave the roads we will have fewer problems. Please submit your plans to the governor for road projects. Each director has a responsibility to talk to the governor, to bring him your projects. With respect to education, we have many schools but they have no students. We must visit each school site to take a survey to know what books and supplies they need and whether they have students. We also have teachers that don't show up. We must set the budget to reflect these realities. We need to make sure our paperwork reflects the real situation. All departments need to work with the governor, he is the chief.

These opening remarks were encouraging and demonstrated to me that the provincial government was at least functioning, had resources, and was somewhat responsive to the needs of the people. The deputy governor continued, "Attorneys and judges need to visit the districts as we discussed at the last meeting. Even though they are concerned about their safety in taking the roads to the districts we must find a solution." Discussion then continued for the next hour and a half and covered the contract for rebuilding the judiciary headquarters, how well the crops were going to be this season due to a wet rainy season, and the need to make sure the directors submitted their agenda items at least three days before the meeting and increased their coordination with the governor. Once the meeting concluded, Scott and I tried to corral a few of the directors to see if they'd be willing to meet with us at FOB Ripley in order to get to know them better and to see how we could help them perform their duties. Several agreed to our request. We were making progress on working more closely with the local government and helping them build their capacity.

As we prepared to depart, I reflected on how much local government had changed since I had last been in the province. One of the major problems we faced when we invaded Afghanistan in 2001 was the almost complete lack of trained civil servants in rural Afghanistan, including our own. Most of our initial efforts to build the Afghan state focused on the central government, and when we started to focus on the provinces through the Provincial Reconstruction Teams, most of our work was on constructing the physical infrastructure of the country. We had very few programs and personnel to actually train local Afghans in budgeting, planning, construction, finance, and other skills. In a strange twist of fate, most of the locals I initially worked with were former communists who had been trained in Kabul or even in the Soviet Union itself in the skills needed to run local government. So many Afghans had missed schooling due to the decades of fighting in the country when they either didn't have time to go to school, had their schools destroyed, or, during the Taliban's rule, had their schools closed and a normal curriculum replaced with solely Qur'anic teachings. Most of the development agencies we worked through, such as the U.S. Department of State and the United States Agency for International Development, were top-down bureaucracies, either administratively too weak to do what was required or focused almost exclusively on spending money on projects with uncertain completion rates and even less certain results. In 2005, I was the only Department of State representative in the province and, along with my colleague Kerry Greene, who worked with USAID, we were the only civilian personnel at the base. It was only in 2009 that we started to see an increase in U.S. government civilians at the provincial level and then, in some areas, the districts.

The U.S. government also embraced the concept of a unitary Afghan state. Virtually all local programs went through a corrupt, generally unresponsive central government that often overlooked the interests of weak and underpopulated provinces like Uruzgan. All governors in the country were appointed, all provincial directors answered to far-off bureaucracies, and elected Provincial Councils had little oversight power and no budget authority. Local judicial efforts were anemic at best, and local warlords, tribal leaders, insurgent-aligned locals, and even criminals had too much influence on local political affairs.

The Afghan government eventually adopted a modest decentralization of power in 2007, but even then it was too little and was simply surface-level. Most Afghans lived in small villages and isolated valleys and rarely saw their government. For many of them, traditional authority structures, Pashtun culture, religious teachings, and tribal practices addressed most of their needs, and our approach to building the Afghan state, which was top-down, only discovered the need to have a complementary bottom-up approach later in the war, when American patience for the whole effort was almost exhausted.

In contrast, the Taliban focused their modest "good governance" efforts on providing a form of sharia-based justice, tribal outreach, and simple construction projects. They largely respected local power structures, although this was often done in order for them to reclaim power, and worked with Afghan culture more than against it. U.S. efforts also suffered from a unique problem of being generally unwilling to meddle in Afghan affairs when even a little pressure and cajoling could have done a lot to redress their more predatory tendencies. The Afghan government's sovereignty was simultaneously being built, contested by the Taliban, and undermined by Afghan corruption. As Scott, Ed, and I departed the meeting, I looked forward to getting to know the current directors much better and to see how local government had improved since I had last served in the province.

✧

One of the great joys of returning to Uruzgan was being able to reconnect with my friend and interpreter Mohibullah Sarwary. Mohib was a local man the Provincial Reconstruction Team had hired in 2004 to work as one of our handful of interpreters at the base. In addition to interpreting meetings for us, he also served as a local guide of sorts to the political terrain and he was my earliest teacher of the tribal names, key personalities of the province, and Afghan culture and history. Even though he had only been in his early twenties, in many respects he was my mentor. Mohib provided me with several advantages when I first started serving in the province. His uncle was the deputy governor of the province during Jan Mohammed Khan's rule, he was from the area, and his tribe, the Mohammedzai, was looked on with favor because the last president of Afghanistan before the Soviet invasion had been Sardar Mohammed Daoud Khan, who came from the same tribe. Daoud Khan had been assassinated in 1978 by political forces aligned with the communists, so his rule is often fondly remembered by Afghans as one of the truly good periods in the country's history before the disaster of the Soviet invasion. It also helped that Mohib's tribe was so small in the province that it had largely escaped all the political intrigue of the major players and that Mohib himself was an honest broker between the various factions. One sign of his high regard and our trust in him was that he slept in the same barracks with our soldiers back in 2005. He was about five feet six, had a short, black beard, always dressed traditionally, and prayed five times a day. As one indicator of our friendship, I purchased two American wedding dresses for his fiancée, who was determined to be married in a U.S. gown, when I had gone on leave in 2005. I bought two mostly to make sure she would at least have a choice of what to wear and some material to adjust the dress accordingly. Mohib dutifully paid me back over a few months. Mohib finished his time with the Provincial Reconstruction Team in 2006 as the Dutch took over and brought their own interpreters with them.

When I returned to the province in early 2012, my early stories of hiring local interpreters and having them live with us, and other tales of friendship and camaraderie usually solicited curious, or, quite frankly, hostile responses from people about my supposed naïveté. It was now the fashion to bring "vetted" Afghans, typically expats who had fled Afghanistan because of the fighting, to serve as our interpreters and advisors. Our primary interpreter at the command was such a person, but she was not Pashtun, the local population of the area, was quite young, and didn't really speak Pashto. She spoke Dari, which was the other official language of Afghanistan although not often well-understood by local officials. She was dedicated and worked hard, but she could never leave the wire without force protection, if she wanted to leave at all, and she took multiple leave breaks, which caused us problems. I worked well with her and admired her dedication, but our efforts to work with the local population suffered. Her gender also was a challenge for us as local mores were more conservative and a Western-dressed woman alone in the province often prompted local rumors. It was a curious aspect of the campaign in Afghanistan that at just the moment we were most directly involved in the affairs of the Afghans, knew the most we could about them, and had clearly become students of their history, culture, behavior, and other practices, we seemed to trust them the least. Some of this tendency, of course, was due to the horrendous effect of insider attacks on building trust by ideologically motivated or disgruntled Afghans against our soldiers. This chasm of ill will hampered our operations throughout 2012 and we now had Guardian Angels, soldiers who came with us as our protection, at most of our meetings with local Afghans in case one of them decided to attack us. It was an unusual time to be in Afghanistan.

Once I was settled in at the SOTF, I e-mailed Mohib about the possibility of meeting, to which he responded favorably. I eventually met him at the front gate of the main base and gave him a bear hug. He looked exactly the same, although both of us had added some weight to our frames (muscle, we told ourselves). "Mohib!" I exclaimed, smiling, "How are you my friend?"

"Sir, I am doing well. I brought you a gift from downtown." He handed me a small, tightly wound pink plastic bag. I quickly opened it and a number of candies tumbled into my hand.

"It is so great to see you, my friend," I said. "I can't believe how big the base is now!" He nodded in agreement. "How is your family?" I asked.

"My father and family are well."

"You must have many children by now."

He smiled sheepishly. "Yes, I have four children now," he mustered.

"Holy cow," I exclaimed. "I hope your wife is doing well."

He indicated that she was, and we both quickly walked through security and then drove off to sit in the dining facility at the base. It was a joy to see Mohib again. He was the bridge for me between my first tour, with all the fresh experiences of the war, and what I had become three tours later. It made me miss my old friends, as much as my old self, from the Provincial Reconstruction Team days. We eventually caught up that afternoon.

He was now working with the local United Nations office as a development advisor and interpreter and was still meeting local Afghan officials about all sorts of projects. He owned a sizable compound downtown, in addition to his own home, that he rented to a nongovernmental organization, and he had his own construction company. I teased him that he should add the appellation "Khan" to his name since he was clearly a man on the make. I enquired about his uncle, who was now retired, and about his various plans. He told me the U.N. office was closing and that he needed additional work. Interestingly, he was eventually offered a job by both Matullah, the police chief, and Shirzad, the governor, even though both men detested each other. This spoke volumes of how highly Mohib was thought of by local leaders. In fact, when Matullah approached him, he referred to him as "Mohibullah Khan." I told him I would do my best to find him a position with the SOTF, and I asked him if he wouldn't mind interpreting for me for some of my meetings. He generously agreed to help.

We eventually turned to local politics, and he helped me catch up on the key events of the province. One of his good friends, a man named Khoshal, was the second son of former provincial chief of police and Barakzai tribal elder Rozi Khan, who had been killed in 2008. I remembered him fondly from my time in 2005 when he had been a middle school student, but he was now grown up and de facto leader of his tribe, even though others were competing with him for power. His older brother had been assassinated in Kabul by men supposedly allied with Matullah and the Populzai tribe. I told Mohib I would like to meet with Khoshal to get to know him better. He agreed to help. He then told me that the Provincial Council was now dominated by allies of Matullah and that the rough tribal balance that had existed when I was there in 2005 was now gone. The police chief was pushing his own candidate for its head, a young Afghan man I had not heard of before. When the United States actively stepped back from overseeing the elections in 2009 and 2010, local Afghan powerbrokers filled the vacuum, and where our involvement ensured a fair and transparent result, the same could not be said of the later elections. I had been the only international elections observer in the province in 2005 when the first Provincial Council had been elected, so it was disheartening to now see a less-than-honest result. He then told me that relations between Matullah and the governor had reached a point that large parts of the government were not even reporting to the provincial administration meetings anymore, which might have explained the meager attendance at the meeting I had attended.

I then asked him about Mullah Hamdullah, the former head of the Provincial Council and a colorful character in local politics. Hamdullah was a local mullah who led one of the mosques in Tarin Kowt and had been a close friend of Jan Mohammed Khan. He and the former governor had fought against the Soviets in multiple battles, and even though he was with the Barakzai tribe, he was a good friend of the governor. Famously, his forehead had caught a bullet in one battle with the Soviets and knocked him out but miraculously missed his brain. He had a gnarly scar on his forehead, an indentation really, and he loved to tease people that he didn't really know if the bullet had been pulled out or not and would shake his head as if it was still there banging around in his skull. He had resigned his position in 2008 over a dispute and was now head of the Haj and Religious Affairs Directorate, which maintained the mosques of the province and paid the salaries of select mullahs. He was also in charge of administering the haj and ran an official lottery to choose who was selected. Governor Shirzad had him under investigation for taking bribes related to administering the lottery. I had heard through the grapevine that he had almost been killed recently when a man chased after him downtown and shot at him several times. Hamdullah had been hit in the thigh and had stumbled to the ground. The assassin then stood over him with the pistol aimed at his head when the weapon malfunctioned. Local police then ran up and the attacker departed. It was a harrowing story and I wanted to make sure he was all right. Mohib pledged to help me reconnect to the mullah as well.

It was great to see Mohib again, and before he departed, I invited him to my room to give him a gift. After I slipped him into the barracks (after all, Afghans were now prohibited from our areas), I gave him a copy of my book about Uruzgan. I flipped to his picture, which he had given me, and showed him the other photos. He was grateful to receive a copy and I signed it for him. As we drove to the front gate I reflected on how generous and kind Mohib was and the risks he had run to work with the United States as well as with the Afghan government. Many aspects of his character were shaped by the traditional Afghan culture he came from. His dedication to his faith, his family, and his country were inspiring. It was great to see how much Uruzgan Province had changed for the better.

As much as we felt we were moving things along in the area and Afghanistan more broadly, it was due to the good work of local Afghans like Mohib who wanted a better future for their country.

SEVEN

The Season of Assassinations

Attacks were launched against government outposts, not to kill government soldiers, but to convince the people that the government could not protect them. Assassinations were carried out, not to eliminate the Viet Cong's enemies, but to prove to the population that the government was unable to prevent them. Each action taken by the Viet Cong and the North Vietnamese had a political objective that far outweighed the military objective, for they had learned long ago that a pure military victory was impossible.

—JOHN L. COOK, *The Advisor*

The general feeling I had of security and stability in the province was in marked contrast to the open warfare I had witnessed in 2006, when it was common for the Taliban to stage conventional military assaults on populated areas in order to seize and hold territory. On this third trip to the province, it was the small details of life that indicated to me that stability was more the norm than the exception. My first impression of being back in Uruzgan was that ever-elusive feeling of stability, that quiet quality that reassures you that normalcy is in fact normal and not a transient feeling. The chaotic urgency of a province in open warfare had been replaced by a community confident in its ability to provide security for its residents. Police wore their uniforms, no small feat, and there were plenty of them throughout the provincial capital and around the area. The town of Tarin Kowt had a bustling bazaar and suffered from rural sprawl due to unplanned development because the

77

paved road linking the province to Kandahar had been extended into the surrounding districts and people were flocking to the capital. The Afghan army had a much larger presence as well and U.S. Special Operations Forces had increased Afghan Local Police in the villages, augmenting the Afghan police presence there too. Even with all these positive security changes, the Taliban were still adapting their strategy. They had replaced conventional assaults with suicide attacks, infantry tactics with political assassinations, and holding territory with using information operations and politics against the government. The war had shifted, and even though I thought we now had the momentum, the Taliban's hidden presence was still among us.

On March 19, my colleagues and I traveled again to the governor's compound, this time to attend the Afghan New Year celebration called Nawruz. A brief sandstorm the day before had threatened the festivities, but the sky was clear when we finally arrived mid-morning. The day's activities were scheduled in the large yellow meeting hall that had been constructed by the Dutch government to the left of the governor's compound as we entered the outer courtyard. It was a large structure with rooms on the second floor, and a sizable stage stood at the front of the main hall as honored guests sat in plush chairs toward the front. Other attendees filled out the room and sat on dozens of simple chairs. A loudspeaker system had been set up and five-foot-tall photos of President Karzai lined the walls. This was going to be Governor Shirzad's show; Matullah was nowhere to be seen. A local mullah began the celebration with a simple prayer, and the governor welcomed us as his guests. I sat next to Mike, who was one of the governor's honored invitees. After welcoming remarks and recognizing visiting dignitaries, celebratory dancing began. Off to the side, several Afghan soldiers shed their body armor, helmets, shoes, and weapons and entered the room in a low, rhythmic trot. They were members of the Afghan commando unit the SEALs worked alongside and mentored. The men were better trained and better equipped than the typical Afghan army soldier and they had a strong esprit de corps. They slowly began to twist their upper bodies in unison and their arms began to rise, and as they finished a twist, they would raise their hands above their head. They danced in a slow circle, each man twisting and singing. It was a sight to behold. Their bare feet gripped the carpets and their green and brown camouflage was in stark contrast with the multicolored rugs. The music eventually wound down and the men fell back to the side of the meeting. One of the governor's aides then approached the podium with a sheaf of papers and began to call people forward to receive certificates from the governor. It was a classic moment for a politician. The governor shook the hand of each man and said a few words of praise, and a cameraman took a picture. Eventually, Mike was called up, and as he ambled back to his seat he had a sheepish grin on his face as he was now the proud owner of his very own set of bright red plastic flowers and a book of Afghan sayings. We teased him mercilessly about the perils of being a SEAL commando undertaking community engagement work. The whole event wound down and we decamped to one of the governor's open-air verandas to sit down for lunch.

A thirty-foot table covered in bright red cloth lined the rectangular room, and the walls were floor to ceiling windows with a pleasant view of the rose gardens and the governor's compound. Our men pulled guard duty and looked after our gear as we all lined up along one side of the table awaiting the governor. All the Afghans filled the remaining forty or so seats and we all sat down after the governor was seated. I always relished these meals with the Afghans, and their hospitality was legendary. A series of glass bowls lined the table and ample dishes of baked chicken, meatballs, beef, and potatoes were stacked all along it with the ubiquitous Afghan rice and flat bread. Great big bowls of large oranges were neatly set in among the dishes, and cans of Coke were available for each participant. There were a number of Afghan faces familiar to me in the room, but one stood out in particular. I had seen him before and I had heard he was in town, so I was prepared to bump into him. His name was Haji Khairo Jan and he was a former member of Parliament who had been elected when I first served in the province.

Khairo Jan was something of a minor legend in Uruzgan Province. As a wizened Populzai tribal elder he was a key figure in the political support network of President Hamid Karzai. He was tall by Afghan standards, about six feet two, and had a kindly face, a gray beard, and a full head of hair. When I first met him he had received the most votes in the province for the Provincial Council and had beaten out more than thirty other candidates. Because he had received the most votes, he was automatically promoted to membership in the Meshrano Jirga, the upper house of Parliament. During the 1980s he had helped the mujahedeen in Uruzgan by collecting intelligence on Soviet military moves as well as providing fighters and logistical support to them when the communists made their few military incursions into the province. When the Taliban arrived in the area in 1994, he was appointed mayor of Tarin Kowt and set out to modernize the small village. To that end, he met with a visiting United Nations team and began to lay out a proper city grid, improved drainage and sewage, and started to look into how to electrify local businesses. But the governor for the province, a man named Sardar, disapproved of Khairo Jan's closeness to the "infidel" outsiders who worked for the UN and threw him in jail. Within twenty-four hours, every single business in Tarin Kowt shut its doors in protest over his imprisonment. There was no clearer sign of support from the people for Khairo Jan. The next day the governor released him and Khairo Jan became a confirmed opponent of the Taliban. When the U.S. invaded in 2001, he joined the resistance and provided advice to then governor Jan Mohammed Khan, who subsequently backed him in his run for office in 2005.

When I prepared to depart Uruzgan in November 2005 I received a message that Khairo Jan was at the front gate and wanted to see me. I quickly made my way to the gate and invited him in and asked, "How are you, my friend? How can I help you?"

He smiled and grasped my hand. "I understand you are going home."

"I am, in a few weeks," I responded.

"I wanted to thank you for all of your hard work and for helping the people of Uruzgan," he said. "To be a young man and to serve here"— he gestured with his hands to the desert valley and spartan mountains of the province—"means so much to us. You were always respectful of our leaders and our people, and as a sign of my thankfulness, I would like to introduce you to President Karzai to tell him the great work you have done, and to buy you some Afghan clothing as a gift."

I was incredibly humbled by his thoughtful and heartfelt comments, and it was touching to see how well received my efforts had been by him and the Afghan people. I shook his hand with both of mine and thanked him for his selfless comments. I asked him if he had a ride to Kabul to the opening session of Afghanistan's reconstituted Parliament. He told me he hadn't, so I mentioned that I would look into whether we could fly him and another newly elected member of Parliament, Mohammed Hanif, to Kabul in the next few days and that I would pass the message on to him through Mohib. He kindly thanked me for my offer. We would eventually fly both of them to Kabul on my way home to the states and introduce them to the U.S. embassy's liaison to the Parliament. While I never got a chance to meet President Karzai, Haji Khairo Jan did return to the embassy that evening with a set of Afghan clothes for me. It was a touching and fitting end to what I thought would be my final experience with Uruzgan.

Seven years later, I made my way over to Haji Khairo Jan, who was chatting with some government officials in a small group once the lunch had finished. People were socializing just outside the meeting room near the governor's offices, and even though Khairo Jan and I had actually seen each other a few times before, he hadn't recognized me since I was now clean shaven and wearing a military uniform. However, this time I brought a small photo album with me from my 2005 tour with plenty of pictures of me in civilian clothes with a beard. Thankfully, Mohib was present and kindly translated for me. I approached Khairo Jan and asked him if he remembered me from 2005 when I had been with the State Department. Mohib translated and Khairo Jan indicated that it had been many years and that he unfortunately did not remember me. I quickly fished my photo album from my pocket and showed him several pictures. Mohib flipped through the book and pointed to me and some of the Afghans he might know. A look of recognition came over Khairo Jan's face and he smiled broadly. He said he did remember me and that I had been his first American friend. He grasped my hand with both of his and spoke quickly to Mohib. Mohib said that Khairo Jan had wondered what had happened to me all these years, and he inquired about my family. I told him my parents were well. He then said that I must have dinner with him as his guest at the governor's compound, which was where he stayed when he was in town. I readily agreed. He then said he had much to discuss with me about events in the province and that my knowledge of the area was so invaluable. I was humbled by his comments. I told him I would be honored to have dinner with him and asked that he pass the information to Mohib, who would get it to me. He readily agreed.

Three days later I made my way back to the governor's compound with Robert Wright, the executive officer of SOTF-SE, and a small force protection detail to have dinner with Haji Khairo Jan and Mohammed Hanif. The late spring heat was now constant even as we arrived in the early evening.

Khairo Jan met us as we approached the governor's office and guided us into a small antechamber for refreshments as the food was being prepared. We settled into the plush chairs, and a buzzing fluorescent light kept the darkness at bay. I asked him about his family and his health and inquired if his daughter was doing well since she had been married in 2005. He was pleased that I remembered and said his daughter was doing well. He then asked if I was married as well and innocently wondered why I hadn't married yet. I said I was too busy helping Afghanistan to settle down just yet. He smiled. We eventually went upstairs to a larger meeting room and sat on dark red pillows that lined the walls as our food was brought out on small plates. The usual Afghan fare was present with baked chicken breasts and legs, small skewers with lamb kebabs, French fries, the traditional rice and bread, and pear slices. Once we had had our fill the conversation turned to politics. Both men were now senior advisors to Governor Shirzad after being defeated for re-election in 2010.

With Governor Jan Mohammed Khan out of office and thus unable to use his position to influence the vote, and the United States taking a back seat to the Afghans as they led the elections process, both men found it hard to get re-elected as other Afghan leaders used their influence to win office.

Both men were interested in sharing with us their perspective on local politics, the security situation, and Taliban influence in the government. They felt that security had significantly improved in the area but that the Taliban were waging a low-level campaign of assassination against supporters of the government of Afghanistan. They were interested in working with Coalition Forces to develop a plan to better protect the friends of the government, but they weren't just worried about the Taliban. They each expressed their concern that current Uruzgan Wolesi Jirga member Haji Obaidullah Barakzai was not only corrupt but was under the influence of either the Taliban or Pakistani intelligence. They said he had spread disinformation about the United States in Kabul and deliberately sought to divide the tribes from the government. They both suggested that we should get involved in some manner to address this Taliban influence. Haji Khairo Jan said he was willing to meet again and bring area tribal elders to the SOTF to address the assassination threat as well as the political influence of the Taliban. I asked him if this was the same Obaidullah who had been the district chief of Chora in 2006 when the Taliban had overrun his headquarters.

Khairo Jan quickly responded, "Yes, yes, it is the same man!"

I then said, "If I remember correctly, wasn't he arrested for collaborating with the Taliban by the governor?"

Khairo Jan nodded his head quickly. "You are right. You do remember!"

I then asked, "Do you feel he is behind these murders?"

Khairo Jan became quiet and cast a quick glance at the Afghan servers. "We cannot talk now but we must talk about this again."

I told him I understood. We talked about how much the province had changed and the upcoming Afghan and U.S. presidential elections. It was clear that the threat to the government did not just come from outside it but from within it as well. Wright and I posed for pictures with both men (a practice I had fallen into because so many of these officials tended to get killed) and we both departed for FOB Ripley.

The next day I was sitting in on one of the interminable video-teleconferences that seemed to dominate our days when Mike Hayes poked his head into the room. After finding me, he gestured for me to come outside. I quickly excused myself and walked into the hallway. The executive officer was there and another sailor and Mike looked at me directly.

"Haji Khairo Jan was just assassinated."

"Whaaat?" I responded, a sense of dread descending upon me.

"He was killed just outside Ripley by an explosion that destroyed his vehicle."

"Where?" I uttered.

"He was in a police vehicle and was driving on the paved road outside our wire when they briefly crossed over an unpaved section. The IED must have been remote controlled and it killed him, another tribal elder, and three policemen."

I muttered, "I can't believe it," as a sense of despondency welled up inside me. "Is this the road that passes right by the guard tower?" I asked.

Mike responded, "I believe it is and we're trying to see if we have any footage of the IED emplacement or the explosion."

I thanked him for telling me, and before they left I asked, "What's going to happen to the bodies?"

Mike said, "The bodies are being prepared for burial, and since the policemen were from northern Afghanistan we will have to find a way to get them home. I believe Khairo Jan will be buried in his village along with the other elder." I nodded my head in understanding.

It was a devastating blow to Haji Khairo Jan's family, and I felt numb for the next few days. I was just so sick of the score settling, blood feuds, and power plays that motivated the perpetrators of these kinds of attacks, and I missed tranquility. I was determined to do what I could to find Haji Khairo Jan's killer. To everyone at the base, he was simply another faceless Afghan killed in the constant drumbeat of death; to me, he was a dear friend.

A few days later, Major Bradley and I met with Haji Khairo Jan's partner, Mohammed Hanif Khan, at our base. Hanif said he didn't specifically know who killed Haji Khairo Jan but felt that since Matullah Khan had not extended a security detail to him and the murder had taken place near Matullah's home that he was likely involved in some manner. He then confirmed a rumor we had heard that Omar Shirzad, the well-meaning but largely undercut governor of Uruzgan, was going to be replaced with another outsider named Amir Mohammed Akunzada. Amir was a former deputy governor of Helmand Province to our west and had also served as a district chief there at some point. He went on to say that he did not know the new governor personally but had worked closely with his brother, Sher Mohammed Akunzada, in Parliament and thought well of him. He did say, however, that Amir was not well-educated and would not govern the province as effectively as Governor Shirzad. Finally, he said he planned to stay in Uruzgan for the change of leadership ceremony at the governor's compound but planned to move back to Kabul with his family for his and their safety. Hanif did mention that he would be willing to advise the new governor if he wanted him to.

It was clear to me that since Khairo Jan was such a significant and influential tribal elder, Matullah had ordered him killed to weaken the governor politically, to send him a message, and to further consolidate his hold on the Populzai tribe. Khairo Jan's family buried him in his home village south of Ripley and then left for Kabul. The three policemen were eventually brought to our base in simple wooden coffins and placed in one of our refrigerator shipping containers that we typically used for food. After going back and forth with our higher command, we eventually prevailed upon them to allow us to fly the coffins to northern Afghanistan. Late one evening Mike and I and a few volunteers transported the bodies into vehicles for the short ride to the flight line. A C-130 cargo plane eventually landed, and a work detail carefully lifted each coffin into the rear of the plane. Mike and I also greeted the friends of the deceased policemen as they carried their belongings in simple knapsacks for the journey. All of them were either Uzbek, Hazaran, or Tajik and were not from Uruzgan.

I've always felt that Haji Khairo Jan had been lured from the governor's compound, where he had benefited from the security detail there, with the promise of police protection. That the men in his security detail were not local likely assured him he would be safe since they had no stake in the political conflicts of the province. It was easy to see him depart the compound since there was only really one road out and they had to go by several different police checkpoints. Matullah likely knew that Khairo Jan would be visiting his home village, and the most convenient route there was the paved road that went by our base as well as by the police chief's home. The IED had to have been placed by police forces or some other government entity since the site was within sight of our guard towers and anyone other than the police would have raised red flags. I wouldn't put it past the Afghan guards there to have been bribed. I've always had a dim view of Matullah from his militia days, but as security improved in the province and his own power increased, he still used the militia to gain power, this time by consolidating his hold on his tribe and getting a governor to his liking. It was a time of great political intrigue and the Afghan people suffered because of it.

A few days later, Mike and I met with Haji Obaidullah Barakzai, one of Uruzgan Province's two male members of Parliament in the Wolesi Jirga, the lower house of the legislative assembly. We met at the Afghan commando's compound, which was near FOB Ripley. Obaidullah had been elected in 2010 and his predecessor, Mohammed Hashim Watanwall, had been assassinated in Kabul in 2011 when visiting his friend former governor Jan Mohammed Khan. I knew Obaidullah's background and was well-acquainted with his savage and incompetent record of leadership. Besides having lost the district of Chora to the Taliban in 2006 when he was district chief, he had previously been in charge of Uruzgan's easternmost district called Khas Uruzgan. He had been involved in a nefarious assassination plot there himself in 2004 and had reportedly ordered the killing of a man who had been running a nongovernmental organization he wanted to control. The man's wife, Hilla, was quite close to the Provincial Reconstruction Team when I was there, and we did what we could to help her situation, but she constantly lived in fear for her life and those of her children. Interestingly, Hilla was elected to Parliament in 2010 as well, so she had more power to do something about her situation and a platform to make her case known. But she also had to suffer the indignity of serving alongside her husband's supposed killer.

With the killing of the well-respected leader of the Barakzai tribe, Rozi Khan, in 2008, the assassination of his first son in 2011 after he had been appointed district chief of Chora in his stead, and the marginalization of his second son Khoshal, the rise of Obaidullah was an interesting development. Since he was a member of Rozi Khan's tribe, one would think he would defer to Khoshal, despite his being a much younger man than Obaidullah, but this was not the case. The leadership of the Barakzai tribe was in turmoil, which was what the Populzai tribe and Matullah, as its local leader, wanted. Obaidullah was only too ready to be supported by Matullah in his quest for power, and now with the influence that came from being a member of Parliament, he was making sure the sons of Rozi Khan never rose up again. I briefed Mike on this sordid history so he would be ready for this quick meeting. We met in a small meeting room in the commando's headquarters, and a small retinue of aides followed Obaidullah as he entered the room. He struck me as an ebullient man, but his eyes betrayed his calculating nature. He was all of five feet four and had a shock of black hair and a pitch black beard. His preference for the ubiquitous black turban of the Barakzai tribe stood in marked contrast to his white garb, and his dark gray vest completed the look. He shook all of our hands and gestured for us to take a seat while his aide filmed us, necessary evidence of his clear power and influence. We all took a seat and Mike let him have it.

"I took this meeting out of respect for your position, but your past record raises more questions for me than answers."

Obaidullah sat silently.

"Special Forces will only work with people who are committed to fighting the Taliban and your past history suggests you might not be a good partner."

Obaidullah squirmed in his chair as Mike's full six-foot-four frame and determined gaze had the intimidating effect he desired. "We will only work with you if you help us find the Taliban and strengthen the government."

Obaidullah slowly nodded and thanked us for meeting. It was clear he was nervous, and he regaled us with stories of the many Americans he had worked with over the years. It was the usual bluster of a politician.

He then said he was principally interested in expanding the Afghan Local Police program in Chora District, with a particular emphasis on six villages in the Barakzai tribal area. He felt that there were too many ALP in Gizab District and that if we were interested in expanding the program to his recommended areas, he would visit Uruzgan from Kabul and facilitate contacts with insurgent groups. He would help us if we helped him. Additionally, if we expanded the Afghan Local Police program to the villages he suggested, he would get credit with the Barakzai tribe for delivering necessary jobs to the area.

Mike then began speaking. "I appreciate your offer but we must build trust if we are to work together. We want insurgents to give up and join the government. If you provide us with the contact information for insurgent leaders in Uruzgan we can then talk about expanding the ALP."

Obaidullah nodded again and said, "I will see what I can find out. Chora is a dangerous place and information is hard to get."

"Yes, but my men are up there and fight the Taliban every day," Mike responded. "The people know where the Taliban are and I know you know where they are as well."

Obaidullah then said, "I will do what I can."

"I'm sure you will." The meeting concluded and we headed out.

We heard that Matullah was at the base getting a medical checkup, so we caught up to him as he was leaving. He told us he had some leads about who had killed Haji Khairo Jan and was following up on them. We never found out who the killers were.

Over the course of my five deployments to Afghanistan and Iraq I've worked with a number of local government, tribal, military, and police officials in the furtherance of our good governance, development, reconstruction, and security goals. Unfortunately, too many have had attempts made on their lives and some, tragically, have been killed. Haji Khairo Jan's death was only the latest in a long line of deaths of officials I had worked alongside. While insurgents often used assassination as a tool of terror, it was also common for various Afghan and Iraqi groups to use it to seize power, destabilize a tribe, send a message, and or settle a vendetta. Many of those killed were going to or coming home from praying at a mosque or from meetings with Coalition Forces. Some were killed at their homes, some on the street in Kabul or Fallujah, others at or near the mosques where they prayed.

Some officials had an amazing amount of luck at escaping death. One of those was Mullah Hamdullah, the head of the Haj and Religious Affairs Directorate in Uruzgan Province, who had had at least seven attempts made on his life. He had been shot a number of times over the years and even had his minbar at his mosque blow up, but he endured.

Taj Mohammed, a judge in Uruzgan, had been killed by an improvised explosive device as he took off his shoes at the entrance to the mosque where he was about to pray. He had been killed by his son, who had joined the Taliban. Others had been killed when someone had used the ruse of friendship or compassion to shoot them, such as Daoud Khan, Rozi Khan's son, who was killed by a friend at his home. Even former Uruzgan governor Jan Mohammed Khan was killed at his home in Kabul along with former member of Parliament Mohammed Hashim Watanwall by two visiting youths from the province asking for charity. Since so much of counterinsurgency work requires working alongside locals and developing a sympathetic understanding of their concerns, these killings could be quite demoralizing for our soldiers, sailors, airmen, and Marines. In some cases, it felt as if you had lost a friend, and because so many of them were involved in building a new future for their country it could also be emotionally debilitating. Below is a list of officials I have worked with in Afghanistan and Iraq who have had attempts made on their lives or who have been killed.

✦

As political infighting increased and rumors about the governor's imminent departure began to look more like a fact, Mike and I met with one of Governor Shirzad's aides, who had requested the meeting and who was also the governor's nephew. We had made a point of reaching out to the governor to express our support for him, so in many respects this meeting was not unexpected. We had heard that a man named Amir Mohammed Akunzada had been selected as governor but we didn't really

Afghans	Position	Method	Lived?
Jan Mohammed Khan	Governor	Shot	No
Mohammed Hashim Watanwall	Member of Parliament	Shot	No
Taj Mohammed	Judge	IED	No
Dr. Abdul Baki	Provincial Shura	Shot	No
Daoud Khan	Tribal leader	Shot	No
Haji Khairo Jan	Member of Parliament	IED	No
Matullah Khan	Provincial chief of police	Shot	No
Mullah Hamdullah	Haj and Religious Affairs	Shot	Yes
Mir Ahmad	Provincial Shura	Shot	No
Haji Mohammad Wali	Provincial Council candidate	Shot	No
Atiqullah Khan	Provincial Council candidate	Shot	No
Iraqis			
Sheik Sami Abdul Amir al-Jumayli	Fallujah City Council chair	Shot	No
Hikmat	Fallujah City Council	Shot	No
Sheik Aifan Saddun al-Issawi	Tribal leader	Suicide vest	No

know until it actually happened. The aide wanted to address the rumors of corruption swirling around the governor, which centered on mishandled condolence money and reintegration payments for encouraging members of the Taliban to join the government. He said the charges were untrue and asked for us to intervene in the dispute. We told him we could not and that the Afghan political and judicial system had to address these problems. We told him we still supported the governor but had to remain neutral. The aide then requested that if Shirzad was going to be removed as governor that he be allowed to continue to govern for three additional months, if only to deny Matullah the satisfaction of having initiated the removal. We told him we would support whoever provided stability to the province and had the support of the people. The aide then said that the rumors were that a Hazaran man from Dai Kundi Province who was close to Matullah might be selected as governor. We asked the aide for the man's name but he didn't know it.

The political intrigue that revolved around officials using their contacts in Kabul to disrupt local governance was just one more example of how a highly centralized government could meddle in affairs that rightfully should be decided at the ballot box by local villagers. Our report that evening indicated our concerns and these were the most relevant passages:

> While these corruption charges are being addressed within the Afghan system, discussion of replacing Shirzad with a Hazaran outsider from Dai Kundi Province could be disruptive to counter-insurgency operations in Uruzgan. The destabilizing effect of naming a Hazaran governor to the largely Pashtun province would not only likely make him ineffective, but would also make him largely dependent on Matullah, upsetting a delicate balance between factions in the area that has promoted stability. Additionally, while the merit of the corruption charges is difficult to judge, there is a long-standing pattern in Uruzgan of outsider governors being undermined by officials with strong local ties such as Matullah and his uncle, the deceased former Governor Jan Mohammed Khan. While the Afghan political system will reach some conclusion to this controversy, I think it is important to consider a few points.
>
> 1. Any charges of corruption should be promptly dealt with and the rule of law should be strictly followed. Political trials of malfeasance undermine stability.
>
> 2. If Governor Shirzad is removed, a popularly supported replacement must immediately be named. When Governor Hamdam was removed in 2010, for example, it took approximately nine months for his replacement to be named.
>
> 3. A system of checks and balances between political leaders in Uruzgan promotes stability and a weak replacement governor could undermine good governance in the area.

4. A change in leadership may lead to other resignations in the provincial government that could further destabilize the province. The head of the Provincial Council, Haji Ibrahim Akunzada, has already threatened to resign if the governor is removed.

5. Changing the governor at the beginning of the fighting season may be disruptive to area stability.

I hoped for the best and wanted to have a governor who was effective, qualified, and got along with Matullah, but still represented the people. Only time would tell if that happened.

EIGHT

Spreading the Faith

It's the people in the end. That's the critical thing of the whole business.

—Gen. Creighton Abrams, U.S. Army.
Quoted in Lewis Sorley, *A Better War:
The Unexamined Victories and Final
Tragedy of America's Last Years in Vietnam*

Even though the Village Stability Operations approach had gained wide support from village elders across Uruzgan Province, there were still areas where it was struggling to gain traction with the local population. One of our teams in the western district of Shahid-e-Hasas was having a great deal of difficulty convincing the elders to support the Afghan Local Police program, and so Mike decided we needed to take Matullah there to convince the elders of the merits of the initiative. I was very interested in seeing how Matullah, a man I had long regarded as more of a threat to stability (at least long-term stability) than a source of it, would interact with the population. The Village Stability Platform we were going to visit, called Khod, was perched on a cliff overlooking a meandering river across from one of twenty villages in the area. The villagers came from five different tribes that were mostly along the riverbanks, although mountains carved them into separate communities. Even though it was still winter you could tell that the valley could be quite lush in the spring, and, although this was to the good fortune of the villagers, the area was also a key infiltration route for the Taliban.

They typically made their way south into Uruzgan after traversing up the Bagran Valley in Helmand Province, entering into Kajran District to the north in Dai Kundi Province, and then down past Khod into Uruzgan proper. The Special Forces team at Khod had struggled mightily to get even one villager to join the Afghan Local Police, but locals were reluctant to volunteer because of the persistent threat of the Taliban, tribal politics, and perhaps the location of the team, which was away from the population. As we prepared to depart Tarin Kowt en route to the northwest area of the province on April 11, I was curious to see this part of Uruzgan I had only seen from helicopters and to witness how Matullah the police chief differed from Matullah the militia leader.

As our Blackhawk helicopters approached the village of Khod, I made out the distinct pattern of Hesco walls surrounding the edge of Village Stability Platform Khod, perched along the upper banks of the main river on a desert plateau. We were to the north of Forward Operating Base Cobra in the district of Shahid-e-Hasas along one of the main river valleys that eventually fed into the great Helmand River to the south. Khod was one of four stability platforms in the area all supported by Cobra, but it was the newest site, having been erected in the previous six months. It was much more mountainous here compared to Tarin Kowt, which sat at the bottom of a desert bowl and was dominated by brown and khaki-colored sand. Closer to the mountains, a kaleidoscope of natural colors dotted the landscape as different rock formations with their distinctive chemical configurations created a hodge-podge of various reds, dark greens, blacks, oranges, and yellows sprinkled throughout the valley. Even though the farmers' fields at this elevation were still barren, it was clear that the valley was naturally quite green since every piece of arable land had already been laid out in grids for planting by local farmers. Like many of our VSP sites, Khod was situated in a rented Afghan compound of adobe set out in a rough rectangle. A number of security improvements had been added, including an exterior Hesco wall, mortar pit, razor wire, a variety of crew-served weapon firing positions, and numerous cameras. The men lived in two makeshift wooden buildings that looked like trailer park homes that we often referred to as "plywood palaces." The isolated nature of the base meant that all its supplies were delivered by air, and so a great heaping mound of parachutes sat just outside the external perimeter. The packages from the planes were called, in keeping with military terminology, containerized delivery systems (CDSs). These boxes carried everything (bullets, food, water, firewood, and spare parts) and they were a lifeline for our isolated and austere bases. Some of the CDS drops would be configured for fuel and so sometimes a pallet of four fifty-gallon drums of fuel would be airdropped as well; it made quite a mess when they landed poorly!

Once the helicopters landed, Mike, Matullah, Major Jacobs, and I approached VSP Khod, the cooler mountain air a welcome contrast to Tarin Kowt, and quickly met Captain Williams, the commanding officer of the site. Williams guided our group to the front gate and said that a number of elders from the area had arrived, some of them from quite a distance, and were eager to meet with Matullah. He then said he and his men had organized a shura with about thirty elders and that they had managed to recruit five ALP in the past week, which was encouraging. The elders were standing to the side as we approached, and Matullah and his aide broke off to meet each man. They all had black turbans and were very dark from working in the sun all the time. They were clearly men of bearing and their wizened features and well-groomed gray-and-white beards indicated their standing in the community. Williams explained to us that they had held countless meetings with these men but had not been able to make any inroads despite the recent success of the five new ALP recruits. He was not optimistic, but I knew Matullah could be persuasive, and he had thus far been supportive of our efforts. We finally entered the wide-open center of the Afghan compound and staked out a corner of the dirt ground. Several gray plastic parachutes were brought out as matting for the meeting, and a series of multicolored blankets and pillows were arranged around the edge of the chute in a square pattern. Matullah and his aide sat in the corner and the men sat in a circle along its edges. This was going to be the classic battle of wits and wills between the Afghan leaders. Mike and I and an interpreter sat nearby while Jacobs and Williams sat toward the front. The shura was a traditional meeting of

Afghan villagers and in a way served as a rough form of democracy, akin to a town hall meeting. All men were eligible to speak and it was common practice to seek accommodation between different groups so that some sort of consensus could be reached. At countless meetings like this around Afghanistan the future of the country was being decided.

Matullah began the meeting by addressing the village elders in a more than frank manner. "I am happy to see you after four years and I'm here to solve your problems."

Villager: "We are happy you are here but we have not seen the government for five years. No one wants to be the first to join the ALP, but we will follow what you decide."

Matullah: "It is the same problems for the last thirty-five years. If you provide security you will have clinics, schools, bridges, and work from the government. You will see development. The Americans want to bring security but they will not stay here forever. The U.S. commandos want to bring security but you don't want it. You should take advantage of their presence."

Villager: "I am happy the U.S. is here and we support them."

Matullah: "Two months ago several men from Khod came to me and told me they wanted Afghan Local Police and would help the U.S. captain. Other Afghans have come here from all over the country to help you and you won't protect yourself [he gestured toward the Afghan security guards]. The Hazarans help you but not the Pashtuns, our own people. They have clinics and schools. You need to help yourself. What do you think?"

Villager: "There are twenty villages here and the biggest village is Khod."

Matullah: "If you give me ten men from each village I will pay for their food, gas, and salaries."

Villager: "The ANSF are good people."

Matullah: "They are here to help Afghanistan and the U.S. needs your help."

Villager: "We are happy you are here!"

Mike: "Special Forces have worked with General Matullah Khan for over ten years. As I travel around Uruzgan I ask myself if this is the best place to use our limited resources. If the people don't want us here we will move. U.S. taxpayers are paying for our salaries and your salaries, our schools and your schools, your roads and our roads. At some point, they will get tired of paying. Young men must volunteer from your villages, to have the honor of standing up for all of Afghanistan. Pakistan wants to keep Afghanistan weak and disabled. If we start with your villages we can work together to join the government. Doing nothing is not an option. As we extend our hand we must have you extend yours to us."

Villager: "The Taliban come from other villages and fight us and we are not happy about it. They put IEDs in front of my house and shoot at the village and then run into the mountains. You should go to their meetings and you will get them. If you talk to the villagers they will tell you where the IEDs are located."

Matullah: "I am happy you told me that the Taliban are doing it because it is then our fault. However, if the Taliban are doing this it is really your fault. You say the Taliban put IEDs near your home and the Taliban are in your village. Are you telling me you don't control your village? You know who they are. You need to show the U.S. where the Taliban are. If there is one Taliban coming from the mountains during the night, the U.S. will shoot them. You are all liars. (Laughter) The Taliban are from your village."

Villager: "We are happy the U.S. is here for the last six months."

Captain Williams: "You know who dug the IEDs, everyone knew it. There were no shuras, no one told us about it. No one came to me today. General Matullah told us you would give us information. Your ears are closed and you are telling lies. Why is Zahir not here?" [His daughter was allegedly sick but this was an important meeting.]

Matullah: "Send a doctor to his home."

Afghan security guard: "We should never come to a shura. All we hear are excuses, lies, and you never tell us about the Taliban. You are always making excuses."

Villager: "We should go to the District Center to talk about ALP."

Matullah: "I'm ashamed of you. The U.S. has been here for six months and you have no clinics or schools and you will have them with security."

Afghan security guard: "The last shura provided five men for the ALP."

Captain Williams: "One village gave up five ALP. Saturday's shura, five guys to Oshay village."

Five Afghan men who had been sitting behind the group then stood up and Williams gestured toward them. Matullah beckoned them over and his assistant unrolled a huge wad of Afghanis (the national currency) and peeled off chunks of it for each man. They walked as a small group to his side while he remained seated and took the cash as he pressed it into their hands. It was an impressive display of power and patronage, used as much for its theatrics as its practical effects.

Matullah: "I will give you one more chance or I will bring my men but I am not responsible for the damages. Then it will be no problem for the U.S."

Villager: "We don't want other men, Hazarans, etc. . . . ."

Matullah: "I will meet with the elders at the District Center in ten days. I will make sure the road is safe and will pay for the gas for men who will join the ALP. It is easy money to make instead of going to Pakistan and Iran."

Villager: "Two men were killed going on that road to Oshay. There are no other men coming from the villages. Need to secure road to Oshay."

Matullah: "Hazarans protect this road, are they better than you?"

Captain Williams: "Checkpoints on the road have created security. The village of Shakana has already given up ALP."

Matullah: "I will bring the regular police. If you provide ALP I will construct the checkpoints. We have had shuras for six months. We must have action now. We can't pressure the people to join ALP. I will bring my own men and the ANSF."

Villager: "Bring Wali Dad [district chief of police]."

Matullah: "Good."

The meeting finally concluded and Williams guided Matullah over to a pile of bundled parachutes that had been brought in and several bags of grain and other foodstuffs. With our cameraman in tow, Matullah handed each new ALP recruit a bag of food, spoke to him a bit, and gestured for him to choose a parachute. The Afghans loved the parachutes because they were water resistant and could be tailored to fit any structure. They were highly sought after by the villagers, and it was not uncommon to see a parachute stretched out over the roof of an Afghan home to prevent rain from coming in. The men eagerly grabbed the gifts and made their way out. Matullah then walked across the courtyard to meet other villagers who had come to the front gate. The crowd gathered around him as if he were a celebrity, and Matullah engaged them all in conversation, sharing a laugh with some and handing out more wads of cash. He even posed for a number of photos, although no selfies. It was clear that Matullah had reached a new level of importance in the area and even though he was a Populzai, a tribe not highly regarded in this Ghilzai-heavy area, he was respected and even feared.

As the Afghans went about their visit, I wandered around VSP Khod to see what life was like this far forward. Even though the site couldn't be supplied via road, the men were still quite well taken care of at the base. An open-air kitchen had been constructed in the corner of the courtyard, two large stainless steel refrigerators hummed quietly in the corner, and the larder was full of cans and boxes of food. A standing counter had also been constructed for the men to eat at. I then went through an arched gateway that had been built in the adobe wall and saw the village of Khod across the river valley. A number of CDS containers rested in this side area and to my left was a containerized shower system that provided the men modern showers in this austere location. It was pretty amazing to witness. Our group eventually rallied at the burn pit in the central courtyard to put our gear back on and wait for our rides. Matullah finished making the rounds and we all strained to hear the faint sound of the helicopters. The helicopters eventually arrived and as we departed I contemplated what I had witnessed and the challenges Khod faced in recruiting Afghan Local Police.

It was clear that the terrain made it difficult for one team to develop a relationship with each of the valley's twenty different villages. The site was also very new, in contrast to FOB Cobra, which had been in Shahid-e-Hasas district for eight years, and its location on a plateau made it difficult for villagers to visit it or to feel the effects of the security it provided. Additionally, their location astride a major ratline the Taliban used to infiltrate Uruzgan Province made it difficult for villagers to feel truly secure from the insurgency. The team also didn't seem to have many other enablers at the site, such as a psychological operations element and civil affairs team. As we flew back to Tarin Kowt, I filed these observations away as I contemplated how we could measure success in these types of operations more effectively.

Two weeks later a Taliban political agent convinced the five ALP members to join with them, and they torched their checkpoint and gave their guns to the Islamist movement. One step forward, many steps backward.

NINE

Return to a New Beginning

A man who has once been a soldier can never be quite a civilian again. A military experience, especially in time of war, leaves a mark upon a man. If we are to understand the veteran, we must learn what he experiences as a soldier.

—WILLARD WALLER, *The Veteran Comes Back*

The political rumblings that had plagued the local government for weeks about the imminent and then delayed and then possibly deferred departure of Governor Shirzad were finally confirmed when his replacement was announced. His name was Amir Mohammed Akunzada and he was in his mid-thirties and seemed to be full of great ambition and energy. Although not originally from the area, he came from the neighboring province of Helmand and was highly regarded largely due to the bravery and exploits of his father against the Soviets. His arrival as Uruzgan's new governor in 2012 came as bit of a surprise since his prior political experiences in Helmand had been so damning. He had previously served as the district chief of a district in Helmand Province and then as deputy governor of the same province after his brother, who had been appointed governor in 2002, had been removed in 2005 for corruption and brutality. He was barred from running for Parliament due to his ties to militias and then famously was found to be storing several tons of opium in his compound when he was district chief. Following his appointment as a tribal advisor to President Karzai in Kabul his future seemed destined to be on a national stage, but Karzai needed a new governor of Uruzgan who had the support of the people, was connected in Kabul, and was determined to do a good job, which largely meant getting along with Matullah. On April 14, I joined my colleagues for a trip to the governor's compound to attend his formal swearing-in. This would be the fourth governor I had worked with in Uruzgan and the sixth overall since 2001, and I was hopeful he would be a success. We had already had a long line of well-meaning but politically emasculated outsiders attempt to govern the area from 2006 to 2012, so it was not certain how he would be different and whether his term would be a success.

The leadership of the SOTF, including Major Jacobs and his command sergeant major Robert Shaner, journeyed down to the governor's compound in the late morning to attend the festivities. It was a clear day and the winter chill was no longer a concern, and as we entered the inner courtyard of the compound, we saw about three hundred or so Afghans seated in a wide, grassy area next to the governor's office. One side of the governor's building had been converted into a small stage with a podium, and several dozen rows of chairs lined the open area. A large Afghan flag about five feet tall and fifty feet long wrapped the side of the building and the photo of President Karzai that usually sat in the provincial administration meeting room had been hauled out and set above the podium on the wall. A loudspeaker system had been set up and several journalists hovered along the edge of the crowd with their cameras to film the event. Three of Uruzgan's members of Parliament, including Obaidullah, the head of the Provincial Council Haji Ibrahim, Police Chief Matullah Khan, and many other members of the provincial government were in attendance. Outgoing governor Shirzad was notably absent. Since we had arrived a bit late, Governor Akunzada was already on the stage and about to deliver his remarks. My colleagues and I grabbed some plastic chairs on the edge of the crowd, and I snagged an interpreter to help me understand the speeches.

Governor Akunzada was relatively short in stature, about five feet four, and had a generous figure and a bald pate even though he was only in his middle to late thirties. He was a carbon copy of his brother Sher Mohammed Akunzada, who had been governor of Helmand Province from 2001 to 2005. In many ways, his brother was the equivalent of Jan Mohammed Khan for Helmand Province: loyal to Karzai, keen to make a buck, and quite willing to go after the Taliban. As I would later learn, the governor had a quick mind, and his eyes always actively scanned the room even when he engaged people in intense conversation. Akunzada was impatient with the rural pace of governance in Uruzgan and sought to provide the modern leadership the province desperately needed. I hoped he would succeed. He was close to General Matullah Khan and, though they were allies, he was sharply critical of his provincial ways even though they shared many of the same objectives for the area. His supreme goal, however, was to rehabilitate his reputation in the eyes of the international community, to demonstrate to them that he was an able public servant who could produce results in even the most backwater province and that he should return to the center stage of national politics. His own history was a great indictment of his character and abilities, but it was difficult to find many Afghans who didn't have some skeletons in their closets. Often those who were most effective had the greatest number of questionable episodes in their past. Conversely, those who had the cleanest backgrounds and thus were most amenable to the international community were frequently the least effective. I looked forward to seeing how Governor Akunzada would execute his duties.

The governor was already at the podium and began to speak.

> It is a new time for Afghanistan. We must build this province, we must work together, and I need your support. As brothers, students, scholars, and elders we must come together and all tribes must be brothers to each other. It is time for our independence. Haji Khairo Jan sacrificed his life for our country and we all want what he wanted, an independent and proud country. We are here to serve and prosper together. We are close friends of the military and we must stick with them. Thanks to the U.S. and Australia for their hard work for this province and we must continue to support and care for their people. They are our guests. We deeply appreciate their help and sacrifice. We must always remember the poor people and we request your help in building education and bringing development to our province. We must also help the widows and the children. We must build stability here and it is not hard if the

people support their government. We have a deep respect for the people and I ask your help in building the government. I ask the Taliban to join the peace program and I ask all scholars and mullahs to talk to the Taliban and teach them the path of peace. We must all work hard to bring progress to our province. We must bring computers here and talented people so that we do not stay behind the other provinces and our country does not stay behind other countries. We appreciate all the help of the foreign advisors as well and welcome their support. President Karzai sent me here to serve and to help you. I will do my best and, from when I was a young boy, I have always had good memories of Uruzgan. I humbly ask for your help and assistance, I need it, and I pray for Uruzgan.

His speech was well-delivered and had the usual Afghan tone of deference and humility, and I appreciated his mention of Khairo Jan. He seemed to have the drive and the energy to do what was right, and the fact that Matullah sat just behind him conveyed Matullah's support for him and, quite possibly, suggested a new era of cooperation in the province. Other Afghan officials soon followed with their remarks.

One of the province's senators began:

We need to work together to build the province. We all know the governor well and he is a good person. His family was involved in the jihad. Governor Shirzad helped a lot and we have more students going to Kabul, all because of his attention and support. We are hoping for the best and we want a good and peaceful province. I will not talk too long. All of Uruzgan are our brothers and we will help the new governor. If we do not help the people we cannot build our hometown. If we have the support of the tribes and the tribal elders we can build this province. We have lots of support for the new governor in Parliament and we must continue to work closely with the security forces.

Senator Obaidullah then followed:

The people of this province fought against communism but this province continues to be poor. Too many of our young students are studying in Pakistan and we must improve education so that they stay here and study in Afghan schools. The new governor is a good man and the president wants to make sure the tribal elders, the provincial government, and the parliament work together for the people. We are here to support you and to bring stability to our community.

The third senator for the province then spoke:

I have known Governor Akunzada a long time and he was here fighting the communists and fighting for the jihad. He is close to God, honest and good, and is not materialistic. He is knowledgeable and talented. If you don't pay attention to and respect the people then God will judge you. We must have honesty and brotherhood. If we are together we are strong. We should follow the Qur'an and seek to improve our lives and educate our children. One brother will not kill another brother.

It was clear that the governor's time in Kabul had been well spent and he had the clear support of most of the senators from Uruzgan. The head of the Provincial Council, a man named Haji Ibrahim whom I had known from 2005 when he had been a district chief of police, then spoke: "I want to welcome everyone and ask that you support the new governor. The Provincial Council will share with him your views and we must bring unity between Uruzgan's leaders." The final speaker was Mullah Hamdullah, a man I knew well from 2005–6, and he began with a prayer. He then turned to his brief remarks: "We have to do everything based on rules and laws. We will face a good or a bad judgment on doomsday. If you do bad you will be badly judged. I want to compliment the new governor as he takes on these new responsibilities." With the speeches over, the crowd dispersed, and several guests of the new governor stayed behind to partake of lunch. It was notable that Matullah walked into the governor's compound to meet with Akunzada. It was certainly a good sign that the provincial government was going to be working better, although one wondered what other things they plotted.

I had long wanted to reconnect with Mullah Hamdullah since our first association in 2005–6. At that time, he had been elected head of the Provincial Shura, an association of tribal elders from around the province, and had also served as a local mullah, or religious leader, in the Tarin Kowt area. He was a close confidant of then governor Jan Mohammed

Khan, and even though he was from the Barakzai tribe, a tribe often in opposition to the governor's Populzai tribe, he was a friend of the governor since they had both fought alongside each other against the Soviets. He was a constant schemer and always seemed to end up on the right side of power. The day before his death, Khairo Jan had related to me an interesting story of Hamdullah from 2001. At that time, Karzai was with his tribal supporters trying to launch an uprising against the Taliban regime. He and his men, including Khairo Jan, were across the river in the Deh Rawud District when the Taliban arrived along with Mullah Hamdullah. Once they had been seen, Hamdullah yelled at the men from across the river, telling them that all their marriages were void since they had sided against the Taliban and their wives were now eligible to be married by members of the Islamist group. It was a curious story since several years later Hamdullah was one of our key contacts in the local government and had actually secured an all-expense paid trip to the United States with the State Department as an international visitor where he had gotten to meet several high-level American officials.

Prior to the U.S. invasion of Afghanistan, Hamdullah had served as a Taliban judge for a number of years before resigning, so he told me, two years before the United States invaded. Hamdullah was eventually elected to the Provincial Council in 2005 but resigned three years later after he and then governor Asadullah Hamdam had gotten into a political dispute. Hamdullah had allegedly slapped a young man over an insult, and to avoid time in jail he had resigned his position. As time went on, he was appointed the director of Haj and religious affairs for the province and administered the salaries of local mullahs. He also maintained the upkeep of the province's mosques and oversaw the lottery to attend the Haj in Saudi Arabia. He and Governor Shirzad were at odds with each other, with the governor accusing him of taking bribes from would-be pilgrims keen to go to Mecca. The fact that he finished Akunzada's inauguration with a prayer and a speech was a clear sign he was back in the fold of provincial power.

In late March I finally had a chance to catch up with Mullah Hamdullah. Mohib once again kindly translated for me. Mullah Malawi

Hamdullah was in his sixties, stood at five feet six, and, as always, was full of energy and intrigue. He always wore a black turban, which was quite common among the Barakzai tribesmen, and his face was ringed with a rich, black beard. His eyes were lined with black khol (a kind of eyeliner popular with the Taliban), and his expressive smile and welcoming demeanor reflected his religious training and secure status in the community. He was sometimes referred to by members of the U.S. forces as the "black mullah." I picked Hamdullah up at the front gate and as we journeyed to FOB Ripley I asked about his health, since I had heard he had recently been shot. He quickly recounted the story of how he had been chased out of his mosque in August 2011 by a man who began shooting at him, eventually hitting him in the thigh. At this point, he hiked up his pant leg and showed me the small scar on his thigh. "What happened next?" I hurriedly asked. He said that the shot had knocked him to the ground and the assassin stood over him but his weapon jammed, which prevented his murder. Hamdullah then related that there had been seven different attempts made on his life. The most notable attempt was when the podium at his mosque exploded but, according to him, miraculously missed damaging the Qur'an. He said, "It was God's will." I asked him how he felt about all of these attempts on his life. "When it is your time, it is your time," he replied.

I began our meeting by jogging his memory about the last time I had been in the province, and I showed him the same photo album I had showed Haji Khairo Jan. He seemed to recognize me but I wasn't sure, so I continued the conversation. I started by asking him why Governor Shirzad and Matullah had not gotten along. He replied that things had started off well between the two men, but their first disagreement surrounded whether prisoners Matullah was capturing were Taliban or not. Matullah wasn't police chief at the time. He was commander of the Afghan Highway Police, but due to the tribal tensions in the province the governor was probably responding to complaints he had received that Matullah was, as always, focusing his "security" efforts on his tribal opponents.

Following the killing of Osama bin Laden on May 2, 2011, a complicated attack was mounted in downtown Tarin Kowt on July 28, 2011, targeting the governor's compound. That such a large attack could take place forced the government of Afghanistan to replace the provincial police chief. Matullah was appointed the new provincial chief of police the next month. Now that he had the highest and most secure local position one could have in security, the tensions between the two men continued and now revolved around issues of corruption, leadership, and, as always, power. It was a familiar story of tension in Uruzgan between an outside governor and the local police chief. A key problem was that the provincial chief of police position did not directly answer to the governor, which inevitably led to tensions. Positive command was replaced with poor coordination.

I asked him what he thought of Governor Akunzada and whether he would get along with Matullah. He said that Akunzada and Matullah had known each other for many years and that their families had known each other even longer. In some respects, I sensed that because both men were in their thirties they had much more in common with each other than did the generationally disconnected Shirzad and Matullah. More cynically, they also had long-standing connections due to ongoing business associations and shared common economic interests. Mullah Hamdullah said that the governor was an honest man and had the support of the people and would work well with Matullah. It certainly seemed encouraging, and with Hamdullah back in the political game I'm sure he was quite pleased with the outcome.

With Governor Shirzad out of the picture and the impending investigation into impropriety in his management of the Haj and Religious Affairs Directorate likely terminated, Hamdullah's political future was as bright as ever. I then asked him about Haji Khairo Jan's killing, and he turned somber and looked down for a brief moment. He expressed genuine sorrow for his death and praised him as a man focused on building Uruzgan. I asked him if he knew who had killed him and he said he did not. Who really knew, I wondered, and would they ever talk? After catching up on a few other topics, our conversation ended. I showed him his picture in *The Valley's Edge* and he seemed genuinely pleased with being included. I walked him to our car and escorted him to the front gate. I thanked him again for coming to the base to visit, and as I watched him walk away I knew I would never see this colorful character again.

TEN

The Western Frontier

Frontier areas are always good places for bandits. If they see the police approaching from one side they can always step across the frontier into the other country.

—JOHN BAGOT GLUBB, *The Story of the Arab Legion*

The great western edge of Uruzgan had long been considered a wild and perhaps untamable land that, through a combination of the then ungoverned Helmand Province to its west, a series of rivers to its east, and the jagged mountain ranges of the Hindu Kush to its north, had created an almost impenetrable safe haven the Taliban had long used to their advantage. Although I had visited the area twice when I had worked in Uruzgan in 2005, they were both limited trips, and I had never crossed over the river into "Taliban country," so when the opportunity came to visit our bases there with Major Jacobs, I jumped at the chance. I had heard that great things had taken place in the area, in part due to the expansion of Village Stability Operations to the region, and also due to the construction of three bridges across the main rivers there. Due to these efforts, a series of checkpoints manned by Afghan Local Police had been built to protect the bridges and main roads as well as the communities. They had been performing quite well as the villagers there embraced the local police. I was curious too about the police chiefs in Deh Rawud and Shahid-e-Hasas Districts, who had been getting rave reviews for their work and were considered competent and able public servants. It had been uncommon to hear any such praise about an Afghan leader in 2005–6 so my curiosity was piqued. As I prepared for the trip, I couldn't believe I would be visiting this obscure part of the province again after it had been buried in my brain for so many years. So many Americans had died there in its isolated valleys where so much fighting, year after grinding year, had taken place. It was also good to escape the political intrigue of Tarin Kowt.

We departed mid-morning from Tarin Kowt aboard Blackhawk helicopters en route to Forward Operating Base Tycz in Deh Rawud District. The helicopters churned forward in a westerly direction after taking off from Ripley and quickly passed over the provincial capital. Spring was now in season and the verdant Tarin Kowt Valley was full of lush green fields, with the farmers actively cultivating their plots. As the helicopters rose in elevation, the spartan brown and mottled gray peaks of the mountains came into view, their sun-blasted and jagged precipices barren from the glaring heat. We followed a valley that cut through the mountains, which had a modest-sized creek winding its way westward as well, eventually flowing into a series of waterways that led to the Helmand River. The mountains dwarfed our "birds," as the helicopters were often referred to, and as soon as we left the mountain range the full expanse of the neighboring valley presented itself. It too was enclosed by a far-off mountain, but the large green belt of cultivated land in its center was enormous, much larger than Tarin Kowt's. It stretched far to the left and right, disappearing into the mountains along a spiderweb of waterways. The combination of several rivers and creeks and various mountain ranges intersecting near the center of Deh Rawud District created a rich alluvial plain and a vital agricultural area for the province. For this reason alone it was the major poppy-producing area of Uruzgan and thus a major source of revenue for the Taliban as much as for government officials. As we approached the eastern edge of this "vegetable emerald," the familiar outline of Firebase Tycz, perched on the edge of the desert and the beginning of the farm belt, presented itself.[1]

The base was the first enduring presence U.S. forces had in Uruzgan. It had been constructed in the summer of 2002 following an unfortunate bombing of a wedding party by U.S. planes in the province on July 1,

2002. This particular episode is detailed in the 2005 book *Hunting al-Qaeda* by Gerald Schumacher. It was thought that a permanent U.S. presence would prevent future mishaps and that a locally based unit could build more bridges, literally and figuratively, to a community than a periodic direct-action raid or kinetic strike. That many senior Taliban leaders also came from the district also informed the decision to build the base. The forward operating base was named "Tycz" after a Third Special Forces Medical Unit soldier, Sgt. 1st Class Peter P. Tycz II, who died on June 12, 2002, on board a U.S. military plane that had crashed in Afghanistan. As the first Coalition Forces base in Uruzgan, it had an unusual design in that it was the only base for many years that had been built solely by U.S. Special Forces. In practice this meant that it had a relaxed and informal style to it. It had been built to resist assaults by insurgent forces, so it had several concentric circles of defense, and because it was so old, it had a haphazard style to it as well. While it was difficult to determine precisely, I figured that probably more than twenty-five military units, mostly Special Forces units and a few conventional, had rotated through the base. Each unit had left its own unique mark on the place, a building constructed here, a mural painted there, or some other improvement, which gave the place a weird mishmash style where doors opened into dead ends, parts of the base had been abandoned, and broken facilities were left to rot as new ones were built. The building motif created an unusual feeling of a complete lack of planning or, using current parlance, it was very organic. Additionally, since the base was constructed in the early days of the war, all the construction had been done by local Afghan contractors instead of large American corporations. This added to the timeworn feel of the place, as overengineering, poor quality concrete, and a jumble of different types of building materials made the firebase feel almost like an outgrowth of the terrain.

Added to this milieu was a healthy application of concrete everywhere, used to control flooding and the mud in the spring while it dampened down dust in the summer. A series of concrete towers and Hescos covered in concertina wire ringed the perimeter, and a smaller ring of wooden ones existed as well but had been abandoned, likely the handiwork of an earlier rotation. A ragtag collection of adobe buildings and makeshift concrete dwellings were haphazardly arranged, and vehicles, various supplies, and construction materials had been dumped into different quarters of the base. Although the firebase was always temporary, it had also become an enduring memorial in a way for the men who had died there over the past ten years. In addition to the occasional portrait of a fallen soldier were names and unit insignias scratched into concrete as well as individual makeshift memorials. One in particular from when I was in Uruzgan in 2005 still stood seven years later. It was dedicated to several 25th Infantry soldiers who had died in Deh Rawud (SSgt. Brian S. Hobbs and Spec. Kyle Ka Eo Fernandez, killed on October 14, 2004, and Cpls. Jacob R. Fleischer and Dale E. Fracker Jr., killed on November 24, 2004), and it had a large American flag painted on the memorial wall and two concrete obelisks with the names affixed to metal plates on the top. It was heartening to see the memorial still there but also discouraging to know that the base would eventually be closed and the memories and memorials along with it would disappear into the deep recesses of the minds of those who had served there.

Forward Operating Base Tycz was the headquarters for the Special Forces Advanced Operations Base for Uruzgan Province. It was led by Maj. Ben Jacobs, who then answered to Special Operations Task Force-South East as his higher command. Jacobs was with the 1st Special Forces Group and had invited me to accompany him on a mission from Tycz in Deh Rawud District to Forward Operating Base Tinsley just to the north in the nearby district of Shahid-e-Hasas. It would be an education for me to travel with him around the western edge of Uruzgan. Since we weren't leaving until the next day, I settled into my "plywood palace," as some liked to call it, which was essentially a quickly erected plywood barracks for soldier housing at forward bases. Jacobs' men were a mix of U.S. Army Special Forces soldiers and U.S. Navy SEALs spread out at nine different locations either at forward operating bases or at Village Stability Platform sites. He controlled three SEAL elements and six different U.S. Army teams. His key tasks for the rotation were to continue to expand the numbers of Afghan Local Police in the area, pacify areas still held by the Taliban, and begin

the process of retrograding or transitioning sites to Afghan forces in order
to move his men down to Zabul Province. These goals were consistent
with the guidance Commander Hayes had given, under which we would
continue to expand security in Uruzgan and then look for opportunities to
divest ourselves of the province and invest in Zabul.

While Tycz was the oldest base in Uruzgan, it was not the only one in
Deh Rawud District. To its south about five hundred meters stood another
base called Forward Operating Base Hadrian, originally built by Dutch
military forces in 2006 but controlled by the Australians since 2012. It
was a great symbol of the kind of dysfunctional war that had long been
fought in Afghanistan, especially after North Atlantic Treaty Organization
(NATO) forces assumed greater control of the military campaign.

When NATO forces expanded to southern Afghanistan beginning
in 2005 and then much more extensively in 2006, they seemed to regard
what was referred to as the Operation Enduring Freedom (OEF) mission
as simply "counterterrorism" and not peace keeping. The then widely
held view among many Europeans was that Americans, being Americans,
lacked the subtler methods of working with the Afghan population that
the NATO peace-keeping mission would bring to the fore. Some aspects
of this critique were correct in that early in the war the emphasis was on
tracking down members of al-Qaeda and the Taliban with little regard for
the sentiments of the population. That Provincial Reconstruction Teams,
a tool expressly designed to work with local populations, had come out
of OEF was conveniently forgotten. The problem for the NATO forces
was that when they had evaluated the war in preparation for the deployment of their troops, they had seen the last quiet year of the war, 2005,
and so when they arrived in 2006 and were confronted by a full-blown
insurgency using conventional military tactics, they were caught completely unawares. Because they didn't want to be associated with the OEF
mission and felt their mission was more consistent with European values,
they built a parallel base next to Tycz that was completely self-sufficient.
So we had the unusual situation of having two bases sitting next to each
other in an isolated Afghan district containing members of two allied

militaries fighting the Taliban in their own uncoordinated way, separated by a common mission.

The Special Forces soldiers were similar to the SEALs in terms of mental outlook (aggressive), tactical ability (efficient and lethal), and physical demeanor (agile and tough), but they differed in certain key respects. While both had been established during President John F. Kennedy's administration as part of his "flexible response" strategy to confront the expansion of communism in the developing world, the U.S. Army Special Forces were expressly designed to partner with indigenous forces, mostly foreign armies, in order to meet U.S. goals by, with, and through the governments of other countries. Largely for these reasons, the Green Berets, or Special Forces as they preferred to be called, were adroit at building rapport with foreign militaries by leveraging their language ability and charismatic personalities to get them to meet U.S. goals. It was a capability developed by the Kennedy administration to leverage U.S. influence without having to resort to U.S. power (i.e., U.S. military invasion). The conceptual complexity required to use an approach that relied on few resources and almost entirely on a foreign military doing what the United States wanted meant that many Special Forces soldiers had developed the highly analytical ability to see things from the perspective of others and to use this to accomplish their goals.

Although this ability is easy to write about and, on a theoretical level, easy to understand, the practical application of this mental outlook was an entirely different matter. In this key respect, the Navy SEALs, primarily designed as a commando strike force, frequently lacked a robust understanding of both indigenous populations and how to defeat insurgencies by leveraging foreign governments to pursue our goals. While many individual SEALs did grasp these fundamental concepts, the community as a whole was still primarily influenced by the tactical requirements of kinetic operations and sometimes grudgingly went through the motions of working by, with, and through indigenous security institutions. My own thinking was more in tune with the Special Forces community than the SEALs since it seemed to focus more on leveraging the Afghans to do more and was holistic in its perspective. The SEALs on this rotation, however, definitely seemed to understand the fundamentals of the war more deeply, in part because of their extensive predeployment training, so change was possible, even in irregular warfare forces.

We departed Tycz in the mid-morning of Wednesday, April 18, in a convoy of four vehicles en route to Forward Operating Base Tinsley/ Cobra in the northern district of Shahid-e-Hasas. The morning was clear and the rich smell of moisture was in the air as we headed out to the gun range to test fire our weapons. As we departed the front gate of Tycz, the open desert, now dotted with sprigs of grass, greeted us, and as it was absorbed by the distant purple mountain range to the front of us, an Afghan on a motorcycle rode by. After a quick test fire at the range and the replacement of a .50-caliber machine gun due to a malfunction, we took a right toward the town of Deh Rawud, en route to a bridge that crossed a nearby river. Our convoy consisted of two MATVs, the replacement vehicle for Humvees, and two Cougars, which are also MRAP (mine-resistant ambush-protected) vehicles. I rode with Major Jacobs in the last vehicle, and although it was still morning the heat of the day was already starting to have an effect.

Due to the great farming wealth of the area, the town of Deh Rawud was modern by Afghan standards. Although most of the district's roads were still dirt, the main town of Deh Rawud was largely paved and most of the key buildings were made of concrete. As we passed by the adobe dwellings of the Afghans, their fields were a green whirl of wheat and poppy interspersed with low adobe walls or an Afghan walking along the road. As our vehicles zipped past and I caught quick, furtive glances, I saw that the flowers of the poppies were already blooming, and their mix of white and pink colors seemed like a Matisse painting. After passing south of the main town we took another right and approached the main bridge. I had visited this same bridge in 2005 when it had been referred to as the "Taliban bridge," in large part because construction of it had begun under the Taliban regime. At the time, it was a bunch of lonely concrete pillars with the river meandering around them, but now it was not only complete but checkpoints guarded both ends and vehicle traffic coursed over its completed surface. What a difference it made to the psychology of the people to know they could cross the river at will and travel southward to Helmand Province if they desired. As we crossed into "Taliban country," the bridge also linked my two memories of the place, one a place of certain death and now, six years later, a place of hope.

Once our convoy crossed over the concrete bridge past the checkpoint guarding its approaches, we wound our way through the remaining villages and started our ascent into the foothills and mountainous terrain forming the Deh Rawud River Valley. The hills were arranged as if a flat bed sheet had been pushed, creating small undulating sheets of rocky terrain. The barren tracks were bereft of foliage as the river disappeared behind us and small collections of villages tucked into the curves of the terrain peeked out, miraculously coaxing water from the ground through makeshift wells. After arriving at the top of the desert plateau overlooking the valley, we briefly stopped to prepare for the longer road ahead. I got out of my truck and surveyed the terrain as a pack of children watched us from a nearby cemetery. Three lonely Soviet armored personnel carriers were set into a lower hill near a village, stripped of their gear and now a part of the terrain themselves. The cemetery, which seemed more like a shrine, was a low, two-story adobe building ringed by a squat wall of large rocks and mud. A slew of flags waved in the breeze on spindly wooden sprigs commemorating the deaths of those who were buried. The various colors signaled how the deceased had been killed—for instance, on jihad or in battle, or some other violent death—and since there were so many different colors I wondered if some also represented different families. We returned to our mission after a few minutes. The dirt road followed the best course of travel in this uneven terrain, and occasionally an Afghan civilian vehicle would pass by, sometimes with a whole family tucked into its small confines. The terrain was bleak and unpopulated, but the Taliban had found ways to use its vast reaches to its advantage. We were approaching Forward Operating Base Tinsley/Cobra from the west, following one of the key rivers and valleys that flowed from Shahid-e-Hasas, and we would eventually turn toward the east as we got closer.

Our trek into this forbidden territory allowed us to approach the first Village Stability Platform we would encounter in Shahid-e-Hasas, a small site called Saraw. As we approached this site, we passed by different check-points manned by Afghan Local Police forces. Most of them were simply a few dirt-filled Hesco barriers arranged into a rectangle, with some ply-wood and sandbags to keep the sun off and enhance security, and the odd motorcycle or vehicle the police used to get around. A small number were more formal buildings or larger concentrations of Hesco barriers, usually where a firefight with the Taliban was more likely.

The checkpoints were frequently built in sight of each other so the police would feel more confident if they encountered any trouble from the Taliban, and they were usually on a terrain feature, such as a small hill or key turn in the road. While we saw many police officers at the check-points, it was not uncommon for them to be cooking or relaxing as they performed their duties. While the checkpoints themselves were not partic-ularly impressive, they had a profound effect on the Taliban. The network of checkpoints along with Afghan Local Police forces severely blunted the freedom of movement of the Taliban along these same roads. The psycho-logical effect of seeing the local population organized in a defensive man-ner was more jarring for the insurgent group. We frequently said that the mystical power of checkpoints made the Taliban go crazy. It was profound to see such simple things have such an impressive effect on the insurgency.

We eventually turned out of the barren escarpment of desert and plunged back into a new river valley, which formed part of an upside down Y of river valleys boxed in by the mountains to the north. Our final destination of Village Stability Platform Tinsley/Cobra was situated on the other side of the Y, and we would travel north to a point where the valleys met and then down the other side to the base. Saraw was a hardscrabble outpost that, while technically a Village Stability Platform, was officially a Village Stability Transition Team, which meant most of its work had been accomplished and it was in the process of being turned over to the Afghans. Although originally created by U.S. Special Forces, it was now led by a conventional infantry unit with three Special Forces soldiers as advisors. There were about thirty U.S. soldiers there along with fifty Afghan National Army (ANA) soldiers and a small collection of interpreters and other camp followers. The team at Saraw oversaw about eighty Afghan Local Police guarding seven checkpoints that protected the local bazaars, main roads, and key geographical features. Although these numbers of ALP and checkpoints appeared modest, it was enough to control the river valley due to the mountainous terrain of the area. The police quota for the area was eighty, which meant the team had completely filled its sourcing requirements and thus the site was ready for transition to Afghan control. The Saraw team was part of four additional Village Stability Platform sites in Shahid-e-Hasas all arrayed throughout the district to protect the main population centers and to link the villages together through safer roads. Our visit was short since we intended to get to Tinsley before nightfall, but it was an illuminating visit for me.

The Saraw team was ensconced in a large, multilayered adobe fort over-looking an outer Hesco perimeter wall where pallets of supplies including diesel, water bottles, wood, and so on were arrayed. After we pulled up with our vehicles we got out to visit the team as well as to walk the ground in the immediate area. The Afghan army was down a dirt road set up in a similar adobe compound, and, due to our being closer to the river, the small hills surrounding the area were covered in a light green carpet. A team of Australian soldiers visiting from Tinsley was set up on a separate hill. The Saraw team was fortunate in that the Afghan army commander for the area was widely considered to be not just competent but forceful in his approach to fighting the Taliban. As we approached his compound, a truck was unloading rough chunks of wood for his men to use for cooking fires near a makeshift guard post of sandbags and plywood. We quickly met with him and his Coalition Forces mentors. They reviewed the security situation since the fighting season had picked up and then talked about logistical support. What was most remarkable to me was that the Afghan soldiers were leading the meeting, with the Afghan commander in clear command of the situation, and the general feeling of safety in the area. The multiday firefights of 2006 had been replaced with a relaxed air of confidence among the soldiers. As my colleagues and I walked between the two bases we didn't wear our armor or helmets, and our weapons were slung over our shoulders or carried by hand. That this area was the scene of constant firefights from 2006 to 2009 spoke volumes about how much had changed due to the Village Stability Operations initiative. We spent about an hour at the site before departing for our final destination for the evening.

Our convoy followed the road that paralleled the river, and the farmsteads grew in number and their fields were lusher. The sea of khakis and browns that had dominated our fields of view as we drove through the arid mountains gave way to the darker colors of rich alluvial soil and loamy fields. The brown-colored rivers also became deeper and flowed with a greater intensity. We made our way north up the river valley, eventually reaching the village of Yakdan, and then turned southeast toward Village Stability Support Area (VSSA) Tinsley. We passed by several checkpoints manned by Afghan Local Police forces and we gained another vehicle from Saraw. It was a Humvee operated by our Civil Mine Reduction Group (CMRG), which were Afghan explosive ordnance disposal (EOD) personnel trained to spot improvised explosive devices, disable them, and destroy them in place. Many of the Afghan personnel who were in the group had found upwards of 1,300 IEDs and had an intuitive sense of where to look for the explosives and an invaluable corporate memory of past insurgent tactics of emplacing them. Even though a constellation of checkpoints knitted the valleys of the district together, there were some blind spots between them. We eventually passed through one of these sections and the CMRG fanned out, walking the route with metal detectors and hardened plastic knives to feel for explosives. They used plastic knives instead of metal to reduce the risk that a static shock might set the device off prematurely. After several hours of creeping along an expansive dry river bed checking for explosives, we eventually made our way out and arrived at Forward Operating Base Tinsley/Cobra in the early evening. We were tired and hot but happy to have arrived safely.

Village Stability Support Area Tinsley/Cobra was the main logistical hub for four Village Stability Platform sites including Saraw, Tagaw, and Khod in the district of Shahid-e-Hasas, as well as a site in Dai Kundi Province called Mushtarak in the district of Kajran. The base had been built by the U.S. Army's 25th Infantry on September 8, 2004, by Charlie Company, Second Battalion, 5th Infantry. It had originally been named

Cobra but had gained the additional name of Tinsley after a Special Forces captain named John Tinsley was killed on August 12, 2009 in the district. The base had been in the area for so long that all the locals still referred to it as Cobra. The commander of the base was a Special Forces soldier, Capt. Mark Simmons, an officer in his early thirties and graduate of the University of California at Davis, who, like all the officers in charge of the base before him, jokingly referred to himself as "Cobra Commander" after the G.I. Joe action figure. Forward Operating Base Cobra was a place of great significance to the Special Forces community since so many men had lost their lives in the isolated valleys and mountain ranges of the surrounding district. It was not uncommon in 2006–9 for the men at this outstation to confront several-hundred-men Taliban fighting formations with little outside assistance other than air support. The valleys were pockmarked with the detritus of past firefights. The craters from bombs dropped from combat aircraft littered the area and leveled compounds brought down by the intensity of firefights were common.

The base itself was similar to Tycz in that it was an odd assortment of Hesco barriers, concertina wire, and concrete. Many of the men lived in modified shipping containers covered over with sandbags surrounding a communal fire pit. The base also had rigid boats to go up and down the rivers plus all the basics of a firebase such as a gym, chow hall, and shower facilities. The men had made it their home and some had done at least four rotations at the same firebase. The men worked out at the "Gonsavles Gym," which was like any gym except it had floor to ceiling pictures of women from men's magazines. Within the past year they had largely been torn down due to concerns about how VIPs would respond to seeing them, but many still remained and were a reminder of life outside the narrow confines of the firebase.

Another key personality at the base was a chief warrant officer named Vince Hatch, a Special Forces soldier and the area's District Augmentation Team member. Hatch was one of those Special Forces soldiers who had been a Green Beret longer than most people had been alive in the U.S. military. He was tough, irascible, and confident; there was little he hadn't seen in Afghanistan and less in the U.S. military. As the District Augmentation

Team (DAT) leader for Shahid-e-Hasas District he was in charge of working with the district governor and the district police chief and acting as a mentor and guide to them. He had been selected to be an Afghan Hand, which meant he had received additional language and cultural training and would be returning to Afghanistan for additional tours.

The whole District Augmentation Team system began at the district level and worked its way up to Kabul through a series of military advisors, and it focused on political/development/security issues. It was a shadow government of sorts to advise Afghan officials and to use personal relationships to leverage influence. In many respects, it was a recognition that the U.S. Department of State and the United States Agency for International Development (USAID) could not do these jobs due to a lack of resources, force protection concerns, and, frankly, imagination. In many respects, due to his experience, gray beard, and longevity in Afghanistan, Hatch was the pre-eminent village elder of the valley. He could walk through the nearby bazaar with just a pistol and no armor, and the people there respected him and sought his advice. Men like him did not end up in Hollywood movies about war because what they did was unglamorous but essential, chipping away at the Taliban insurgency by emulating its ways. Hatch knew more about the tribes, personalities, and valleys of the district than any Taliban leader seeking to cause trouble.

The district of Shahid-e-Hasas was located along the Helmand River in northwestern Uruzgan Province and had between 20,000 and 25,000 residents.[2] The soldiers sometimes referred to it as "shitty hot sauce." The district was divided by two large rivers that flowed northeast to southwest and met in the center of the district, where they flowed south together, dividing the district into three large sections. These areas were incredibly mountainous, as the whole region was on the edge of the Hindu Kush range, and the people there eked out a subsistence living where their farms hugged the banks of the rivers. Unlike Uruzgan's other districts, it was the only one that was predominantly Ghilzai, with its Noorzai subtribe the strongest in the area, and had historically been neglected by the provincial government, which was dominated by the Durrani tribal confederation and its Populzai subtribe. The district was traditionally isolated both politically and economically because of a lack of tribal connections in the provincial capital as well as by a surfeit of bridges and passable roads.

While farmers benefited from yearly water access from the rivers, their main source of revenue in the area was growing poppies, the central ingredient of heroin. Shahid-e-Hasas bordered the predominantly Pashtun province of Helmand to its west and the predominantly Hazaran province of Dai Kundi to its north and was the forward edge of Uruzgan in the area. Due to its isolation, rugged terrain, tribal orientation, and lack of sufficient numbers of Coalition and Afghan troops in the district and the surrounding provinces, Shahid-e-Hasas had long been considered a Taliban safe haven since the invasion of Afghanistan by U.S. forces in 2001. But this began to change in 2010 as the U.S. shifted its strategy in the area and made a determined effort to reclaim the district from Taliban forces using a strategy informed by the insurgency and then turned against it.

U.S. military forces did not create an enduring presence in Shahid-e-Hasas until 2004, when they established Forward Operating Base Cobra. While occasional raids had been conducted in the area before the base's construction, U.S. forces were largely concentrated in either the provincial capital of Tarin Kowt, which was southeast of the district, or at Forward Operating Base Tycz to the south. Villagers in the area rarely saw U.S. troops from 2001 to 2004, and local security, what there was of it, was administered by militia forces that had become official police forces. The Afghan National Police (ANP) in the area were either imported from outside the district or came from one local faction loyal to the provincial government, which was then dominated by local warlord and Populzai strongman Jan Mohammed Khan. Governor Jan Mohammed Khan's strategy for securing Uruzgan during his tenure as governor (2002–6) was to place trusted friends and tribal and family members at the head of ANP forces in each of the province's then five districts. He would also use the Afghan Highway Police, which had also formerly been his militia, to conduct raids against Taliban forces alongside U.S. troops and as a means of maintaining his position in the province.

The predatory behavior of many of these forces on the local population generated a significant amount of resentment against the government and alienated the population. Conventional and U.S. Special Forces units operated out of FOB Tinsley/Cobra and conducted raids, presence patrols, and clearing operations in the district to keep the Taliban at bay, and they partnered with the local ANP to build their capacity. Since nearby Helmand Province was not effectively secured until 2011, insurgent forces were always able to replenish their numbers in the district even though U.S. forces were successful in their operations. While Coalition and Afghan forces were successful in improving security conditions in the area, absent a strategy that enlisted the community in its own defense that also pacified the surrounding provinces, its effects were not enduring.

When conventional forces pulled out of Uruzgan Province in 2005, leaving the whole area including Shahid-e-Hasas under Special Forces control, the Taliban prepared to reassert itself in the area. With the arrival of NATO forces to southern Afghanistan in 2005 and 2006, the Taliban prepared an offensive across the region that sought not just to diminish the will of U.S. and NATO forces to succeed, but to actually seize territory and fight in conventional battles. The Taliban took advantage of NATO's inexperience with counterinsurgency, soft political support for the Afghan mission at home, and risk-averse behavior to make the war in Afghanistan decidedly more kinetic. The district center of Chora, just east of Shahid-e-Hasas, for example, fell to the Taliban in 2006, was retaken, and almost fell again in 2007. Similar operations were also attempted in Shahid-e-Hasas.

While the numbers of Taliban increased all over the province, their tactics, techniques, and procedures had also gone through a small revolution. In addition to greater discipline as a fighting force, the Taliban increasingly partnered with foreign fighters who brought special skills such as sniping, bomb making, and leadership to the conflict as well as extra funding. The first suicide vest and car bomb attack in the area since the U.S. invasion took place in the provincial capital of Tarin Kowt in 2006. All of these changes were felt in Shahid-e-Hasas.

Since FOB Tinsley/Cobra was limited to a small Special Forces team and partnered Afghan National Army soldiers, it had enough men to have a presence in the district but not enough to pacify it. Lacking security in the surrounding provinces and a local force to partner with, the Special Forces were exclusively focused on fighting and survival, not being able to establish an enduring security presence that would last beyond their rotation or exist beyond sight of their base. Afghan National Police forces were largely from outside the district and so were perceived as being almost as foreign as U.S. troops. Lacking any enduring local security as well as an ability to resist the Taliban, local villagers tolerated the presence of the Islamists or enlisted with them as a means of preventing the predatory behavior of Durrani government officials. One Special Forces rotation in Shahid-e-Hasas in 2006, for example, had twenty-two casualties and seven men killed in action. While they made great gains in degrading the insurgency, they were unable to defeat it. A new approach was required, but its form and substance was still unknown.

By the end of 2006, FOB Tinsley/Cobra was surrounded by the insurgency, the main roads leading from the base to the surrounding district were mined, and insurgent fighters were emboldened by greater numbers and greater discipline as well as by the advantages foreign fighters brought to the battlefield. Local villagers had either fled the area, enlisted with the Taliban, or were forced to work with them through coerced collusion.

Beginning in 2010, a concerted effort was made by U.S. and Afghan forces to push out beyond FOB Tinsley/Cobra, to engage with local leaders, and raise an Afghan Local Police (ALP) force. It began by increasing the number of Special Forces teams in the area from one to four and establishing small operating bases throughout the district's valleys and mountain passes. These men operated as the forward edge of FOB Tinsley/Cobra, engaging local communities and establishing an enduring presence in areas that had never known it. After constant contact with village elders, the recruiting process began for the ALP, and regular shuras were convened with area villages to explain the initiative and to identify sources of tribal, economic, and village grievances that alienated the people from their government. As the work progressed, what began in fits and starts became a deluge as area villagers joined the ALP program, accepting a regular paycheck, embracing the pride of wearing the uniform of a respected force, and using their local knowledge to protect their own community. As checkpoints were established at bridge crossings, valley choke points, and bazaar shop entrances, as well as in key villages, the Taliban were slowly squeezed out of the area. The district chief of police, a man named Wali Dad, who was from the area and had previously worked in Tarin Kowt as a police officer, led the Afghan National Police and the Afghan Local Police. He visited local shuras to promote the program and was respected by area elders as one of their own.

Unlike the past, the police chief had resources. The ALP went to him for pay, weapons, and other support, and he had the respect of the community that came from having the resources to directly help the people. As the ALP program simultaneously grew in surrounding districts, roads that had been impassable due to the insurgency opened up, commerce that had been stunted grew, and the signs of a community wresting off insurgent oppression abounded. As much as the ALP program removed the freedom of movement for insurgent fighters through constructing and manning a network of checkpoints, it also enlisted the population in its own defense, robbing the insurgency of a ready-made recruiting pool of poor and unemployed military-age males. Additionally, the creation of the Village Stability Operations framework and the development of a system of military, political, and cultural advisors from the village to the province to the capital complemented a village approach to security by knitting together a holistic and vertically integrated system of political influence.

By 2012 the district of Shahid-e-Hasas had largely been pacified due to the success of the Village Stability Operations program. There were more than 380 Afghan Local Police in the district working alongside 120 Afghan National Police, and there were 60 Afghan National Army soldiers working at more than 40 checkpoints at bazaars, key geographical points, and major roads. Efforts were under way to raise the authorized local police levels from 400 to around 450. Although some work remained to be done north of the district in Dai Kundi Province, the area was largely free of the Taliban, and while the insurgents still attempted to get traction with the villagers, the fact that the local population enthusiastically participated in the Village Stability Operations program really demonstrated who was winning. The checkpoints and Afghan Local Police forces had cleared the roads down to Deh Rawud District as well as to Tarin Kowt, so commerce increased substantially in the area and the villagers were able to bring their crops to market in the provincial capital and return with the manufactured goods they needed. Just prior to our visit, the Afghan phone company Roshan finished building its last cell phone towers in the area, bringing this last part of the province into the fold of connectivity to the outside world. It was certainly heartening to see such profound and sustainable progress in the area knowing that just six years previously it had been completely controlled by the Taliban, with dozens of their fighters involved in ambushes alongside foreign jihadists, and that Firebase Cobra had been as isolated as the Alamo.

We departed for Tycz on April 19, taking an alternate route back to the forward operating base, and, like our trip north, it was guarded by Afghan Local Police forces manning different checkpoints along the route. There were two additional bridges we crossed that hadn't existed six years ago. If I had taken the same route in 2006 it would certainly have involved several ambushes and firefights and we would likely have lost several trucks, and perhaps American lives, to improvised explosive devices.

On April 20, we traveled to the district center building of Deh Rawud and met briefly with Omar Khan, the district chief of police. He had risen to his position through his close association with U.S. Special Forces and had, through this relationship, amassed substantial local power, power that others wanted. Unlike most Afghans, he was clean-shaven and his mop of black hair was thick and unkempt. He looked almost like one of the Beatles, and he wore a tactical police shirt similar to those U.S. Special Operations Forces wore. He seemed responsible and motivated and, based upon what others had told me, he largely performed his duties as required and was widely supported by the local villagers. Unlike the hardscrabble police force I had visited in Deh Rawud in 2005, where none of them had worn their uniform, their compound was an old adobe building, and the prison was filthy and unkempt, the visit this time was dramatically different. Police Chief Omar Khan not only wore his uniform but now commanded a force of Afghan National Police who were logistically supported with weapons, ammunition, vehicles, and pay. He presided over not just his own immediate men but also the Afghan Local Police in the district, who were similarly arrayed around the district of Deh Rawud as they had been in Shahid-e-Hasas. He was smart and personally brave, and since he presided over such a substantial force, numbering around four hundred men, he had most of the resources he needed through Afghan channels to govern his own affairs. He was quite close to Major Jacobs and they both teased each other mercilessly. Outside of a few motorcycle bomb attacks in the district, security was good in the area, and the Taliban were hard-pressed to muster even a token force of men to fight the Afghan security forces.

It was becoming clear that the combination of Afghan Local Police, Afghan National Police, and Afghan National Army soldiers along with Afghan intelligence officials were a deadly mix of capabilities the Taliban found difficult to overcome. These forces, as well as improved roads, bridges, and cell phone connectivity, had opened up the Taliban safe havens in these districts to Afghan and Coalition forces. Positive leadership from the chiefs of police and district governors and the active assistance of tribal elders through Village Stability Operations had fundamentally changed the local dynamics of the insurgency to the Taliban's great disadvantage. The enduring challenge going forward was how these forces would operate once U.S. troops had withdrawn from the country and whether the Afghan government would be able to sustain them and retain the support of local villagers. At least for now, the Taliban insurgency had largely been beaten back, and although challenges remained, the Islamist movement was no longer the mortal threat to the government and the Afghan people it had once been. I remained at the base another day exploring old memories and then departed in a convoy back to Tarin Kowt.

Even though security had improved dramatically throughout Uruzgan, violence still lurked beyond our base's walls and was a constant drumbeat. Below is a rough record I kept of some key events in the area over eight months. The actual violence levels were significantly higher than these brief notes indicate, and this shouldn't be used as a "final" record of all major events. Indirect fire, suicide attacks, firefights, and improvised explosive devices were a constant reality. The key acronyms are TIC: troops in contact (with the enemy); IDF: indirect fire; IED: improvised explosive device; KIA: killed in action; RCIED: remote-controlled IED; and VBIED: vehicle-borne IED. Many more of these types of events took place over the course of the tour, but these are representative examples of the normal routine of an Afghan deployment.

February 2012

February 4, 2012	Arrived in Afghanistan
February 9, 2012	Two rockets launched against FOB Ripley. One struck the Camp Holland dining facility (DFAC) and another landed outside the base
February 11, 2012	Two mortars. One hit the end of the runway. Helmets and vests today
February 14, 2012	Met with Mohib
February 16, 2012	Helmet painted
February 16, 2012	Met with PRT Commander Kosnar
February 17, 2012	Snowed in Tarin Kowt
February 23, 2012	VBIED arrived at Tarin Kowt
February 26, 2012	VBIED captured in Tarin Kowt (same location as July 2011 attack)
February 27, 2012	Rocket attack on MNBTK. 1 X 107mm rocket 500 meters southwest of MNBTK
February 28, 2012	Rocket attack on MNBTK
February 28, 2012	ALP in Shahid-e-Hasas capture Pakistani putting IED in the road
February 28, 2012	Several hundred protesters in TK because of Qur'an burning at Bagram Airfield (BAF)

March 2012

March 2, 2012	National Directorate for Security (NDS) colonel assassinated outside his home by two men on motorcycles. Three shots: shoulder, kidney, and leg

March 3, 2012	Spring has arrived
March 8, 2012	PRT transfer of authority at Camp Holland
March 10, 2012	Met with Mohib
March 11, 2012	Went to Tarin Kowt (TK) bazaar on camp
March 11, 2012	U.S. soldier kills local Afghans after dressing as Afghan
March 12, 2012	Jordan Special Operations Forces (JORSOF) soldier kicked off C-130 plane because he was Arab
March 12, 2012	Deh Rawud (DRW) ambush of CF patrol
March 13, 2012	Six-year-old picks up UXO (unexploded ordnance), it blows up in his hands, both hands amputated
March 17, 2012	Got sick
March 18, 2012	Truck with gravel in it tried to get on base with explosives. Driver detained and parts of truck blown up in place. False alarm. Some insurgents found frozen to death in refrigerator truck trying to get on base.
March 18, 2012	Chlamydia outbreak in village
March 19, 2012	Sandstorm
March 20, 2012	Nawruz celebration at the governor's compound
March 21, 2012	Met with new Combined Team Uruzgan (CTU) leadership. Colonel Hadley had read my book.
March 23, 2012	Met with former member of Parliament Haji Khairo Jan for dinner at governor's compound
March 24, 2012	Haji Khairo Jan killed by IED along with four members of the Afghan National Police
March 24, 2012	Dinner with CO/XO/General Matullah at Ripley and then with SEALs
March 26, 2012	Suicide vest attack in Chora by fourteen-year-old boy. AusAID and U.S. Marine injured along with two Navy PRT members
March 30, 2012	Met with Shirzad's aide and colleagues to discuss governor's removal
March 30, 2012	Combined Joint Special Operations Task Force–Afghanistan (CJSOTF-A) orders all DAT and PAT personnel to shave their beards

April 2012

April 2, 2012	New Uruzgan governor announced
April 2, 2012	Two rockets launched at the base. One hit Camp Holland and the other hit the base's entry control point
April 7, 2012	Mortar attack, bombed compound
April 8, 2012	FOB Ripley picnic
April 8, 2012	Kajran TIC and follow on checkpoint construction
April 9, 2012	SEAL assistant officer in charge (AOIC) at VSP Bagh shot in thigh, no bone or artery. Full recovery
April 14, 2012	New Uruzgan governor ceremony
April 27, 2012	Mujahedeen Day, 500–700 attend events in Tarin Kowt
April 17–21, 2012	Trip to Tycz, Saraw, Tinsley/Cobra, Tycz
April 24, 2012	Met with Uruzgan director of Civil Service Commission
April 25, 2012	ALP members shot in stomach brought to Ripley clinic
April 25, 2012	IED injures Navy EOD member at VSP Bagh
April 25, 2012	ANA soldiers shoot four Special Forces in Kandahar, one U.S. KIA
April 26, 2012	"Found" two old landmines outside wall of FOB Ripley. EOD called. Turns out they were old pipes
April 29, 2012	Visit VSP Bagh
April 30, 2012	TIC at VSP Shobar, three children KIA

May 2012

May 1, 2012	Met with director of communications
May 1, 2012	Field Surgical Team U.S. Army captain dies in his room while talking to wife on Skype
May 1, 2012	Rocket/mortar attack on MNBTK
May 2, 2012	Rocket/mortar attack on MNBTK
May 3, 2012	VSP Kajran TIC, nine Taliban killed
May 4, 2012	Rocket/mortar attack on MNBTK. Lands three hundred meters outside wire
May 4, 2012	Memorial for U.S. Army captain
May 4, 2012	FOB Tinsley checkpoints attacked
May 6, 2012	TIC at VSP Shobar

May 7, 2012	TIC at checkpoint at VSP Bagh
May 7, 2012	Gen. John R. Allen, commanding general of ISAF, visits
May 8, 2012	TIC at VSSA Anaconda checkpoint, ALP quick reaction force
May 9, 2012	Visit FOB Mogensen/VSP Shobar
May 10–11, 2012	ANA commando operation near VSP Shobar
May 11, 2012	Threat to Khoshal (Rozi Khan's son), he moves to Kabul
May 13, 2012	President Karzai announces Uruzgan transition
May 13, 2012	TIC at VSP Bagh, one U.S. soldier shot in leg
May 15, 2012	TIC at VSP Bagh
May 20, 2012	Suicide vest attack at Uruzgan provincial police headquarters, two U.S. killed, attended ramp ceremony
May 22–23, 2012	Battlefield Circulation (BFC) with Captain Szymanski to VSP Shobar, etc.
May 24, 2012	Kush Kadir ambush, two CMRG (civil mine reduction group) KIA, two insurgents KIA
May 28, 2012	Uruzgan provincial administration meeting canceled due to car bomb threat in Tarin Kowt
May 28, 2012	TIC at VSP Mushtarak, one CF slightly wounded
May 28, 2012	RCIED injures two and kills one approximately 1 km west of Tarin Kowt traffic circle
May 29, 2012	Provincial Augmentation Team member Maj. Scott Bradley goes home
May 30, 2012	TIC at VSP Nawbahar, one PKM machine gun approximately 2 km out

June 2012

June 3, 2012	VSP Kalach retrograde will be complete
June 13, 2012	IDF attack at MNBTK
June 13, 2012	TIC at VSP Shobar
June 15, 2012	TIC at VSP Choar, Lamar (light) Operation
June 15, 2012	TIC at VSP Bagh, route clearance
June 19, 2012	TIC at VSP Shobar, IDF

June 21, 2012	Three Taliban placing an IED near an ALP checkpoint. Dropped bomb and killed two after they left.
June 22, 2012	VSP Gizab closing today
June 26, 2012	IED at Uruzgan police headquarters

July 2012

July 2, 2012	Task Force (TF) XX loses one soldier KIA
July 2, 2012	Car bomb threat in Tarin Kowt, trip to Ulema conference canceled
July 4, 2012	TIC at VSP Sayagez
July 5, 2012	Ramp ceremony for TF 66 soldier
July 7, 2012	TIC at VSP Sayagez
July 9–11, 2012	Kabul/IJC Trip
July 17, 2012	Uruzgan transitions to Afghan government control
July 17, 2012	FOB Ripley guard detained, making fake CTU and FOB Ripley IDs
July 18, 2012	SOCS Whitmore leaves Afghanistan with two wounded SEALs
July 29, 2012	IDF attack at MNBTK
July 30, 2012	Taj Mohammed killed by IED at mosque placed by his son in the village of Khayro Karez
July 31, 2012	Special Forces Operational Detachment Alpha (ODA) soldier shot in the head

August 2012

August 6, 2012	VSSA Tinsley TIC
August 7, 2012	VSP Khod TIC
August 8, 2012	ALP checkpoint commander killed by IED, lost both legs
August 10, 2012	VSP Sayagez TIC
August 11, 2012	Third trip to Abdul Samad's house
August 12, 2012	LMAR (light) operation
August 14, 2012	VBIED blown up in place at VSP Chora

August 15, 2012	Threat to attack VSP Chora
August 17, 2012	VSP Mushtarak retrograde finished
August 20, 2012	IDF attack at MNBTK
August 24, 2012	Trip to VSP Chora
August 27, 2012	Visit to SOTF-SE of Regional Command-South commander, Major General Huggins and his replacement Major General Abrams
August 30, 2012	Five Australian soldiers killed, three green-on-blue, two TF XX when helicopter rolls on to them

September 2012

September 1, 2012	Australia (AUS) ramp ceremony, five killed
September 9, 2012	Child suicide vest attack near U.S. embassy in Kabul
September 15, 2012	Attack at FOB Bastion kills several Marines and destroys several jet fighters
September 5, 2012	Temperature begins to drop
September 20, 2012	Last U.S. surge troops leave
September 21, 2012	CJSOTF-A Commanding Officer Fletcher arrives at SOTF-SE
September 28, 2012	Rocket-propelled grenade (RPG) shot at Chinook at it arrived at VSP Sayagez, exploded three hundred meters away
September 25, 2012	VSSA Anaconda trip to visit Hazarans
September 26, 2012	U.S. Army Capt. Paul Martin is injured along with his interpreter when an IED goes off near their RAZR at VSSA Tinsley
September 27, 2012	TIC at VSP Sayagez
September 27, 2012	Met with Mohib and Khoshal at Camp Holland cafe
September 28, 2012	Tarnak-Wa-Jaldak trip with NBC
September 29, 2012	Met with Mohib and Khoshal at PRT House
September 29, 2012	SEAL Team Two (ST2) relieved by ST4 at 7 p.m.

View of river valley in Shahid-e-Hasas District in Uruzgan Province in 2012. *Author collection*

Front gate of Village Stability Platform site Walan Rabat in Zabul Province in 2012.
Author collection

Former Uruzgan Province governor Jan Mohammed Khan,
who served from 2002 to 2006 and was assassinated in 2011.
Author collection

Author visiting Uruzgan provincial governor's compound in 2012. *Author collection*

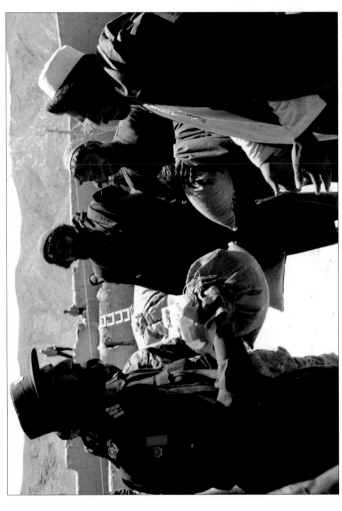

Uruzgan provincial chief of police General Matullah Khan distributes foodstuffs to new Afghan Local Police recruits at Village Stability Platform Khod in 2012. *U.S. Navy*

Uruzgan governor Amir Mohammed Akunzada (second from left, with turban) participates in road-opening ceremony in Tarin Kowt in 2012. *Author collection*

Lt. (jg) Edward Crawford meets with United Nations Development advisor Mohib (center) and Barakzai tribal leader Khoshal at Camp Holland in Tarin Kowt, Uruzgan Province, in 2012. *Author collection*

U.S. Navy SEAL officer crosses the Arghandab River in Zabul Province during clearing operation against the Taliban in preparation for the insertion of Village Stability Platform Sayagez in 2012. *U.S. Navy*

Uruzgan provincial chief of police Matullah Khan convenes a shura with elders from the village of Khod in Shahid-e-Hasas District, Uruzgan Province, in 2012. *U.S. Navy*

Afghan Local Police recruits begin their physical and tactical training after recommendation by village elders and vetting by U.S. and Afghan forces in 2012. *U.S. Navy*

Taliban commander Abdul Samad (right) participates in a reintegration ceremony at the governor's compound in Uruzgan Province in 2012. *U.S. Navy*

Aerial view of U.S. Navy SEAL Village Stability Platform Chora in Uruzgan Province in 2012.
Author collection

Afghan Army Special Forces soldier addresses villagers at the transition ceremony of Village Stability Platform Mushtaarak from U.S. to Afghan control in Kajran District, Dai Kundi Province, in 2012.

U.S. Navy

Author (left) with U.S. Navy SEAL Lt. Magnus Norton at Forward Operating Base Ripley in Uruzgan Province in 2012. *Author collection*

Vehicle from Village Stability Platform Gizab crosses a bridge in northern Uruzgan Province in 2012. *U.S. Navy*

Local bridge built by U.S. Navy SEAL Village Stability Platform Sayagez in Zabul Province in 2012. *U.S. Navy*

ELEVEN

The Eastern Frontier

Overidentification with one or another faction triggers
intricate patterns of rivalry and often creates complication.
Alliances with one or the other group often result in antago-
nizing rival blocs.

—AKBAR S. AHMED, *Resistance
and Control in Pakistan*

After being sworn in as governor of Uruzgan Province just two
weeks earlier, Governor Akunzada decided to make his first trip
to the eastern vastness of Uruzgan and our solitary base there
called Anaconda. It had been named after the unit that had originally
built it in 2004, A Company of the 25th Infantry Division. Anaconda
was nestled deep into the mountains of Khas Uruzgan next to the town
of Khas Uruzgan, which was also its district capital and had previously
served as the province's capital before the province had been split into
two on March 28, 2004. The team there was with the U.S. Army Special
Forces, and the challenges they faced were enormous. Due to its isolation
Anaconda could realistically expect little or no support from Coalition
Forces units if its members got into trouble, outside of aircraft, which
would take time to arrive on station. Additionally, the neighboring districts
to its south and east in Zabul and Ghazni Provinces had no U.S. forces or
were too far away to make a difference.

The real challenge for the soldiers at Anaconda was navigating the
minefield of sectarian and ethnic politics between the Sunni Pashtuns and

135

Shiite Hazaran populations. Both groups had historically been at odds over such issues as access to water, arable land, and respect, and the Taliban relentlessly exploited these frictions to present what might have been solvable problems as earth-shattering questions of identity, prestige, and respect between the two groups. With the growth of cell phone towers and the media in Afghanistan, what were often local disputes became national questions rooted in the worst aspects of ethnic politics. Any perceived affront was frequently blown to epic proportions by Pashtun politicians currying favor with the public. What the Taliban lacked in numbers of men in the district they made up for in the use of propaganda. They constantly played the Pashtuns off the Hazarans and tied the province's local officials up in knots, as they did with our own units, which constantly had to respond to or investigate all sorts of various rumors.

We departed in the early morning from Tarin Kowt on April 27 and, due to the size of our group, flew in Chinooks accompanied by Blackhawk helicopters. In addition to its political aspect, allowing the governor to meet the residents and leaders of the area, the trip was also intended to be a show of strength by the provincial government. Governor Akunzada wanted to demonstrate that his government in Tarin Kowt cared about the interests of the people and that he wanted to seriously address the problems between the Pashtun and Hazaran communities. To this end, he also brought Matullah, a man named Khan Mohammed Khan, who was head of the local National Directorate for Security (NDS), and the chief judge of the province, among other security and judicial officials. The tensions between the two ethnic communities were also complicated by the fact that each had its own Afghan Local Police commander who also effectively served as the political leader of their respective group. Thus the tensions in the district had simultaneous political and security dimensions, which were also rooted in economic competition. Against this backdrop of local conflict, the Taliban lurked, looking for opportunities to strike at local ALP commanders, to attack our forces, and to leverage community sentiment in its favor.

While the Hazaran population was reliably anti-Taliban and their villages served as a natural northern limit to Taliban expansion in the area, the surrounding districts in Zabul and Ghazni Provinces were virtual safe havens for the enemy. We had a small team in the district of Deh Chopan just across the border from Khas Uruzgan in Zabul Province, but it was a pinprick compared to the district's size and mountainous terrain. Additionally, the Taliban used ratlines from Pakistan that crossed through Zabul Province and terminated in Khas Uruzgan District, which allowed them to pull off a number of complex operations against our forces even in such a remote area. The district also served as a vital thoroughfare for the Taliban into Uruzgan Province, so we had to do our best to secure the region. When the Taliban returned with a vengeance in 2006–7, a multi-day firefight took place in and around Forward Operating Base Anaconda as several hundred Taliban attempted to seize it. It was rumored that Mullah Omar himself had ordered it taken. Interestingly, the base had initially been slated to be turned over to Afghan forces, and our men were going to shift to a new location just before the Taliban launched their attacks in the summer of 2007. It took eleven days to fight the Taliban off and some estimates put the Taliban fighting strength at 250 to 300 fighters. The ability to transport so many men to such a remote area was another reminder of how dedicated the Taliban were to their cause and of their relentless ingenuity. It was further evidence that without an effective strategy to enlist the population in their own defense we would never be able to simultaneously blunt the Taliban's offensives while protecting the people.

The dominant feature of Khas Uruzgan was its mountainous terrain and deep valleys; its tallest peaks rose to roughly eight thousand feet in elevation. It was customary to see snow on the highest summits even in the hottest parts of the summer. Due to the area's deep valleys, the population lived along the mountains' creek beds, and when spring arrived, the snow melt created torrential floods. Like clockwork, these floods occurred every year despite the best efforts of the provincial government to address them. Some parts of the district were so isolated that in 2005 we had to send emergency foodstuffs to a village at the end of a long valley that had been cut off when the single road that led to it had been covered by fifteen to twenty feet of snow.

As our helicopter ascended toward Village Stability Support Area Anaconda in 2012, the warm spring air gave way to the coolness of the mountain peaks. The terrain was jagged and bereft of vegetation, and a multitude of colored rocks and dirt, some reddish, some black, and others a lush green sprinkled the landscape, an unusual coloration created by the tectonic shifts that had created the Hindu Kush Mountains. The brisk, clean air was refreshing and it invigorated my senses as we departed the dust bowl that was Tarin Kowt. As we approached Anaconda you could make out the neatly laid streets of the former provincial capital, and a number of buildings were made of concrete, which was a rarity. A large river coursed through town carrying the snowmelt, and a ring of distant mountains dominated the landscape. A large mosque stood on the edge of the village and the whole place had the feel of a frontier town. After making a pass of the town, our helicopters circled back around and approached Anaconda, a place I hadn't visited in seven years.

Forward Operating Base Anaconda had been around for more than eight years, and like many of our bases built early in the war it had largely been constructed using local materials, labor, and designs, which gave it a rough but durable look. The base itself was set at the edge of a small range of hills, and the local police force occupied a slightly higher perch on the hill overlooking it and the town of Khas Uruzgan. The base had a small clinic that handled the daily Afghan walk-ins as well as the more dire emergency medical cases of our soldiers. The soldiers lived in concrete barracks with the usual Pakistani steel I-beams in the ceilings interspersed with ornate concrete tiles. A row of Humvees and MRAPs were arrayed in a line facing the front courtyard/landing strip under a metal overhang. There was also a specially modified vehicle that had been designed to climb steep mountains. It had the v-shaped hull of the MRAP but was much higher off the ground and was largely unarmored, which made it much lighter. I was later told it had been brought in so the team could traverse the mountainsides and deep rivers much better. It was just the latest example of how the Special Operations community was marching in its own direction, going lighter, leaner, and faster while the big military machine was embracing MRAPs with all of their limitations on

movement. A central building that had been built by the Afghans served
as the tactical operations center, and a makeshift chow hall sat thirty feet
away from it. Other guard towers ringed this inner courtyard, and toward
the back of the simple base stood an open pen where the team's horses
had once stayed. About a dozen feed troughs still ringed the edge of the
area. Ever since the base had been built the men there had used horses to
traverse the Hazaran areas, which was a welcome change from sitting in a
Humvee all day, but the days of this kind of expeditionary warfare seemed
to be behind us. The horses had been sold off to the locals within the past
year or so. The outer edge of the base was enclosed by a large concrete wall
with guard towers on each corner, and as our helicopters landed in the
expansive courtyard, we seemed like a collection of black bugs landing on
the spine of the earth.

The men at Anaconda were led by a U.S. Army Special Forces captain
named Trevor Erickson. He presided over a team of ten Special Forces
soldiers along with six regular infantry soldiers and four civil affairs
soldiers. Their Afghan Civil Mine Reduction Group was substantial, forty-
one people, which led me to believe they also functioned as a guard force
and a ready pool of bodies to thicken out the Special Forces patrols. Most
of these men were Hazaran, which created some difficulties with the local
population. This relatively small force presided over 260 Afghan Local
Police in the district set out at a number of checkpoints, and they also
mentored the local Afghan National Police force, liaised with the district
chief, and conducted shuras with village elders, all the while fighting the
Taliban. Their responsibilities were enormous but they seemed to juggle
them all quite well. In addition to these various responsibilities, Captain
Erickson also supported a local who had once been with the Taliban but
had switched sides to support the Coalition. His name was Abdul Samad
and he controlled the Sultan Mohammed Nawa Valley from his village of
Dahane Sangu, roughly thirty kilometers northeast of Forward Operating
Base Anaconda. He had fought U.S. soldiers for many years but was now
our nominal ally after turning against the Taliban in his area (see chapter
15). Erickson's other responsibility was managing the complex relationship
between the largely Pashtun police force led by the district chief of police

Haji Rashid. This included the local police led by Kayhl Mohammed, also a Pashtun, and the Hazaran ALP force led by a man named Shujayee.

Through an unusual mix of widespread illiteracy, competition between ethnic groups, and the village rumor network, all stoked by the Taliban of course, Shujayee was seen as the devil incarnate in the isolated world of Khas Uruzgan. To hear some of the Pashtuns talk about him, Shujayee was ten feet tall and slew Pashtuns left and right while leveling villages as he put the fear of God in the Taliban. The truth was naturally far different, but Shujayee was as elusive as a ghost. There had been many reported sightings of him, but I had never seen him in the flesh. He was officially a member of the Afghan Local Police and received a regular paycheck from them as well as other resources, and he largely confined his activities to his valley. We had heard through the rumor mill, however, that he was not going to visit our base or even travel to Tarin Kowt because he was worried we would detain him or that he might be arrested by the Afghan police. The little we knew about his situation often came from rumors, although he would occasionally communicate with our men at Anaconda or through a local Hazaran politician named Mohammed Salari, who was the director of the province's counternarcotics program. As you can imagine, with the Pashtun population up in arms against him and frustrated by their inability to get to him, we often took the blame for sheltering him, or we would even be accused of building a "Hazaran militia." We would frequently get calls from our higher-ups trying to figure out this whole situation in Uruzgan after they had received complaints about it in Kabul. It was a curious thing to be held accountable for the actions of a man who received a regular salary from the police, which is to say from General Matullah Khan, when he could have easily stopped paying him or supplying him with weapons and ammunition. Interestingly, even though Matullah had a reputation as a ruthless killer of his tribal opponents, he had a strong relationship with the Hazarans who he knew would be keenly anti-Taliban. However it worked out, accusations, recriminations, and hallucinations would continue to reverberate around the province and would cause occasional flare-ups.

After arriving at Anaconda, we collected the Afghan officials and made our way over to the town of Khas Uruzgan, just outside the base's wall. Mike Hayes and the SEALs walked with the governor and his men while Captain Erickson spoke with Mike. As we made our way down the path, we passed by the mosque we had seen from the air. In 2005, the 25th Infantry Company at Anaconda had undertaken a number of civil affairs projects in the area but had deliberately avoided the mosque so as not to cause any offense through a misunderstanding. The main mosque was a fairly large white structure with a couple of minarets surrounded by a low, enclosed wall. The locals had noticed that no projects had been done at the main mosque in the area, and a rumor developed in the community that the "Americans" did not like Islam or did not respect their culture. Interestingly, out of a heartfelt desire not to offend the Afghans we had inadvertently offended some of them. The U.S. Army unit there then decided to spend a few dollars to purchase new megaphones for the minarets so that the call to prayer could be heard, a number of additional prayer rugs, foodstuffs the imam could distribute to the poor, and a fresh coat of paint for the whole building. Almost instantaneously the community's views of our soldiers turned around and the base was beset with locals offering to help them, giving them tips on the Taliban, and inviting them to their villages. It was an early lesson for the unit as well as for me on how to work with local communities and how our avoidance of certain cultural flashpoints could actually contribute to a fait accompli of misunderstandings if we weren't wise about how we interacted with the locals. As we walked past the mosque I reflected on how much had changed in the war and how a spirit of mistrust due to insider attacks had intruded upon our relatively easygoing ways with the Afghans not that long ago.

Our collection of Afghan officials and U.S. soldiers eventually wound its way to the local high school on the edge of town. Even though it was spring, a slight chill filled the air as the governor and Matullah chatted amiably with the local government officials. We passed by a collection of stores carrying pots and pans, foodstuffs, and farming equipment, and we went past a bakery as most of the locals looked upon us. We finally reached the edge of the high school and passed underneath an impressive arch as a phalanx of Afghan officials and prominent locals lined the governor's path. The governor and Matullah shook the hands of the various men, who were all dressed in the usual turbans and *salwar kameez* of the Pashtuns. It was a sea of browns, grays, blacks, and dark greens, the men covered with extra shawls against the residual winter chill. Not too long after our arrival, word had gotten out that the governor and his entourage were there, and local men streamed into the open field next to the high school. There were about 250 or so once everyone had gathered and settled down. The school's volleyball court was quickly converted into a makeshift gathering area, and a table and chairs were procured for the visiting officials. Locals began to sit in a group in front of the dignitaries as the police formed an outer perimeter and climbed onto the roofs of the nearby buildings. A gentle wind blew through the area as the district governor rose to speak, and the nearby volleyball nets swayed ever so slightly.

The local chieftain began to address the crowd.

> We face many tribal and personal challenges. The tribal leaders are tired of fighting and they must play a positive role and unify the province. They are trying their best but they need our help. We are receiving more leaders because of better security. Give them your advice. We are now able to open more schools. We need skilled people to resolve the issues of the people. We want better security. There are some challenges between the tribes and the government. We must try to bring them together. We greatly appreciate the efforts of the Coalition Forces. Our youth are still unemployed. Elders had local shuras with tribal leaders to discuss the problems of the district. Tell your problems to the governor today. We must be open with him.

As he sat down the crowd politely cheered.

Although the governor was diminutive in stature, he had a strong presence as someone long used to having others follow his commands. His brown turban matched his beard, and as he spoke his hands would gesture to make a point, always returning to his mid-chest area as they formed a small peak.

> I am very happy to be here but also sad. Good because we are here to bring development to your villages. Whatever you say, we will do it.

You know us, we respect you and want your advice. We must work to unify the tribes and the government and to stop the fighting between the tribes. The leadership of the government is here to serve you and we will do our best. These leaders are your people, they belong to you and are your servants. All are trying the best to bring peace, prosperity and the rule of law. They try to do their best. If we do not do the right thing the people will not support us. These young men are here to serve you as well. The system of Islam is for the people. The Coalition Forces work with us and the government of Afghanistan to build the rule of law, it is what we want. We need the Coalition Forces to make Afghanistan strong and to help build bridges between the people and their government. If we build security we can bring development. We must stay strong and work together and not allow those with personal agendas to stop us. They do not want to have a good government, they don't want education. You are poor, unfortunately. There is little development in this province. I need your help and I don't want to promise you anything if I cannot deliver it.

His words seemed well received, and the crowd of Pashtuns and Hazarans clapped again. It was encouraging to see how well his comments were received.

The chief justice of the province then rose to address the crowd.

Blessings go to the nations who do not kill needlessly. Don't kill for the small greed. You play your role, will receive blessings. No justice for suicide attackers. Jihad is allowed if someone is trying to take your land, property from the Qur'an, what Islam is all about. Government and constitution is supported by the Qur'an, we must implement them. We must take care of each other. We must advise the president about the rule of law. Coalition Forces came here to support the people and fought our enemies and brought projects. Partnership is authorized by the Qur'an. Islam and the constitution don't allow people to fight for personal greed.

It was a rousing speech that seemed partially rooted in law as well as in the Qur'an. Many of the people nodded their heads as he spoke, punctuating his points one at a time with his hands. As he sat down a donkey made a braying sound in the background.

Following their speeches, the floor was opened up to the public, and while many men spoke, two stood out the most. The first man to speak was a local Pashtun elder.

> The people have suffered for the last ten years, we have had no government representatives visit us. We are very happy you are here today. Please hear our problems, solve them. That is leadership. We want our local leaders to bring security, stop crime. We are all children of Islam, there are no Pashtuns or Hazarans. If you provide security, the people will be with you. To have security in the district we need more police, more ANA, no personal issues, they will not benefit anyone. There is no work for the youth. We need your help. Little development in this district. The district chief of police and provincial chief of police are good, they have helped open the road from Tarin Kowt to Khas Uruzgan.

In collaboration with the Afghan National Army, Matullah and his men had cleared the road from the provincial capital to Khas Uruzgan and had erected a series of checkpoints along the route as well as small bases to support them. Our forces had assisted but it had largely been an Afghan affair. The man continued, "If we do wrong, we must follow the rule of law. Bad, then kill them if you need to. If the police don't follow the rules, distance is created between the people and the government of Afghanistan."

Once he sat down a local Hazaran elder then stood up.

> We must follow the rule of law in order to become a civilized country. We must try our best to bring security to the people. We must bring brotherhood and support the government and the people. The governor is a good man, God bless him and bring him courage. People have suffered a long time, the governor's word is good. We support the district chief of police and provincial chief of police all the way. The government of Afghanistan is trying its best. The Qur'an tells us that we must follow the law and be honest and when we do this we will be successful.

The meeting continued but the main points had been raised. What was most remarkable to me was that the Afghan system, for what it was, was genuinely trying to do the right thing and the leaders and the people were emphasizing the right points. The Afghan government was still quite weak and struggled with corruption, a lack of talented civil servants, and the ever-present challenge of the Taliban, but it had made a great deal of progress. While it would take a while to evaluate the governor's record, I was encouraged by his actions, and he seemed much better than the first governor I had worked with in Uruzgan, Jan Mohammed Khan. Only time would tell if he would be a great governor. As the meeting broke up, the governor, Matullah, and other officials moved over to the boys' school and found a room in which to meet. After concluding the public aspects of his job, it was now time for the governor to work through the issues of the police and Shujayee. Both the district chief and the district chief of police were there and as we sat around the outer edge of the barren room on pillows, lunch was being procured. Commander Hayes was there as well as Maj. Ben Jacobs. Jacobs was in charge of the Special Forces Advanced Operations Base for Uruzgan Province and was best placed to address these various issues since his men worked directly with Afghan officials every day. We had also brought along the new commander in charge of Combined Team Uruzgan (CTU), who was a welcome change from his predecessor.

The governor sat near the far corner of the twenty-five-foot by thirty-foot blue room with Matullah by his side as the district officials sat across from them on the brown carpet. The governor began the conversation. "What are the problems in the area? Are they just between the ANP and the ALP? Is your *tashkeil* big enough? The NDS chief gave me a report on security in the area. We must do something."

The district chief of Khas Uruzgan spoke up: "We always work with the security forces. Security is good, and we work together and work very hard."

The district chief of police then responded plaintively, "I have no power or authority over the police. I can do nothing. ALP don't respect me or follow me."

"Why not capture these people?"

"Eighty percent of ALP are out of my control. My request is to abolish the ALP."

The governor was shocked and asked, "Who does these crimes? Shujayee? Isn't he under your command?"

"No, he does not respect me," the police chief responded.

Matullah then weighed in. "We must respect the rules and the law. Nobody does if you don't enforce the rules. If they break the law, then you must put them in jail. Judges should hear the cases."

The governor, clearly a bit frustrated, his expression exasperated, said, "We have heard many accusations and complaints. The cases are ready to be heard."

Matullah echoed these sentiments. "MOI has ordered the detention of Shujayee. The people request it but we cannot find him. I will resign if I cannot get him. We must go to Karzai and make our case to him."

The colonel in charge of Combined Team Uruzgan then spoke up: "It is good to talk about these issues. No one is taking ownership of anything. The ALP get their supplies from the ANP. Why not discuss with the ANP then?"

Matullah then uttered his view: "Coalition Forces pay him, support him."

An incensed Major Jacobs spoke up. "These men work for you [gesturing to Matullah]. MOI is paying them. We are here to help you [pointing at the chief of police]. You cannot say these are our guys; they are your guys. You can't handle them, need to talk to the police chief and must want security in your area. You must do it. We are here to help you, but only if you take responsibility for it. If not, I can't help you."

Matullah responded, "We have the responsibility but not the authority."

The governor then asked, "Can't we bring him here? We have all the people here. What to do?"

"We have many human rights complaints about Shujayee," Mutallah said. "The attorney general must find out what is true. If he is good, he will be let go. If not, he will be arrested."

"Karzai gave him a letter of release," the governor said. "Your job [to Matullah] is to find out if the ALP still answer to the ANP. I'm the governor of Uruzgan, what should I say to Karzai when I call him? ALP built by SOF, given to ANP to manage. Never heard these kinds of problems before [Marjah, etc.]. It is a very good program."

Jacobs agreed. "You are right. It is a local program that is defensive in structure, vetted by the local shura. ALP is subordinate to the ANP. We don't give them fuel, weapons, ammunition, etc. They get it through the PCOP and DCOP. We focus on security, governance, and development. All three must take place. There needs to be a fair process of law for Shujayee. The Taliban do things in Khas Uruzgan. They are good at starting rumors and causing problems. I support the provincial chief of police and governor as long as the province follows the rule of law."

Matullah then said defensively, "All the ALP and ANP are under my command, I'm responsible; no one else. I send the case to the judge and prosecutors, etc. . . . No official document to get Shujayee; he is my soldier. I will pay him and give him food. He works for me. Respect the law, it is the rule of the land. No respect for the law, not work for me."

The governor, nodding his head, said, "The ALP's job is to respect the people. What is left for the people? How do they answer to the people? The Taliban are using rumor, I know that. We must have an honest investigation."

"Our justice system should work like those of other countries," the judge responded. "We should all work together, not allow other organizations to influence us. We all know our job."

Hayes finished the meeting by stating, "It is good to talk about our problems and discuss the issues. Everyone wants peace and security in Khas Uruzgan. We all want one thing. All the discussion has been about Shujayee. Don't put people in jail for rumors. Justice must be quick. Criminals should go to jail for a set time. We must do the right thing."

The meeting had certainly clarified who was responsible for resolving this issue: General Matullah Khan. It had also revealed that the district chief of police, Haji Rashid, who had been appointed to his position in March, had not yet consolidated his position in the district and that other local police officials did not respect him or his authority. Once again, no matter how well-resourced someone might be and how much they were trying to do the right thing, no amount of good intentions could overcome poor leadership. There was broad agreement that a second trip should be made to Anaconda made up of security and judicial officials to question the ALP commanders and to attempt to resolve the issue. While no resolution was arrived at, a consensus, at least among the Afghan officials, seemed to develop that the accused ALP commanders must be brought to Tarin Kowt for questioning and that criminal charges should be filed. The process continued.

The complexity of the situation in Khas Uruzgan was extremely challenging to navigate, and our unit there, as well as our people in Tarin Kowt, tried to make the best of it. It was also another example to me of how our presence as honest brokers and facilitators helped the Afghan system function better. This is not to say we had to stay indefinitely, but that our presence could be beneficial if structured the right way. It was also useful to see that however successful the ALP was in the district, ethnic and religious tensions could make it less effective and nearby Taliban safe havens made it even more difficult. We finally departed Khas Uruzgan for Tarin Kowt in the mid-afternoon, and it was heartening to see that even though problems continued in the area, significant progress had been made, much of it I would never have expected.

The Hazaran community had long supported Coalition Forces throughout Afghanistan and especially in Uruzgan Province. As Shiite Muslims they had suffered mightily under the Taliban's rule and were resolute in their opposition to the Islamist movement. Asiatic in appearance and allegedly descended from Genghis Khan, the Hazarans were a dependable community loyal to the Afghan government. Their leaders were wise in the ways of how power operated in Afghanistan and had long cultivated ties with U.S. units in their home areas. In the district of Khas Uruzgan, for example, this relationship included a Hazaran security force at Forward Operating Base Anaconda and a robust presence in the Afghan Local Police. Unlike Dai Kundi Province to the north, which was predominantly

Hazaran, Khas Uruzgan was the only district in Uruzgan that had a sizable population of Hazarans other than when Gizab was added as a district in 2006. While opinions differed over their actual numbers, they were enough of a substantial presence that one of their leaders, Mohammed Salari, had been the only Hazaran elected in the 2005 Uruzgan Provincial Council elections. He had also served as the only Hazaran district chief in Uruzgan and now, in 2012, was the director of poppy eradication. Salari was a bespectacled man in his early fifties with a propensity for wearing a white *salwar kameez* with a dark gray vest and turban with a red and black cap. He had a close relationship with Matullah and they often collaborated with each other on Hazaran/Pashtun issues, but even then Matullah could not be seen as being too supportive of the Hazaran population.

In mid-September, I sat down with Mohammed Salari to discuss not only his political situation in the province but also his views on Hazaran and Pashtun relations. My colleague Scott and I had met with him before to discuss his role as head of the counternarcotics directorate in the province, but he also wore the hat of the leader of the Hazaran community in the province. One reason he was most likely chosen to head the counternarcotics office was that as a Hazaran, he might be regarded as more neutral in his administration of such a sensitive job when so many Pashtuns were involved in cultivating poppies. Additionally, it didn't hurt that he was connected to Matullah, so I'm sure he looked out for his interests as well. In 2005, Salari had been elected to the Provincial Council but could not accept the position due to his being the district chief of Uruzgan; one couldn't hold a government office and run for the Provincial Council. It was a testament to his support that he was able to win a seat in his own right in such a deeply Pashtun province. We met at FOB Ripley in our meeting room for local officials and exchanged pleasantries. He was his usual upbeat self and had the bearing and gravitas of a community leader with significant responsibilities. In his opinion, the Hazaran people had not received as much development assistance as the Pashtuns even though they were loyal to the government of Afghanistan. He then mentioned that some Hazaran leaders in the province were considering the possibility of creating a separate Hazaran-only district carved out of present-day Khas Uruzgan. He mentioned that these discussions were preliminary and he had no specific details of where the border of such a district would be located, but there was community interest in the idea.

Salari also discussed the inability of the Hazarans to travel to the Khas Uruzgan district center because the Taliban controlled the roads to it. It was true that as a rule the Coalition did not usually spend much development money in areas that were safe, preferring to focus our efforts on Taliban-contested areas as a way of winning the support of the population. Additionally, the largely Pashtun provincial government would not naturally have a sensitivity to Hazaran interests and, due to their lack of representation in the government, no real advocates for their interests. His advocacy of a separate district for the Hazarans was fascinating, and the fact that such a district could come about peacefully was a real testament to how a political process could lead to positive and peaceful results. His ideas required further study.

We eventually concluded the meeting and Salari expressed his desire to have the SOTF visit the Hazaran areas of Khas Uruzgan to greater familiarize ourselves with his community's concerns. I was hopeful we could make the trip.

✧

After much prodding from Salari, on September 25 the leadership of Special Operations Task Force-South East and I finally made a trip to his village in Khas Uruzgan, which was nestled deep in the heartland of the Hazarans. Unlike almost all our other trips around the province when we had met with Afghan leaders, we had decided not to invite any of the province's officials to accompany us. The issue of what to do with Shujayee continued to percolate as the Taliban summer offensive cranked away and efforts by the Afghan government to arrest Shujayee continued. The fact that certain local officials were killing their own tribal opponents prompted little action by the government, but inter-ethnic/sectarian violence always caused a swift reaction. In early August, the Taliban had attacked Shujayee's men, and while the Hazarans killed eight of the Islamists, two of Shujayee's men had been beheaded by the Taliban. It was an unusually bloody action for them to do, but it seemed calculated to prompt a retaliatory action by Shujayee. "Conveniently," a few Pashtun locals were killed in the ambush, although it was difficult to ascertain whether they were fighting alongside the Taliban, and bloody pictures of their bodies began to circulate. The allegations of civilian casualties by the ALP once again regained the attention of district and provincial officials as well as members of Parliament, the national government, and international media. Some media reports stressed that Shujayee was a criminal and Special Operations Forces units had played a role in preventing his facing justice. Others stated that even though Shujayee was officially an ALP commander, his men functioned more like a militia led by a warlord rather than a defensively oriented local protective force. Other media reports quoted local Khas Uruzgan officials as stating that SOF unilaterally stood up Shujayee's men without the support of the community and that Shujayee was from Ghazni Province and not Uruzgan. As you can imagine, things were not going well for us or for Shujayee, and we did what we could by meeting with the provincial officials in Tarin Kowt to iron out some sort of solution, but it was to no avail.

As events swirled around us, Hayes decided to make this final trip to the Hazaran heartland to visit with them and to demonstrate our support more broadly. If the Shujayee issue was ever going to be addressed, it would be with the new team at this late stage in our tour. We took off from Tarin Kowt in the late morning and initially stopped at Anaconda to pick up more men and to wait for a link up with Salari. The main challenge we had was simply locating his village since he and his community were in such a remote area. This required us to communicate with him, which was also problematic among the steep mountain passes. After a good while we finally arranged everything and a smaller element of our party went out first to secure the area by vehicle and then our main effort flew in by Chinook. As we approached their mountain redoubt, we could see several thousand people milling about what seemed to be a school set among the barren hillsides. We finally landed in a nearby field and made our way up a small hill, where we were greeted as conquering heroes. The local villagers lined both sides of the road toward the school for well over a mile and clapped and welcomed us. As our group walked toward the school, a few Hazarans were filming us—film that would likely be used to demonstrate U.S. interest in their cause. We finally made our way to the school, and a loud chanting began to take place: "Welcome, welcome, honored guests! Welcome, welcome, honored guests! Welcome, welcome, honored guests!" The high-pitched chants in English were coming from about twenty-five young Hazaran schoolchildren who were also clapping in sequence with their chant. The SEALs and the Special Forces soldiers fanned out into the courtyard to take up positions and Hayes and his replacement from SEAL Team Four, Job Price, were ushered toward the front of the growing crowd.

A long table was set up in back of the school and a banner had been hung welcoming the Americans and pledging the support of the Hazarans for peace and stability. An honor guard of Afghan Local Police stood behind the table on the steps of the school as a loudspeaker was used to communicate to the crowd. The chanting of the children began to die down as Hayes and Price took their positions of honor along with the Special Forces AOB commander and the commander of Forward Operating Base Anaconda. Salari was there helping to guide the event, and then Shujayee showed up. He wore round-rimmed glasses and had a small, wispy beard, and he was in total command of the situation. He was physically diminutive and short in stature but was clearly respected. A number of the Hazarans had seen him arrive and had registered their curiosity about the "savior of the Hazarans" with quick glances. The hero of the moment had arrived. The Hazaran leaders made a number of speeches and not only praised the Coalition Forces for our support but also shared their concerns about their future with us in a smaller meeting afterwards. As the sun began to set, the last few remarks were made and the Hazarans presented Hayes and Price as well as the Special Forces leaders with gifts. The Hazarans tightly wrapped each of their heads in turbans and hung large brown Afghan overcoats on them while presenting them with flowers and other small gifts. To see two SEAL team commanders dressed in native garb was priceless and really served as a testament to how much the Naval Special Warfare community had adapted to fulfill the Village Stability Operations mission. While the days of the SEALs kicking in doors hadn't really gone away, it was heartening to see their transformation to fighting the war with a strategy that was more likely to work for the long term. As the evening began to set in, we finally made our way back to the field and waited for our helicopters. They eventually arrived and we departed the Hazarans for one last time, hoping they would find some measure of peace in the Afghanistan of the future.

TWELVE

Twilight Zone

Books about war psychology ought to contain a chapter on "medal-reflexes" and "decoration complexes." Much might be written, even here, about medals and their stimulating effects on those who really risked their lives for them. But the safest thing to be said is that nobody knew how much a decoration was worth except the man who received it.

—SIEGFRIED SASSOON, *Memoirs of an Infantry Officer*

Kandahar Air Field (KAF) in Kandahar Province was the central hub for all activities in Regional Command-South, including all of the provinces Special Operations Task Force-South East was responsible for, which included Dai Kundi, Uruzgan, and Zabul. I had last visited KAF during the fall of 2010, albeit quite briefly, and it was already becoming a bustling little America surrounded by a scorching desert. When the opportunity presented itself to visit again in 2012 with my colleague Major Bradley to meet and brief his replacement, I jumped at the chance to see this iconic base and how our presence had changed there. Scott and I arrived on the far runway of the base on May 16 on board a C-130 for a three-day trip, which was in a way also a rest break. As the commuter shuttle that picked us up creaked along the unpaved road and the hot blast of desert air periodically pierced our protective air conditioning bubble, I slowly took in all the changes that had been wrought since I had first visited KAF in 2005.

My first impressions were of a still bustling airfield but suffering from urban sprawl and overcrowding. The base was choked with vehicles of all types and sizes, and the ubiquitous blast walls I had seen in my Iraq tour in 2007 were the greatest addition to the base's décor. Every structure was surrounded by a twenty-five-foot rectangular blast wall, and, while dust was still kicked up as the shuttle labored around the flight line, an unbroken view of gray concrete interspersed with a touch of camouflage of a passing soldier dominated one's perspective. As the bus pulled on to one of the main roads leading to Camp Brevard, the Special Operations base at KAF, we passed the Regional Command-South headquarters, which had been a few "temporary" plywood shacks in 2006 but was now a mix of shipping containers, blast walls, and a hodgepodge of other structures that blocked what had once been an open road.

Passing on the left was an airport terminal, which still retained its eponymously named "Taliban last stand" where you can fly a U.S. flag up the flagpole through the hole a U.S. bomb had made in the middle of the building back in 2001. Quite naturally this name was shown not to be entirely true years later. We eventually pulled into the front gate of Camp Brevard, a safe haven, if you will, from the frenetic energy of the airfield, where Special Operations Task Force-South was located.

Major Bradley and I finally dropped off our gear in our plywood hooches, checked in with the staff of the Village Stability Coordination Center (VSCC), and made our way to the infamous boardwalk. The VSCC was sort of the home office for Scott and the other Provincial Augmentation Teams. It was charged with supporting their efforts in the provinces by providing research support, liaison and advocacy with the Village Stability National Coordination Center (VSNCC) in Kabul, and administrative support, among other tasks. They maintained a constantly updated database of key political, tribal, religious, and economic Afghan leaders throughout southern Afghanistan and sought to evaluate who helped build good governance and who didn't. In many respects, this was the natural opposite of our usual intelligence gathering efforts, which tended to focus almost solely on the enemy's situation.

The center would also interact with its higher headquarters in Kabul, which had a number of Afghan government liaisons. These liaisons worked in the Afghan bureaucracies each day and knew the administrative, financial, budgeting, and resource terrain of each government entity. These officers would then advocate for removing a particularly corrupt official, chase down some program or leader to help solve a problem one of our DATs or PATs were working on, and pass information, as well as gossip, down the chain of command to keep our efforts informed. In many ways, this whole infrastructure existed because the U.S. Department of State didn't have the resources or, often, the conceptual tools to work on the political tasks required to defeat the Taliban's political program. Additionally, because many of the personnel who performed this type of work were Afghan Hands, often trained in the language and with repeated tours in Afghanistan, they also tried to exert positive influence where they could to stop some of the Afghan government's more pernicious activities and bolster those who wanted genuine reform.

One of the challenges in an insurgency environment is that a foreign nation's sovereignty is obviously weak because the insurgent exists, but the insurgent exists in part because of the poor policies and bad behavior of the national government. Additionally, the insurgent is undermining the host government's sovereignty while trying to establish the sovereignty of its own nascent cause and country. The work of Scott and the whole political advocacy effort was undertaken to address these exact problems.

When you have been working in an austere location for months at a time where deprivation is the rule, and you get the opportunity to visit Kandahar Air Field, a number of images come to mind. In so many ways, KAF is the Las Vegas of southern Afghanistan. It is surrounded by a vast desert that stretches to the horizon, was built by the mob (in this case, heavily connected tribes that operate like the Mafia), everyone is from somewhere else, and you lose all your money there. Tales of endless salsa-dancing classes, countless food courts, shipping container housing, alcohol on the sly, a bottomless pit of tobacco, and a more equitable gender ratio all fed the imaginations of the soldiers. We used to joke that KAF was where all your dreams came true and every road was "paved with gold."

The other side of KAF was that because it was the headquarters for our operations in southern Afghanistan it also had all the characteristics of a base back at home, which meant speeding tickets, reflective belts, lots of saluting, and plenty of regulations. One phrase that was quite popular was that "I went to war and a garrison broke out." In some circles it was a badge of honor to have a speeding ticket from the police at KAF.

The place to visit at KAF was the infamous boardwalk, a several-acre section of the base where a square, wooden-covered walkway provided endless shopping pleasures. In 2005, the original boardwalk was a much smaller and simpler structure near the flight line, with a Pizza Hut, Burger King, Green Beans Coffee, a modest Post Exchange, and a few other shops to cater to the visiting soldier. At that time, the base was still quite small and several tons worth of old Soviet helicopters, jets, and other junk still had to be removed. Of course, the senior-most officer in southern Afghanistan at that time was an Army colonel who was responsible for six provinces. The senior officer by 2012 was a two-star general in charge of four provinces. Times had certainly changed. Below is a list of the rules the commanding officer of Kandahar Air Field had posted to govern our behavior on his base.

COMKAF [Commander, Kandahar Air Field]
TOP 10 LIST

10. No alcohol, pornography, or controlled substances. What would grandma think??!!

9. If it walks, talks and looks like a duck, then it probably is a duck. If not, it's probably an officer. Please extend proper military courtesies.

8. Wear a clean uniform or PT [physical training] gear in the DFAC. No one wants to sit next to the Poo Pond life guard.

7. Talking trash is great . . . picking up trash is not. Clean up after yourselves!

6. Just because you THINK you're "the bomb" on KAF doesn't mean you can't be hurt by one; during a rocket attack, lie on the ground for 2 minutes before seeking shelter.

5. Hope your iPod has the song "Danger Zone" loaded because if you are plugged in while walking or running on the streets, then you are living in one. No wearing of ear phones while jogging outdoors.

4. You may feel like Dale Earnhardt today, but you better be "Driving Miss Daisy" on the streets of KAF. Speed limits are posted for our safety 20 KMH unless otherwise posted. Just humor us on this one . . .

3. There are approximately 4,000 crosswalks on KAF—Please find one to use BEFORE crossing a street.

2. "Badges? We don't need no stinkin' badges!" Well . . . on KAF, you do. Please display it properly.

1. "What is it that cannot be seen, cannot be heard, but can double as a hood ornament or hub cap?" YOU, without a reflective belt . . . wear one during hours of low visibility and darkness.

The boardwalk of 2012 was a sight to behold. It could probably be seen from space. The center courtyard had a plush faux grass soccer field, an outdoor rink for hockey, several volleyball nets, a running track, and the ubiquitous bomb shelters for incoming rockets and mortars. The shops ran the gamut of fast food such as pizzeria Mamma Mia, Kandahar Fresh Deli & Pizza, and an actual TGIF. Other shops included the Majib Bicycle & Motor Bike Shop, Fresh Juice Bar, and a mothballed Tim Hortons, the famous Canadian food chain that had closed when most Canadian forces had been withdrawn from Afghanistan. There was also your usual assortment of military gear stores (got to get another pouch and knife!) and your standard Afghan souvenir shop. It was the goal of nearly every soldier in Afghanistan to acquire an old firearm, preferably British, or something new such as a fully automatic AK-47. Every Afghan knew someone who could get one for a price, and it was common for soldiers to talk about trying to "piece out" an AK-47 and get it home by trying to mail it, pack it, or stash it somewhere. There was always a grizzled soldier who would recount stories of bringing back "truckloads" of AK-47s back in the early days of the war or how they had stumbled upon a mother lode of old British rifles that you simply couldn't get these days. Soldiers had different collecting preferences; some only wanted bayonets, others wanted any

Soviet bric-a-brac, some wanted only "ancient" weapons like pikes, axes, and helmets. There was always the odd soldier who instantly became a gem expert, constantly parlaying with the Afghan merchants over the "right" cut of a jewel. Some of the more enterprising souls actually had gem weights and other instruments to determine the "actual" quality and worth of a gem.

Going to the boardwalk was such a common pastime at the base that some soldiers would have made good candidates for the show "Hoarders." All in all, it was an orgy of consumerism and so many soldiers long accustomed to privation spent their hard-earned dollars on all these baubles, fast-food, and junk that it created its own sort of postshopping euphoria.

The other main terrain feature at the base was the famous "poo pond," which was part of the sewage-management system at the base. When I had visited this unfortunate landmark in 2005 it was on the edge of civilization at the base, but as the years went on and more and more troops came to Afghanistan, the poo pond became engulfed in sprawl. It was now used as a reference point by the residents of KAF to offer directions to a visitor or to set up a future meeting. A few examples: "take a right at the poo pond and it should be on your left" or "if you get to the poo pond you've gone too far." It even spawned its own set of T-shirts such as "I was a life-guard at the poo pond" and "I survived the poo pond," which were available for purchase at the higher-end stores of Kandahar Air Field.

Another aspect of the base's sprawl was that in addition to the soldiers and civilians, a small army of "third country nationals" operated at the base, ran its chow halls, cleaned up the place, and simply made life bearable. This interesting term of "third country nationals" usually meant Filipinos, Indians, Bangladeshis, Indonesians, and so many other countries that one lost track. Different parts of the base were unofficially assigned to them, and due to the great number of people at the base and the constant churn of bodies coming and going, an underground social order had been created. There were many tales of various contractors closing shop and not transporting their workers back home, and these same workers stayed at the base and fed themselves off the free chow, undertook odd jobs for their friends, and built small communities there. Countless babies had unofficially been born at the base, and parts of it looked more like a developing country slum than a proper U.S. military base. Homelessness was actually a problem at the base. An old rule of thumb when you served in Afghanistan was that you should prepare to lose from ten to twenty pounds; these days, more soldiers wondered how much they would gain.

There was often such an air of unreality at KAF that one wondered if we were all participating in the same war. A rumor circulated that when Gen. Stanley McChrystal first visited KAF upon becoming ISAF commander in 2009 (keep in mind, he had initially been there in 2001), he allegedly said, upon looking around, that "this is what defeat looks like." Not too far off the mark. In many respects, KAF in 2012 reminded me of the great excesses of the Iraq War, and these "Ugly American" tendencies were simply a central feature of how our country waged war. Too much money was being spent, too few risks were being taken to win, bureaucracy had arrived large and in charge, and the constant rotation of soldiers meant wisdom about the war was often a rare commodity.

All these tendencies eventually showed up in places like Uruzgan Province, where reflective belts were now required at night, shopping amenities now existed at the base, and rules were rigidly enforced even if common sense suggested otherwise. Even though sexual assault is a major problem that must be stopped, it didn't seem to make much sense to issue the SEAL team members a rape whistle since the odds of any its members being sexually assaulted was essentially zero. I informally referred to all these developments as my "reflective belt and paved sidewalk" theory of military defeat. You knew you weren't winning when paved sidewalks and reflective belts started to show up, because that was when you were more concerned about events inside the wire rather than outside it. A whole other book will have to be written to figure out how things got so bad. Once Scott and I partook of the "forbidden" pleasures of KAF and picked up his replacement, a Major Williams, we returned to Uruzgan and FOB Ripley recharged from our sojourn and ready to return to our duties.

THIRTEEN

Transition to Victory

I have often found that when I was afraid, the best course was
to advance towards the enemy.

—JOHN BAGOT GLUBB, *The Story of the Arab Legion*

The district of Gizab in northern Uruzgan is a place of special
significance to the SOF community because in June 2010 the
villagers there took security into their own hands and kicked
the Taliban out of the area. A U.S. Special Forces team was then quickly
dispatched to the district to partner with the villagers, and even though
it was only a local revolt, it had strategic implications well beyond the
small isolated district. It indicated that the Afghans were not willing to
just absorb the abuses of the Taliban but would stand against them given
the right conditions. In this way, Gizab became the first Village Stability
Platform site in the country and a catchphrase for the successful partnership between U.S. Special Forces and the Afghan population.

The far northern district of Gizab is divided into Hazaran and Pashtun
populations and is set into the great mountains of the Hindu Kush. Due
to the district's mountainous terrain the community's initial efforts to kick
out the Taliban were relatively easy to achieve and maintain through con-
trolling the small number of key passes that allowed the insurgents access
to the villages. The local Hazaran population was also reliably anti-Taliban.
On June 20, I traveled with Commander Hayes and the Combined Team
Uruzgan leadership to Gizab to witness the conclusion of the process of
raising an Afghan Local Police force capable of defending itself. We would

be transferring the site from American to Afghan control and preparing to move the embedded team there to a new location. Gizab was one of those anonymous "fly over" areas of Afghanistan that I had long dreamed of visiting, but when I departed the area in August 2006 I thought my moment had come and gone. As we left that warm sunny Wednesday in 2012, I couldn't believe my good fortune to visit this place and to witness not only the transition ceremony but also the first site that helped begin this process of helping the Afghans turn against the Taliban insurgency.

Unlike Uruzgan's other districts, Gizab had several advantages that made it the safest part of the province. In addition to the district's remote location and mountainous terrain, the nearby Hazaran province of Dai Kundi bordered it to the north, as well as the Khas Uruzgan District to its east and the Kajran District to its west, which also had Hazaran populations. The district had essentially been dropped in a demographic cul-de-sac that protected its population from three directions.

The Hazarans were implacable foes of the Taliban and were much better organized at resisting the Taliban than were the Pashtuns. Many of them had fled to Iran and other parts of Central Asia during Taliban rule. After they were driven from their homes, they had worked to make sure it never happened again. Many had acquired military training, had expanded their education, and established extensive networks they could draw upon when they returned to Afghanistan after 2001. All these factors helped the Hazaran community continually repel Taliban incursions. A substantial river also coursed through Gizab District and a wide-open plane of small rivulets branched out from the main body of water, establishing the basic division of the district east to west.

While the barren deserts and spartan mountains were bereft of vegetation, the residents of the area had been able to cultivate substantial farm holdings, so they were well-fed and lived in a thriving and viable community. What was most notable was that even though the community was split between the Sunni Pashtuns and the Shiite Hazarans, they seemed to largely get along. The four-hundred-strong Afghan Local Police force was multiethnic and multireligious and led by a local Pashtun leader. In many ways, the simple rural life of the area and the generally comfortable living arrangements prevented any real need for competition between the communities. The physical isolation of the region also made it difficult for the Taliban to insert a sectarian element to the situation. More people saw themselves as proud residents of Gizab rather than members of different religious communities. It also probably helped that large numbers from both groups tended to live with each other in mixed areas.

The district chief of police was a local named Lala (la-lay) who ran the area with a firm but balanced hand. There was no doubt he was in charge, and he was as aggressive against the Taliban as was Matullah, which is one reason they sometimes clashed as two strong-willed leaders. Chief Lala had once burned down a Taliban bazaar in the southernmost part of the district as a warning sign not only to them but to any locals who even thought of supporting the insurgency. The chief also personally led his resupply missions to Tarin Kowt to pick up pay, ammunition, uniforms, and other equipment from Matullah. He was a force in Gizab, and he was able to impose his writ due to the greater resources he had under VSO, which was yet another example of how important the program was in empowering local leaders to solve their own security, governance, and development problems. Even though the trip to Gizab was a celebration of success as the Village Stability Platform transitioned to Afghan control, the locals were still nervous about the Taliban and were keen on making sure we and the Afghan government didn't forget them. As our helicopters approached Gizab, we noticed a small group of official-looking Afghans waiting near the landing site. Several of them wore police uniforms, which suggested Chief Lala was among them.

The landing zone was a large square of rocks that had been assembled to keep the dust down and was located next to a looming mountain ridge that defined the northern portion of the district. Our Blackhawk helicopters quickly landed and Mike, Matullah, the deputy governor Haji Kuday Rahim Khan, and a phalanx of SEALs exited toward the assembled local dignitaries. Matullah went directly to Chief Lala and shook his hand and chatted a bit before shaking the hands of all the other assembled men. Several of the local police had assembled in a small formation with the leader holding an Afghan flag on a pole as spectators hovered around our group from a distance. Matullah was definitely doing his job, and his authority now stretched throughout the province, albeit due to our help, versus in the past when the police chief was mostly confined to the Tarin Kowt area.

Lieutenant Anderson of the U.S. Army, the head of Village Stability Transition Team Gizab, greeted us as well and told us the plan of the day. Once we had dropped our gear off at the base, we would assemble right behind it for the transition ceremony and then decamp to Chief Lala's house for lunch. Anderson was a West Point graduate and former college wrestler who led the VSTT along with a few Navy SEALs. Once the ceremony was over he and his team would break down the site, drive overland to FOB Ripley, and then refit and prepare to be deployed to a new location. The compound the team lived in had been rented and was made of adobe, but it had several improvements added to it, which usually entailed heavy concrete treatments. While they got their supplies, including bottles of water, via parachute drops, they also had a well with an old-fashioned bucket and rope to descend to its darkest depths. It was quite a spartan location.

We finally arrived behind the small headquarters for the team while some last-minute arrangements were still being put into place. A giant camouflage parachute had been attached to the back wall, which was also ringed with sandbags and supported by bamboo poles to create a canopy. The floor was made up of the discarded hard plastic bottoms of the airdrops, and empty oil drums were arrayed along the back to create a small wall. A wooden podium stood toward the front. Some carpets were laid around for the dignitaries, along with some chairs plus a table for tea and treats. One of the hosts poured tea for Hayes, Matullah, and the deputy governor, and the other guests sat at the front as the local community sat on the ground in their usual manner. Chief Lala's men hovered along the fringes with their AK-47s hanging along their chests and with chest rigs full of extra magazines. A large Afghan flag was hung from the wall along with prominently displayed pictures of President Karzai and Matullah.

First Lieutenant Anderson began by welcoming his guests. He said, "This is the first district to transition in all of Afghanistan. This is due to our collective efforts. It is a proud day for Gizab and for Afghanistan." He then introduced Commander Hayes, who said, "This is a celebration. A celebration of the work we did together. As we transition this site to your community, we will no longer be with you step by step but will be right behind you supporting you. As we close Gizab we will continue to come back. The Special Forces are never leaving Afghanistan because you are our brothers." His comments were well-received.

The deputy governor, a proud local official, then stood up to give his remarks.

> The provincial government is completely behind you. This is a good moment for the Afghan nation to demonstrate to the world that we are a responsible people and are making progress. We must continue to build trust with the people by showing them respect. Our country has suffered a long time. With the help of the police we took the district back from the insurgents. We used to run from our homes due to the dangers but now we can fight the Taliban and we can build peaceful, civilized lives. Important for our leaders to always be open to negotiation. We truly appreciate from the bottom of our heart all of the hard work of the U.S. This is an important day as we claim our security and we must continue to improve coordination and cooperation. The Coalition Forces have sacrificed big time in this country. We must give the Afghan National Police the capabilities, the training, and the weapons they need to keep us safe. I ask the district leaders to send your requests to Tarin Kowt so we can help you. We need people to serve who can read and write to help with proper planning. I feel good about Gizab, it has been loyal to the country. We cannot take a leader by his words. His actions show his true intentions. We need to maintain security. The new governor is trying very hard and is very active. He has been taking our case to the central government, and the president is happy so far. He is showing no favoritism to anyone and is treating everyone equally. We will never forget you. When I go back, I will take your message to the other districts. You are united and I will also talk to the president of Afghanistan.

His words were welcomed heartily by the crowd and they clapped loudly.

The local district chief then stood up and said:

> We are happy to have you visit us. Gizab is the first to transition. Iran and Pakistan want to keep us divided but we are ready and able to handle our area and to help keep our country united as one nation. I only ask that you consider giving Gizab to Dai Kundi Province because Tarin Kowt is so far away from us. We need your help and support. The Kush Kadir Valley [we recently transitioned a VSP there] is very important to us because it keeps the road open to Tarin Kowt.

The next speaker was a senior representative of the Afghan National Police. He spoke while Matullah remained seated.

> All of Uruzgan salutes you. Without any support you fought the Taliban and you took it to the insurgents. You earned your freedom and are better than anyone else. You are the first to transition and the first to get your freedom. You have no Afghan army, no Coalition Forces and yet you defended yourselves. It is important that you continue to coordinate and cooperate with the Afghan National Police; it is key. General Matullah Khan will not forget you. He has asked the Central Government for one hundred more Afghan National Police and two hundred Afghan Local Police for Gizab and to increase the *tashkeil*. This is a proud moment for Uruzgan.

The community loved his full-throated speech and his respect for all they had accomplished. A local mullah then expressed his sincere gratitude for the U.S. presence in Afghanistan the past eleven years and stated that the transition of Gizab to Afghan control would free up U.S. forces to go where the Taliban still were.

The final speaker was the U.S. commander of Combined Team Uruzgan, ostensibly in charge of the whole province. "Friends, I would like to close with a prayer. Peace and prosperity for Gizab. A prayer for our leaders, the provincial chief of police, the district governor, the district chief of police. Please help the good people of Uruzgan and Gizab. We will never say goodbye but only until we meet again." With these concluding remarks the simple ceremony was over and Matullah posed for pictures with the Afghan National Police and Afghan Local Police in the area, reminding me again of how much of a local celebrity he had become.

The whole group slowly meandered its way over to Chief Lala's home, where he was hosting us for lunch. As we made our way there, we noticed that a number of traffic barriers surrounded his house. Unlike the normal concrete structure these were actually half-buried empty oil drums that had been filled with dirt with concertina wire strung between them. This was another example of Afghan ingenuity, where nothing went to waste. Every single piece of a containerized delivery system was used including the parachute, the hard plastic top and bottom, the wooden frame, the cardboard box, and everything that came with it. Lala's house was a fortified compound with sandbagged positions on each corner and men at attention as we entered. Like most men of power in Afghanistan, Lala had an outside pavilion for entertaining. It was covered in plush carpets and pillows and there were two bamboo curtains at either end supplemented with dried bushes. The bushes would be drenched with water as the meeting went on so that the air temperature would be reduced due to evaporation. It was a simple but effective method of air conditioning.

A small creek flowed by the pavilion and a series of small trees provided shade. Lala's home overlooked a wide field that led to the large open valley and terminated at the distant mountains. Additional guard posts were along the back wall, and several parachutes had been tailored there to provide shade from the sun and rain. Men with AK-47s and PKM machine guns stood guard in their police uniforms, reminding me that the term "police" was understood a little differently in Afghanistan, where they often seemed more like military units.

As the featured guest, Matullah sat at the front of the rectangular structure and Deputy Governor Rahim Khan sat to his side. Hayes and the CTU leadership also sat to the side as Chief Lala and other ANP officials sat across from them. As the food was being prepared the men chatted a bit and talked about the future. Even though the day's event was a celebration, the practical reality was that the district was isolated and difficult to resource and the vital road connecting it to Tarin Kowt had to be kept open. Just prior to Gizab we had transitioned a VSP called Kalach, which was just to the south of Gizab and straddled a vital valley connecting the district to the provincial capital. While Chief Lala had stated his strong interest in procuring more heavy weapons, he definitely wanted to have Kalach's ALP added to the Gizab *tashkeil*. Even though he recognized that his *tashkeil* was full, he felt that because the residents of Gizab wanted a safe route they would be more willing to secure the area than would the Chora police. The deputy governor then mentioned that Governor Akunzada was planning to go to Kabul to request one hundred additional ANP for Gizab as well as two hundred ALP. Chief Lala greatly welcomed this news and a smile broke out from beneath his thick black beard since it suggested that perhaps he would have Kalach after all. Hayes also pledged to continue to support Chief Lala and Gizab and promised frequent visits.

As we departed Gizab for the last time and the team broke down the base to move to Tarin Kowt, I reflected upon why Gizab was successful. In many respects, its situation was unique, but clearly the terrain played a key factor in that the mountains did the work of several hundred more ALP to prevent insurgent intimidation. Additionally, the reduced number of entrances to the area allowed fewer ALP to have a greater effect. The leadership of Chief Lala was also crucial, along with the isolated nature of the district, which made it difficult for the Taliban to access. The Hazarans were helpful as well since they strongly disliked the Taliban. The economic situation seemed positive, which diminished local grievances. Finally, there was largely one tribe in the area, the Achikzai, which made organizing the population much easier.

All these factors weighed on my mind, but the real determinant for success going forward was the long-term sustainability of the area through continued logistical support from Tarin Kowt. Our presence and activity could do a lot to help Afghans turn against and resist the Taliban, but we couldn't and wouldn't be there forever. It was essential to make sure that Afghan pay, logistical, and other back office support continued to determine long-term success in the conflict.

A month later, the season of transition was still among us. I traveled down to the governor's compound for the official transition of the province to Afghan government control. While the Afghans had always been in charge of things no matter how much we thought we had a handle on everything, this formal ceremony was significant on so many levels. In many ways, it signaled our departure from Afghanistan and the end of the U.S. experience there. To personally witness the event after having been at the Pentagon on 9/11 was especially poignant even though the transition in practice versus in theory would take longer.

The ceremony took place in the great yellow meeting hall of the governor's compound and was quite the event. A number of Afghan officials attended, including the minister of defense for Afghanistan, the director of the Independent Directorate for Local Governance, the director of the National Directorate for Security, and three deputy ministers from the ministries of health, education, and agriculture. Governor Akunzada, three members of Parliament from the province, and a number of provincial officials, including most of the central ministries' local directors, were present. The Australian ambassador to Afghanistan, a U.S. ambassador from the U.S. embassy in Kabul, the commanding general of Regional Command-South, and representatives of the government of the Netherlands also attended.

In addition to the usual round of speeches by the attendees, a formal flag-raising ceremony concluded the day's events. A brass band festooned in red livery stood to the side, ready to perform, and an American and an Australian soldier stood at attention as they held their respective flags. A line of Afghan soldiers and police in their formal uniforms stood at attention and the Afghan officials filed out after the speeches to raise the Afghan flag. As the flag was raised, the band began to play, and the drums and cymbals beat and clanged away as the brass instruments belted out their tune. After the flag had been raised, the official party departed and met again at the governor's compound, followed by the line of uniformed men marching in as close to unison as possible. While the speeches universally praised the transition, with a great deal of emphasis placed on Afghans now being ready to shoulder the burden of greater responsibility, concern was expressed that the Afghan government needed to better meet the expectations of the people for justice, services, and good governance.

A common theme among several speakers was the need for Kabul to follow through on its repeated promises of services and projects to Uruzgan. One speaker mentioned that many ministers visit foreign countries with more regularity than they visit Uruzgan. Another speaker mentioned that the three key events in Afghanistan's recent history were (1) the withdrawal of Soviet troops from Afghanistan, (2) the attacks of September 11, which brought Karzai to power, and (3) today's transition of Uruzgan Province. The Afghans had a certain poetic sensibility about things, and it was touching to see how important this ceremony was and how deeply it affected them. While full transition would be undertaken in a phased manner, not just in Uruzgan but all over the country, Afghan officials seemed aware of the burden of responsibility they were assuming and, while keen to take on greater authority, were mindful of the remaining challenges they had to meet to satisfy the expectations of the people. So much blood and treasure had been expended in Uruzgan to get to this point, and while I was hopeful and optimistic, a sense of Afghan fatalism had set in over the years. I was braced for disappointment.

✧

After visiting a number of our sites in Uruzgan, Dai Kundi, and Zabul Provinces, I had gained enough insight into how the Village Stability Operations program functioned to speak with Mike about what success looked like. As I listened to each brief of a team leader at a Village Stability Platform, heard the Afghans speak about the successes and challenges of the program, and then compared this knowledge against my own experiences from three previous tours, I arrived at a key insight.

So much of how we thought and talked about the war revolved around what we did *to* the Afghans rather than what came *from* them. We were good about counting how many enemy *we* had killed, how many shuras *we* had attended with the Afghans, how much money *we* had spent on development, and other measures of "success," but what did it all matter if the Afghans continued to be on the sidelines? Additionally, the real measure of the totality of our efforts was what the Afghans did on their own in security, development, and governance. When we got the right balance of kinetic and nonkinetic efforts in an area (for example, enemy killed, local police recruited, community leaders bolstered), the Afghans themselves would make a cost/benefit calculation and either stay at home or take positive steps to improve their situation by siding with the government.

One of the missing components of our whole strategy in Afghanistan had been this locally based "on-ramp" that allowed Afghans to be part of the solution in their own villages. Furthermore, after you reached a community's tipping point, where it not only had risen up against the Taliban but had organized against it in a sustained manner, you also saw the community holding regular governance meetings and investing in the development of their community. When we had sufficiently protected a local community and it had reached its security tipping point, the Afghans would demonstrate our success through the positive actions they took. In the end, we protected a community while the Taliban controlled it. It was a subtle distinction, but it had enormous repercussions.

I stopped by Mike's office again to discuss my thoughts on how we could measure success in this type of warfare. "Come in, come in," he said as he ushered me in with his outstretched arm.

I commented, "I think I've figured out how we can measure success."

"Excellent! What have you found out?"

"Well, a lot of how we usually measure success is dependent on a conventional warfare way of seeing combat," I said. "We can measure all sorts of inputs and outputs such as enemy killed, territory taken, IEDs found, for example. We even measure our good governance and development efforts in the same way, in terms of how many meetings we had and how much money we had spent."

He nodded in agreement.

"These are important measures for sure," I continued, "but they aren't the fundamental ones. The central measure of our success is what we prompt the Afghans to do at the end of the day. Are more joining the ALP, building new businesses because they feel safer, engaging with government leaders, or informing on the insurgents? This truly measures the success or failure of our efforts."

Mike said, "I like how you put that, 'what comes from the Afghans matters more than what we do to them.'"

"I think the missing piece has been an on-ramp for them to do something about their situation," I said. "They weren't going to join the army and leave their village, they weren't necessarily going to join the police full-time, especially if it was controlled by another tribe, and they had no legal manner to protect themselves. Without protection, they couldn't do much else in terms of working with the local government or improving their economic situation. I feel as if looking at things from this perspective allows us to compare the actions of different units and locales better. This would put the usual statistics, for example, enemy killed, in perspective so it didn't matter necessarily how many Taliban you killed but only as much as those deaths prompted a community to join the Afghan Local Police."

"I think this is a very useful way of thinking about the problem set," Mike stated. "I like how you framed the whole situation, but I wonder how we could measure governance and development or even security using this reframing of our desired outcomes? I also know that each VSP is on the hook to recruit three hundred Afghan Local Police regardless of local conditions and I wonder if the tipping points change that much."

"I will have to work on how we could measure this accurately and fairly," I said, "and the idea of why some VSPs are able to recruit three hundred ALP while others struggle to do so also intrigues me."

"Exactly, if you can also help me understand why some succeed and others struggle that would be very useful as well."

"I will need to put this all together and probably use a statistical program to figure it all out."

"Sounds good. Keep up the great work, Dan!"

The more I thought about the various VSPs I had visited, as well as reflecting on my own experience serving in Fallujah during the Anbar Awakening (when I had seen the city turn against al-Qaeda), the more I wondered what were the sets of variables that had to come together to achieve success.

It was clear that the capabilities of each VSP, the quality of local Afghan leadership, and the terrain played key roles. Additionally, the number of tribes in an area mattered, as did proximity to the border with Pakistan and whether surrounding districts had a Coalition Forces presence as well. The amount of time each VSP had been there also seemed to matter, as did the presence of Afghan National Police and the Afghan National Army. These and other variables floated around in my mind as I also thought about how one measured the actions of the Afghans. Additionally, if I could figure out what was important to measure, how could I systematically collect this sort of information?

One of the insights I had picked up was that as security improved, local economics improved. Prices went down for products and more bazaar shops opened up. Another metric was when Afghans went to the district center to involve the district chief in an important matter. By extension, this could include the number of people applying to go on the Haj or even how many were getting married or acquiring a second, third, or fourth wife. Both of these activities required money, a sense of security and faith in the future, and interaction with the Afghan government.

As I thought more about how to measure all these interactions, I also wondered if I could statistically measure them by assessing all the VSP sites in Afghanistan in a systematic way that could give us useful insights into how Afghan communities operated. I definitely had my work cut out for me.

FOURTEEN

The Great Wall of Chora

Here, on the borders of death, life follows an amazingly simple course, it is limited to what is most necessary, all else lies buried in gloomy sleep;—in that lies our primitiveness and our survival.

—Erich Maria Remarque,
All Quiet on the Western Front

Having seen the great success of Village Stability Operations in Gizab District, I was curious about how it was doing in the district of Chora. The district was just east of Uruzgan Province's capital of Tarin Kowt and south of Gizab and sat along the Karmisan River, which flowed southwest, eventually flowing past Tarin Kowt and feeding into the Helmand River.[1] It was largely made up of barren deserts and stark mountains, and the population lived along densely packed green swaths of farmland where local residents eked out a basic existence cultivating the soil that collected in the river basin and at the bases of the mountains. The district's approximately 20,000 residents were divided into two sections by a mountain range that bisected the middle of the district east to west. The whole area was predominantly Pashtun and was mostly divided into the Barakzai and Achikzai tribes in the northern portion and the Populzai in the south around the village of Chenartu. Hazaran and Baluch ethnic communities were also present, with the Hazaran population in larger numbers in the northern areas closer to the predominantly Hazaran province of Dai Kundi. The district bordered Zabul Province to the south and Dai Kundi to the north and the Uruzgan districts of Khas Uruzgan to the east, Tarin Kowt to the south, and Shahid-e-Hasas to the west.

The Chora area had long served as a transit hub for insurgents from either Helmand or Zabul Provinces, where they poured into the districts respectively west and east of Chora and then transited, finally, to the provincial capital of Tarin Kowt. The population was generally anti-Taliban because of their largely Durrani Pashtun tribal affiliation (the Taliban were typically affiliated with the Ghilzai tribal confederation) and were more naturally inclined to support the government of the Islamic Republic of Afghanistan.

I had last visited the district in July 2006 when I had been with the Provincial Reconstruction Team, and it had only been liberated from the Taliban a month or so prior. Our forces had never had a permanent presence there, so when the Taliban returned in the summer of 2006 in much larger numbers than before, the area fell fairly quickly to their fighters. In many respects it was much easier for them because the then district chief, Haji Obaidullah, had done little to prevent their assault, and rumors abounded that he had actually helped them take the area. He would eventually be arrested for his behavior, but this did little to prevent his political ambition and he was now, six years later, a member of Parliament for the province; even in Afghanistan, politics was sometimes the last refuge of a scoundrel. When I had visited the area the Taliban had only recently been pushed out but their forces were still strong in the district. Our mission was to address some of the humanitarian concerns of the population as well as to assess the battle damage for possible development projects. We held a medical outreach event in the area and treated dozens of local residents, and then assessed the damage the next day. The Taliban had tried to burn down the boys school in the area and had also tried to bring down the district center building by placing a mine against the central pillar. They didn't succeed in either of these goals, but both buildings had substantial damage. The Islamists torched the vehicles of the police and looted what they could. We eventually met with the local leaders, who directed our attention to three wounded Taliban in the local clinic, whom we transported back to our base. On the way back to Tarin Kowt we were ambushed and had a two-and-a-half-hour firefight with the Taliban, eventually killing almost thirty of them. There was no significant damage to our side. The conventional-sized assault of the Taliban on Chora shook my confidence in our overall strategy at that time; we had largely viewed the Taliban as a spent force.

In late June 2012, I had an opportunity to visit our team there to see how security and other matters had progressed. Village Stability Platform Chora had only recently been established and the team there had come from another section of the district just west of the district center called Kush Kadir, where they had also run a VSP location. That base had been transitioned to Afghan control and the team now focused on reclaiming the Chora area from the Taliban. The unit that was responsible for the site was led by Navy SEAL officer Lt. Sam Dean. At six feet one he had a full beard and the muscular frame of a competitive swimmer, which he had been at the College of William & Mary, as well as captain of the team, and he was, as I would soon learn, as much a thinker as a doer. In addition to the usual gear one brings on deployment, he had also brought along a steamer trunk full of books on counterinsurgency, stability operations, and Afghanistan, among other subjects. A conceptual thinker, he always sought to take his ideas and concepts about how to defeat the enemy and bring them to fruition. He had been selected by Commander Hayes for an intensive training program called Mirror Image, which puts its students through a roughly ten-day course where they lived and fought like insurgents and received academic lectures about insurgency and terrorism from experts with firsthand experience. The whole goal of the training was to force the student to think like an insurgent and to move beyond Western conceptions of how to solve problems. Dean saw the insurgency for what it was and knew when to set aside force to engage in diplomacy, tribal outreach, and community engagement, but his focus was always on defeating the insurgency and never letting convenience override duty. I was looking forward to this first visit to his site, and I was grateful he invited me to see it.

Lieutenant Dean and his men had visited Tarin Kowt to resupply their stores and to meet with General Matullah Khan to discuss the situation in Chora. I accompanied him to his meeting with the police chief on June 20 at his compound right outside our front gate. Matullah graciously welcomed us and we went to his usual meeting room for visiting guests. Dean's team had established themselves in Chora the previous month and had aggressively been going after the Taliban. The surface-level stability they had initially encountered was only due to the Taliban's control of the area and the complicity or ignorance of other units in the region that did not contest this reality. Over the course of several missions, the newly arrived SEALs killed dozens of Taliban in the area, and the team itself suffered some injuries including one who lost a leg there, another who had been blasted in the face, and an Afghan commando who had been shot in the head. Having pushed the enemy back and cleared several area villages that had been historic Taliban strongholds, Dean's team established several checkpoints in the Chora District village of Deh Rafshan for the Afghan National Police. They now sought Matullah's advice on where to place additional checkpoints as well as recommendations as to which elders they should work with. They also sought his permission to visit the commanders of his checkpoints. Asking for Matullah's permission was a smart gesture by Dean since it showed respect for the police chief's position and was a humbler approach than simply telling him what our men were going to do. Matullah greatly welcomed the recent clearing operations of Chora and also supported the continued construction of checkpoints in the Chora area. He recommended a village elder named Gul Borka Khan as a reliable candidate to be the ALP commander in the area, and he welcomed the news that the SEAL team had established a strong working relationship with Nimatullah, the district chief of police. Matullah then expressed his view that the ANA commanders in the Chora area were collaborating with the Taliban and were not aggressively pursuing them. He agreed that action needed to be taken to change this situation and said he planned to speak with Afghan National Army commander General Zafar as well as Governor Akunzada about the situation. He then recommended that an Afghan National Army base be built near the Kalach area in Chora

District so that the local police would feel secure (the Kalach ALP had threatened to resign following the receipt of their next paycheck). Dean and Matullah agreed that building a new army base would take too much time, so Matullah agreed to send twenty ANP to Kalach with the ALP's pay to bolster their confidence and prevent their mass exodus. It was a productive meeting and demonstrated once again how essential it was to cultivate local leaders, to work with them, and to build Afghan institutions.

After finishing a round of meetings with Matullah, the staff of the SOTF, and Barakzai tribal elders who had been visiting the provincial capital, Dean and his men departed from FOB Ripley in the early afternoon. The full heat of the summer was in effect. His convoy contained as many supplies as he and his men could jam into their vehicles or drag behind them for their VSP and included a huge fuel tank, extra external lights with generators, empty Hescos, and other supplies. I joined Dean in his MRAP and we slowly crept our way out of the base, heavily laden down with our additional baggage. Since the road had been paved out of Tarin Kowt all the way to Chora, which was new since I had last served there, it was a pretty easy ride, and we soon passed by the Rozi Khan mosque, named after and dedicated to the famous Barakzai tribal leader who been accidentally killed by Australian forces in 2008. Just as we arrived on the outskirts of the village of Chora, our convoy halted. A small stretch of road between two Afghan army outposts had long given the team problems. Even though the Afghan army "controlled" the road, it was constantly seeded with IEDs, and from my vantage point you could see that the road had been blown into Swiss cheese at several points. Once we stopped, a small group of SEALs and our Afghan partners stepped out to survey the scene. The Afghans were part of a group we called the Civil Mine Reduction Group (CMRG) and they were local hires whose sole job was to find IEDs and destroy them for our team. What was interesting about them was that because they had worked in the Uruzgan area for multiple rotations and since they were Afghans, they knew how the insurgents thought and the strategies they used to emplace the deadly explosives. After a few minutes of conferring, one of the Afghan men walked out to a small culvert and poked around for an explosive. He eventually found one, returned to our convoy to get explosives, and then returned to the site, where he then placed the charges. He slowly walked back to our convoy and then, from behind cover, exploded the IED, launching chunks of rock into the air along with a giant dust plume. It was a sight to behold. We had long suspected the Afghan army soldiers of colluding with the Taliban, not out of any sympathy for their cause but because most of the army came from other parts of the country and were ethnically different from the local Pashtun population. They simply wanted to survive their tour and didn't really have any emotional connections to the communities they served in. As you can imagine, that one of our ostensible allies might be colluding with the enemy complicated things immensely for the Chora team. We eventually arrived at the site by early evening and offloaded our supplies.

Like most of our other Village Stability Platform sites, the Chora team was in a rented Afghan compound, which they had improved with Hescos and other security upgrades. Their modest site was on the edge of town and had a spartan mountain range behind it bereft of foliage. A couple of plywood shacks had been erected by the Navy Seabees as well as a couple of Alaskan tents for the men to live in, and small piles of sandbags were on the roofs of the shacks to make sure the tarpaper as well as the roof itself didn't blow off when helicopters came to land near the site (unfortunately, this lesson had been learned the hard way). Countless Chigo air conditioning units hummed away as they worked to keep the constant heat at bay. An outside gym had been built and the kitchen had modern amenities such as shiny metal refrigerators and freezers. While the men had MRAPs and Humvees to use, they also had Razors, which were souped-up golf carts that had been tactically modified for Afghanistan with rugged tires, khaki camouflage, and gun mounts. The team used three different compounds for their base and created an external wall of Hescos to link them behind a protective barrier. The SEALs lived in their own plywood palace that had a modified team room in its front where each man had his gear stowed in small wooden lockers, ready to go at a moment's notice. The "techs" lived in another shack across the way from them, and a fire pit and couches were between them. In keeping with the tradition of the Special Operations community, the team was small but powerful. There were only twelve SEALs there, two explosive ordnance disposal members, two Military Information Operations officers, four Army infantry soldiers, two Navy Seabees, one communications specialist, and one intelligence officer. On the Afghan side, there were seventeen CMRGs and four interpreters. This small base of twenty-five Americans and twenty-one Afghans waged war on the unseen enemy, the Taliban. Their selection, training, motivation, and creativity more than made up for their small numbers.

The Afghan team lived in a nearby compound, where they cooked. I stowed my gear in an unoccupied Alaskan tent, got my bearings, grabbed a snack, and checked in with Dean. He invited me to dinner at the Afghan compound and said he would be meeting with the district chief of police the next day. He also planned a mission to reconnoiter a possible checkpoint location for the Afghan Local Police. A little while later I was picking my way through the pitch-black darkness of Chora, following Dean to the Afghan side of the base. Unlike Tarin Kowt, I could make out all the stars in the sky here that were washed out in the provincial capital due to streetlights. The Afghans lived in a rough-and-tumble compound with a large courtyard strewn with rubble, with parts of trucks and other odd pieces of things set in among the rocks. I followed Dean into a low building at the back of the compound and we joined the Afghan crew as they prepared dinner. Some of the other SEALs and support crew stopped by, as did the district chief of police, which was a great surprise. He apparently stayed at the compound in the evening and then went back to the police station during the day. It was just this kind of support that these small teams of Special Operations Forces provided to the local police so they would feel confident and safe enough to do their jobs. Additionally, living among the Afghans both in a VSP in Chora as well as with the CMRG created bonds of friendship and brotherhood that transcended the differences between us. Things seemed to be going well, and as I dozed off that evening I thought about Chora and its many challenges.

The district of Chora had been considered the safest in Uruzgan Province in late 2005, and although it didn't have a Coalition Forces base in its district center, the active patrolling of the 25th Infantry in Khas Uruzgan district to its east as well as patrols from the provincial capital of Tarin Kowt dissuaded the Taliban from establishing a presence in the area.[2] The key tribal chiefs of the Barakzai and Achikzai tribes in the area were substantial leaders in the province with the former a provincial chief of police and the latter a member of Parliament. Although both tribes were influential in their own way, they were largely excluded from the political power of the provincial government, which was dominated by members of the governor's Populzai tribe. The leaders of the Populzai in southern Chora had benefited greatly from the provincial government's largesse, and although they lived in much poorer circumstances than their district neighbors to the north, they had more influence with key leaders in the capital. The province's Provincial Reconstruction Team and 25th Infantry made frequent trips to the district center and the village of Chenartu to its south, and through projects such as a new district center, traffic circle, and smaller-scale projects such as wells, the population received some development assistance. When the fighting season began in early 2006, this tranquil spot of Uruzgan, whose residents supported the government of the Islamic Republic of Afghanistan (GIRoA), was overrun by the Taliban, with the district center falling to their control. The Taliban's offensive was not a limited operation consisting of a small number of fighters; instead, it was a conventional assault with the goal of holding the area and repulsing any subsequent GIRoA effort to take it back. The departure of the 25th Infantry in the summer of 2005, in part due to a perception the province was largely secured, facilitated the resurgence of the Taliban in the area. Gone were the days of limited Taliban attacks on the margins of the province; the province was now effectively split into two. The insurgents poured into Chora from Uruzgan's western district of Shahid-e-Hasas, which bordered the then-insurgent-controlled province of Helmand, and used the cultivated fields of the river basins to mask their movements. While a determined offensive of U.S. and Afghan forces retook Chora not long after it had fallen in 2006, it was now clear that occasional patrols, raids, and the feeling that the population's support for GIRoA was sufficient to stop the Taliban from holding the area were tragically wrong. A new approach was required for the area, one in which a persistent presence of security forces would protect the population from insurgent intimidation.

In the intervening years, new efforts had been undertaken to provide the sustained security Chora required and to better link it to the provincial capital. A series of patrol bases were constructed from the provincial capital of Tarin Kowt that occupied key lines of communication along and within the river basin up to the Chora area. The patrol bases occupied key geographical points insurgents had used for attacks, protected main roads and population centers, and provided areas for the Afghan National Army and the Afghan National Police to stage out of to patrol the region. Subsequently, a new military base was constructed in Chora, which meant that only one district in the province did not have an enduring Coalition Forces presence. This forward operating base also became a hub for the ANA and a means of support to Chora's chief of police as well as district governor. These additional forces performed a crucial role in preventing a second Taliban attempt to overrun the district center in 2007. Additionally, as security improved in the area, a new paved road was built linking Chora to Tarin Kowt and to Gizab, the northernmost district of Uruzgan. When the government of the Netherlands arrived in 2006 to assume responsibility for Uruzgan, their greater development focus on the province, added to the Australian government's efforts that had started after their arrival in late 2005, greatly improved living conditions in the Chora area. A new bridge was constructed that better linked the district to Tarin Kowt, an electrification project was completed, more schools were constructed, and additional water project improvements were finished along with other economic improvements.

Although security had improved through the placement and growth of formal security forces, the community was still not enlisted in its own defense. The absence of violence did not mean violence was absent. The ANA was made up of soldiers from all over Afghanistan and so lacked a local connection to the people, and the ANP, though largely drawn from Uruzgan, were either not from the Chora area or were predominantly loyal to the Populzai-dominated government in Tarin Kowt, which meant there was a sense of antipathy between them and the people as well. It is diffi-cult for a community to embrace a police force that is regarded, at least in part, as an occupation force. Additionally, Special Operations Forces had established two Village Stability Platform sites north of the Chora district center and along the Tarin Kowt/Chora/Gizab Road. These sites increased the numbers of Afghan Local Police in their area, thus ensuring that the road remained secure up to the northern district of Gizab and that the small population centers along them were now better able to resist Taliban intimidation. While security had stabilized in the area, the tribal situation had become markedly more fluid.

Following his removal as provincial chief of police in 2006, Barakzai tribal leader Rozi Khan was elected district governor of Chora, a rare example of local democracy in action; all such positions were usually appointed by the central government. In the summer of 2008, he was accidentally killed by Coalition Forces in a nighttime operation. His death destabilized the Barakzai tribe, a tribe of much influence in Chora, but his son, Mohammed Daoud Khan, assumed the leadership mantle and continued on as the district chief of Chora and head of his family until his removal from office by GIRoA in late 2010. The assassination of Daoud Khan in late 2011, in part in retaliation for the assassination of Populzai tribal leader and former governor Jan Mohammed Khan in Kabul in late summer 2011, further weakened the Barakzai tribe's leadership. It was widely thought within the Populzai tribe that Mohammed Daoud Khan was to blame for the killing of Jan Mohammed Khan, although this was never proven. Rozi Khan's next youngest son, Khoshal, assumed the leadership of the Barakzai tribe, but since he and his older brother were in their twenties, their tribal position was contested by other Barakzai elders seeking to improve their tribal, political, and economic situation. The Achikzai tribal leader, who had originally been district governor of Chora in 2001–2, had subsequently been elected as the province's representa-tive to the Wolesi Jirga, Afghanistan's lower house of Parliament. As a political opponent of then governor Jan Mohammed Khan, his election to Parliament in 2005 came as bit of a surprise, and his alliance with Rozi Khan acted as an effective check on any predatory tendencies of the Populzai-dominated provincial government. It also ensured that their respective tribal members had strong representation in tribal and government affairs. His subsequent defeat in 2010, in part orchestrated through an election process that fell short of international standards of transparency, prompted him to depart the province and reside in Kabul. His new residence protected him from any local assassination attempts organized by his tribal opponents, but it also weakened his local tribe's power because he was not as able to protect their interests while he was away.

In this context of weakened tribal leadership and enhanced but temporary security, the Taliban were able to increase their foothold in the Chora region. While the ANA undertook occasional patrols in the area, they had negotiated nonaggression pacts with the Taliban, so their routes and schedules were already known by the enemy. Additionally, while the ANP were more reliably anti-Taliban, that many of them had come from Tarin Kowt, which meant they were outsiders to Chora, prevented them from having as close a relationship with local residents as they could. This tendency was especially acute since there remained a lingering perception that the ANP were simply outgrowths of Populzai tribal power seeking to encroach into other tribal areas. That said, the ANP were able to construct four ALP checkpoints on their own, protecting some population centers, but not enough to deny the Taliban access to the population. They lacked the manpower to do so. The Taliban took advantage of this tribal power vacuum, compromised ANA, and insufficient ANP to expand their power base in the area. By constantly attacking the ANP through direct attacks, suicide vest attacks, and car bombs, the Taliban kept the police force hobbled. Following the transition of the two Village Stability Platform sites in northern Chora due to their success in recruiting ALP, the Special Operations Forces team that arrived in Chora's district center prepared to shift the balance of power away from the Taliban and toward GIRoA. Unlike the district of Shahid-e-Hasas, the team's approach required more than simply growing Afghan Local Police. It required a proactive approach to push the Taliban out, rehabilitate and empower tribal structures, reassure Afghan allies, and shape the physical terrain to inhibit the Taliban's infiltration routes.

When Dean and his team established Village Stability Platform Chora in late spring 2012 after transitioning VSP Kush Kadir, the insurgency had effectively curtailed the ability of the local police to operate, and the insurgents were acting with impunity against the population and the district government. Dean and his men quickly determined they had to create breathing space for tribal engagement to take place and for local officials to begin to see the seriousness of the VSP's intention to push the Taliban out.[3] There had long been a view held by locals in the area that Coalition Forces had a "live and let live" attitude when it came to confronting the Taliban insurgency. Clearing operations began soon after the team's arrival and were a mix of partnered Afghan commando raids, determined clearing operations with similarly partnered Afghan National Army units, and embedded mentoring with the Afghan National Police. As these operations pushed the Taliban back, the team began an active round of community engagement, principally with Barakzai tribal elders, to begin the process of recruiting local military-age males to serve as Afghan Local Police. This process uncovered a certain elder who, with his sons, was working with the Taliban to extend their personal power in the region but had enough plausible deniability to seek contracts with the Coalition and political influence with GIRoA. This local spoiler could not be killed unless he engaged in hostile acts, but he could be marginalized. His true intentions were discerned through his early suggestion of building a checkpoint in an area that he thought would take the team months to complete but was accomplished within a few days. When he was pressed for ALP recruits, he demurred and left the area. This hidden hand of the insurgency, partly political and partly tribal, helped serve as the backbone of the Taliban's shadow government in the area. The team established a checkpoint near the man's residence to put pressure on him and his family to either turn away from the insurgency or at least remain neutral. Subsequent engagements with area elders signaled an interest by the community to join the ALP but also concern with how enduring the SOF presence would be and whether Taliban control would return. The team sought to remove these concerns through active patrolling, playing a leading role in the weekly security coordination meeting with the ANA and ANP, and having the ANP chief live at their base.

Over the next four days, I accompanied Dean and his men on a foot patrol to the police headquarters and to the same district center building I had visited six years before, and on a convoy to visit with the local ALP commander. Much like I had witnessed in my other trips around the province, the police wore their uniforms, seemed to have the resources they needed, and greatly welcomed the relationship they had with the Special Operations Forces. Dean and his men had been aggressively pushing the Taliban presence back, and through their efforts at tribal engagement they had been able to recruit dozens more Afghan Local Police. While both ANP and ALP numbers increased, the ALP increasing from 40 in the town of Chora to 155, the insurgents were still utilizing the lush undergrowth of the river valley to move between checkpoints, attack the police and SOF at times of their choosing, and conceal their activities. One day, as we journeyed to meet the local ALP commander, his vehicle struck an IED that cut his truck in half, instantly killing him and his son along with four local police. His son's mangled body dangled from the branches of a nearby tree. The SEALs and the CMRG fanned out to search nearby compounds and found a man they thought was the trigger man. He was eventually detained and the SEALs consulted with the local police about where to place a new checkpoint. The SEALs dropped off the Hesco supplies as well as shovels and helped erect some of the shelter for the checkpoint. We departed in the early evening, and as we wound our way through the green zone of the river valley I thought about how different the SEALs were in undertaking this mission of Village Stability Operations compared to the direct action they mostly took part in when I had served in Iraq in 2007. It was a real testament to their ability to transition to this new mission set and to the leadership of the team to implement this new approach to fighting the war. I soon departed for Tarin Kowt and came away impressed with the balanced and flexible approach the team was pursuing in the Chora area; the team soon undertook an incredibly bold and imaginative strategy to fight the Taliban in the next few weeks.

Many of the attacks against the police were traced to a village called Nyazi, southwest of Chora proper and just over the border in Tarin Kowt District. Dean and his men came up with a plan to stem this flow of fighters and to stop their logistical support, but it would be unorthodox and fraught with risk. The idea was simple and without precedent in the area, and it was difficult to gauge how the community would react. Following continued insurgent attacks against ALP members and the ANP and its leadership, and at least one successful and several thwarted suicide vest and suicide motorcycle attacks, VSP Chora decided to physically cut the green zone of vegetation in half through the construction of a wall: the great wall of Chora. The wall would cut off Nyazi village, the center of Taliban activity, from Tarin Kowt to the south and, through the growth of ALP from Chora and the mere existence of the wall, prevent insurgent infiltration up from Tarin Kowt or down from Chora. It would span the entire width of the valley and use the barren mountains that followed the river valley as natural walls to prevent insurgent infiltration.

Clearing operations in the area opened the way and the SOF team began construction of the great wall. In total, the wall would consume more than one hundred Hesco wire and fabric baskets (filled with rock and dirt) that form a bulletproof barrier, and multiple spools of concertina wire. The team brought out earth-moving vehicles and shovels and began their work in earnest, creating an unbroken barrier at the narrowest point of the cultivated land. They soon discovered that the land they had selected was not only owned by one family, which simplified compensation payments for land use, but that the family supported the GIRoA. The leading brother had in fact been teaching school privately in his own home out of fear that the Taliban would further repress him if he became more public with his activities. As the wall was constructed, the brothers volunteered to fill the Hescos and, following their actions, so did other members of the community. Once the wall was completed after two days of work, the leading landowner who was running the secret school requested that he be named the commander of the wall. The SOF team gave him one of their patches with the future promise of a sheriff's badge purchased from the online retailer Amazon.com. It was becoming clear that the community embraced this unorthodox security strategy. Each end of the wall had a checkpoint and a third checkpoint was at its center. Two barren mountains formed natural barriers around the river valley, which forced road traffic past the two checkpoints at either end of the wall. Any foot traffic through the fields would have to pass by the central checkpoint. The wall had an immediate and dramatic effect on security. Once a Taliban probing patrol against the wall had been intercepted by the SOF team and killed, more villagers joined the ALP, and the ANP became more confident to conduct their own operations. As security improved, a more determined clearing operation commenced, which discovered a Taliban command center in the village and, later, two suicide vests that were later destroyed.

Security conditions in the district of Chora began to turn around when Special Operations Forces in the area launched aggressive offensive operations to push the Taliban back. In so doing, they reassured local Afghan allies about U.S. determination to defeat the Taliban in the area instead of coexist with them. This was followed by a robust embedded partnering plan with the Afghan National Police and increased support for their efforts facilitated by VSP Chora's liaising with the provincial chief of police to ensure greater materiel and logistical support and to improve the morale of the battered force. A community engagement strategy of partnering with and empowering tribal elders to both raise Afghan Local Police forces and to get them more involved in local political affairs had an extremely positive effect and furthered the rehabilitation of tribal leadership structures. Additionally, the subsequent removal of an ineffective district governor and the marginalization of a Taliban sympathizer demonstrated to other locals that GIRoA was serious about bringing security *and* governance to their community. The construction of the "Great Wall of Chora" not only brought security to the villages of Nyazi and Chora through shaping the physical terrain of the Chora Valley, it also stemmed insurgent infiltration into the provincial capital of Tarin Kowt and secured a section of the Tarin Kowt/Chora/Gizab road, which had long been the subject of improvised explosive device attacks. Its sheer presence also demonstrated to local villagers, GIRoA officials, and tribal leaders that security could be established and could become an enduring condition instead of a temporary, unsustainable effect. The growth of Afghan Local Police forces as well as the Afghan National Police and the construction of a series of checkpoints throughout Chora dramatically improved security in the area and physically pushed the Taliban out of the area. When Dean and his men transitioned VSP Chora to the next SEAL team, they had been able to recruit and oversee 284 Afghan Local Police out of the 400 their district had been assigned, and they had dramatically improved the security of the area. A balanced approach of using kinetic and nonkinetic strategies greatly enhanced security in the greater Chora Valley and demonstrated that a determined U.S. military unit can sufficiently degrade if not defeat the local Taliban insurgency given the right approach. If residents are actively enlisted in their own defense by participating in local security forces and playing an active role in community institutions, both facilitated by U.S. efforts, the Taliban insurgency is unable to physically intimidate the population, entice it to its cause through payments, or take advantage of its grievances to separate the people from their government.

FIFTEEN

"He's Our Taliban"

These men are hard as nails; they live on little, carry nothing but a rifle and a few cartridges, a knife and a bit of food, and they are shod for quick and sure movement.

—GENERAL SIR ANDREW SKEEN, *Passing It On: Short Talks on Tribal Fighting on the North-West Frontier of India*

The only way to defeat guerillas is with better guerillas, not by the methods of regular warfare.

—JOHN BAGOT GLUBB, *The Story of the Arab Legion*

Friction between American officers is especially noticeable when regular army officers and army special forces officers are working in the same area. A lot of regular officers resent the glamour and irregularity of the special forces men, and many of the special forces men feel the regular army just doesn't understand the problem in Viet Nam.

—MALCOLM W. BROWNE, *The New Face of War*

In early 2012, Special Operations Task Force–South East began to receive reports about a split between local Taliban forces in the Uruzgan district of Khas Uruzgan. As more information was gathered, it became evident that not only was there a rift between different insurgent factions but it had reached the point that they had actually fought each other with losses on both sides. Special Operations Forces in the district reached out to one faction in the quarrel, an Uruzgan local and Taliban commander named Abdul Samad, and sought a meeting with him. Surprisingly, he began to communicate with the team through intermediaries, seeking an opportunity to visit them and possibly join with the government of Afghanistan. Samad was not only a Taliban commander but an influential elder in the village of Dahane Sangu in the Sultan Mohammed Nawa Valley, thirty kilometers northeast of Forward Operating Base Anaconda. He led several dozen Taliban fighters, almost all of whom were from Uruzgan, and had participated in many firefights against U.S. forces over the years in the area. I wasn't sure if any of our men had been killed by his forces, but many guys on this rotation had had past experiences fighting him. As he continued to communicate with the SOF team, it became clear that a split had developed between Samad's forces, who were ostensibly local, and foreign Taliban elements, including a member of Pakistani intelligence. The locus of the dispute centered on the ability of Hazaran villagers—who lived in Samad's valley, were follows of Shia Islam, and were ethnically different from the Pashtuns—to travel down the Sultan Mohammed Nawa Valley to the district center and its shops in Khas Uruzgan village. The Taliban not only opposed the travel of the Hazarans but wanted to kill them because they were, from their perspective, not Muslims and thus unbelievers.

The Taliban began to harass the Hazarans even though Samad protected them as his people, and events reached a point where this provocation and others resulted in a firefight between Samad's men and the Taliban. The lead Taliban commander, who also worked for the Pakistani government, was killed in this engagement along with several other insurgents, and the remaining Taliban vowed to avenge the deaths of their leader and colleagues. The challenge for Samad was that even though he had now turned against the Taliban, he was isolated from the government of Afghanistan and Coalition Forces, which were still technically interested in killing him. Because his village was set deep into a valley with high surrounding mountains, his ability to travel to the district center southwest of his location was difficult; the main road was blocked by Taliban forces residing in the village of Marghunday. Additionally, the Taliban occupied villages north of Samad's village as well, boxing him in by using the surrounding mountains as walls. The SOF team in Khas Uruzgan took advantage of this split within the Taliban to build a relationship with Samad and to secure not only a tactical victory but an information operations victory as well, demonstrating to the Afghan people that even members of the Taliban were interested in joining with the Afghan government. However, several steps still needed to be taken to realize this goal.

On February 7, I traveled to the governor's compound with Commander Hayes to witness a unique event in Uruzgan's history. After several days of journey from eastern Uruzgan, Abdul Samad and roughly a dozen of his men presented themselves to the provincial government to reintegrate with the government of Afghanistan. They were turning their backs on the Taliban movement, rejecting its message and political goals, and siding with their country against them. In many respects, Samad had no other option but to come over to the government's side. He was now a hunted man by the Taliban, and he had always been a hunted man by U.S. forces. His village was surrounded by the Taliban, he was running low on ammunition and guns, and his home and village had suffered significant battle damage. Mike and I stood to the side of a large contingent of Afghan officials who waited for the arrival of Samad and his men. The governor was there, representatives of the Afghan police and the National Directorate of Security, as well as central government officials who had traveled from Kabul for the event. Since it was still winter, all of us were bundled up against the chill. In many respects, Samad's journey from the far eastern corner of the province was all the more impressive since his village and valley in the high elevation of the Hindu Kush were blanketed by snow. He was clearly determined to make this trip to Tarin Kowt. The Afghans were dressed in their usual assortment of black, gray, brown, and white turbans and were bundled up against the cold with additional layers of great cloaks.

Not too long after we arrived and the Afghan officials had gotten into place, Samad led a procession of fifteen of his men toward the group. He carried a large Afghan flag that fluttered from a makeshift flagpole in the cool winter air, and an AK-47 was slung over his shoulder. He had an almost regal bearing and walked in an assured and self-confident manner. It was almost as if we were guests at an event *he* was hosting! He wore a white turban and had a well-groomed black beard along with gold-rimmed aviator sunglasses. A large green cloak was wrapped tightly around him as he strode toward the crowd. He was gaunt with prominent cheekbones and his skin was a dark brown, and each of his men had a rangy, wild-eyed look about him. They had been so accustomed to being hunted or being the hunter that the stately and somewhat sedate surroundings of the governor's compound must have been jarring to them. Each had his own AK-47 slung over his shoulder, and two were carrying a banner behind Samad, as if in a parade, with the green, red, and black colors of the Afghan flag on it. Various Afghan officials filmed the procession and many had smart phones as well to document the important event. In many respects, Samad was coming home.

Once he arrived, an Afghan army soldier took the flag from Samad, and the Taliban commander then turned his AK-47 over to a waiting police officer. A member of the Taliban reintegration committee approached him and, as Samad leaned forward, removed his white turban and wrapped his head in a new black and gray one, a symbolic gesture of a new beginning. A second member of the reintegration committee walked forward and gave Samad a new, red-trimmed Qur'an, which he took with both hands and pressed to his forehead in a sign of deep respect and reverence. Each of Samad's men repeated the steps, turning in their weapons, receiving a new turban, and accepting the Qur'an. Each of the weapons were displayed along with a rocket-propelled grenade launcher on a white tablecloth spread on top of a table in one of the governor's outdoor pavilions. The event began quite solemnly but as it went on the Afghans became more relaxed and they smiled as each Afghan official sought to be the next one to place a turban on a member of the Taliban. It was a fascinating event for me since the Taliban had always been elusive specters, and we were more likely to see the effects of their action rather than the fighters themselves. In 2006 I had a chance to see three Taliban fighters we had captured when I had visited Chora, but I never would have expected to see an actual Taliban commander. The only commanders I had ever seen were in photos of their dead corpses.

As much as Samad and his men were being forced by circumstances to join the Afghan government, they were also intrigued by the possibility of becoming Afghan Local Police. While it was unclear what exactly motivated Samad to join the Taliban, he had originally been a truck driver making delivery runs between the provincial capital of Tarin Kowt to Khas Uruzgan in the east. He was from Uruzgan Province and a local boy, so it stood to reason that he might find the Village Stability Operations program appealing as a way to maintain his leadership position, protect his village, take care of his men, and make some money as well. One of the aspects of the VSO program, however, was that it was not a program designed to reward Taliban who joined the government but was intended to help villagers resist Taliban intimidation. You never really knew if a member of the Taliban was reintegrating simply to make some money, take a break from fighting, and gain some intelligence about Afghan and U.S. forces, only to return to the movement afterwards. Additionally, a dedicated reintegration program already existed to encourage commanders like Samad to come over to the government's side. It was a several-step program that provided payments to the men, training, and resources, as well as opportunities to fully declare their Taliban activities. But the reintegration program was oddly bureaucratic and cumbersome, even though few Taliban had taken advantage of it, and it was not quick enough to capitalize on these discrete reintegration events.

In this gap between the reality of Samad's situation, with the Taliban looking to settle scores with him, and the slow pace of the reintegration effort, strode the SOTF. Once it had become clear that we needed to help Samad's tactical situation now, our team in Khas Uruzgan at Forward Operating Base Anaconda began making regular trips to Samad's house. We provided him ammunition, sandbags, construction material, a regular communications capability, as well as weapons. We also began to provide him cash payments for small projects in his village so he could rebuild battle damage, maintain the support of his community, and help pay his men. Hayes also assigned a newly arrived Navy commander on his first tour as our dedicated reintegration officer to ride herd on the process. He was also our liaison to an Air Force officer at Task Force Uruzgan, the

higher command in charge of the province, who was in charge of reintegration for them and was an Afghan Hand. He was a most interesting
person because he took his duties so seriously that he adopted the mien
of an actual Afghan. He had the usual beard of many of our soldiers keen
on working with the local population, but he frequently wore Afghan
clothing, including a turban. When Gen. John R. Allen, commanding
general of ISAF, visited our base he was asked a question by this officer
dressed in full Afghan regalia. The general was a bit uncertain as to whether
he was being addressed by an Afghan or an American. Interestingly, this
was this officer's first tour in Afghanistan and his normal job was in public
affairs. It was not uncommon for some foreigners in Afghanistan to
completely lose themselves in the drama of the Afghan war as well as the
culture of the Afghans. We were dealing with some heavy subjects, and
the results of our actions always had the potential to be significant. His
example spawned an expression, "You never go full Afghan" as a paean to
the "war" movie *Tropic Thunder*. The officer resented our having our own
reintegration effort and honestly felt that the usual lethargic Afghan way
of running the reintegration effort was more agreeable to their culture. We
disagreed of course and moved full steam ahead, making sure Samad was
taken care of as we brought more Taliban over to the government's side.
This was another example of how Special Operations Forces didn't allow
the slow pace of bureaucracy to get in the way of accomplishing the job.

Samad's joining the Afghan government's side was so significant and
unique in Afghanistan that it frequently merited comment from our
higher-ups. In some respects, Samad became the symbol of what success
looked like in Afghanistan when the right mix of resources, leadership, and
strategy prompted the Taliban to reject the movement. But Samad's case
was unique and it was a challenge to find other Taliban willing to come
over. When General Allen visited our base in May, he said that "Samad is
unique in the whole country" and that "Samad is a great achievement."
The commander of Regional Command-South, Major General Huggins,
also told us that "reintegration is operational defeat for the Taliban." When
I had served in Fallujah in 2007, insurgents were falling over themselves to
join the side of the government, and thousands reintegrated either through

the formal reintegration effort or effectively by joining the tribal security forces we were helping to raise, train, equip, and deploy. You knew you were winning when the insurgents lost more men to defections than they could recruit. We had one instance where an insurgent bomb maker was desperately trying to get out of his al-Qaeda cell. He would build fake bombs and leave them in fairly obvious locations where we would find them, and he would leave lists of the members of his cell in them. He did this so we would, after we had exploited the bomb for intelligence value, discover the lists and kill the members of his group, and he would then be free to rejoin the government. This particular episode, though, took place when the Anbar Awakening was really crushing al-Qaeda and all sorts of insurgents were trying to escape the inevitable. Even as we continued to expand the numbers of Afghan Local Police, transition some sites, open new ones, and launch combat operations against the Taliban, we were achieving significant results. General Allen even commented that in Uruzgan "here is success and here is the future" of Afghanistan.

After several frustrating months of hoping the reintegration program of money, projects, and support for Samad would go into effect, we finally decided we couldn't wait any more for results. While our base in Khas Uruzgan had done a lot to support Samad through short-term support such as ammunition, weapons, and construction material (they even undertook an overland mission to his home), we needed to visit Samad's home directly. On July 15, we took several members of the reintegration committee to Samad's house to speak with him face to face, to demonstrate our continued support for him, and to see what the SOTF could do in light of the Afghan bureaucracy's lethargy. We departed in the late morning aboard helicopters from FOB Ripley in Tarin Kowt and began the long trip to Samad's home and valley. Since he was north of our base in Khas Uruzgan, he was squarely in the steep mountains of the Hindu Kush. The morning was clear and as the helicopter ascended it became much cooler. This trip was uncharted territory for me because even though I had visited Forward Operating Base Anaconda before, this part of Khas Uruzgan District was completely unknown to me. Additionally, the idea that we would be visiting a former Taliban commander's home, village, and valley, as his guests no less, was surreal, and so even though our mission was ostensibly peaceful, Mike was ever mindful of the ubiquitous and varied threats, and he made sure to bring additional SEALs for protection. In addition to the reintegration committee members we also took Captain Hernandez, who was in charge of our civil affairs program, with us to discuss projects with Samad.

After about a forty-five-minute journey, our Chinook helicopter circled over Samad's house as Apaches provided protection. The house was perched on the border of the green zone, a rich valley of farmland that followed the river between the mountains, and the barren escarpment of the mountains, which were a mix of khaki and brown colors. Our helicopter touched down, about three hundred yards from Samad's imposing fortress, and we decamped from the back of the Chinook. Several of the SEALs fanned out as the talcum powder dust churned about and we made our way to Samad's home. The Chinook quickly took off, to return when we were ready to depart. Samad's men were also in their fighting positions providing us protection. It was quickly evident that a number of tactical improvements had been made to Samad's house and that our units in Khas Uruzgan had been busy helping his situation. A series of fighting positions had been dug around his compound, and khaki sandbags were arranged along their edges in a neat U to provide additional cover. One of Samad's men was perched on the ridgeline less than two hundred yards away, which provided a useful perch for observing the Taliban. Not too long ago, these men would have been targets, but now they were our protectors.

Samad's compound was two stories tall but quite expansive, and it was made in the usual Afghan style of thick adobe with a healthy placement of rocks for the base and a wooden roof. The window frames, doors, and stairs had all been made from roughly hewn wood. A water well had been built just outside the front door, and a fifty-gallon drum formed the cover with an old tire placed around its base. A makeshift pulley system had been erected to lower the bucket directly to the water table, and the whole mechanism balanced precariously off a rough contraption of wood.

Though simple by our standards, the compound was quite regal judging by local conditions. Several of our men occupied the newly dug fighting positions as Mike and I along with Hernandez and the reintegration committee members ascended the outdoor steps of Samad's house to join him in his meeting room. The room had a nice second-floor view over the green valley and was covered in rough red carpets ringed with pillows for the guests. In keeping with Afghan tradition, Samad offered us tea and snacks and welcomed us to his home. Mike sat near the window close to Samad, and the reintegration committee leadership sat near him as well. Captain Erickson sat directly across from Samad and the rest of us lined the walls listening to the translation. We quickly got down to business after pleasantries were expressed, with Samad beginning the conversation.

Samad began the meeting. "Thank you for visiting me. It has been a long time since we have met. Many months ago, the Taliban ambushed me and my men. We didn't know about the ambush but we killed many more of them than they killed of us. They then killed my brother when he went to visit his family on a motorcycle. I told him about the Taliban in the area but he went anyway. I'm a Pashtun, I'm with you, I'm loyal. I'm tired of the Taliban. Last year I was fighting with the Taliban because I was helping my people. I now want to help my people by helping you."

Hayes reacted positively. "We don't want to fight, we want to build."

Samad continued, "I recently gathered all of my friends and have invited the Taliban to speak about peace. I will speak to them tonight. If they want peace, I will help them get it. If they don't want peace, then we will fight them. We have taken the first step."

"We must bring more peace to Khas Uruzgan," Hayes said, nodding his head in agreement.

Samad continued. "The Taliban are not fighting for Islam. They are fighting for money, collecting taxes, talking on the radio, and then collecting money. I have killed eleven Taliban. I know them."

Hayes steered the conversation to the Afghan officials he had brought with him. "I have brought men who can do projects for your village."

A member of the Afghan reintegration committee then spoke. "We were talking about more projects for Samad. The community is divided between Samad and the Taliban. We must work to convince these people. Our process is slow and very tiring. We must be active and start working on behalf of Samad. He needs our help and support and we must encourage him. We can help lots of people if we build mosques, schools, roads, etc."

Samad seemed pleased. "I agree with you. I have received nothing yet but only three thousand Afghani. Captain Erickson has given me ammunition, weapons, and over seven to eight thousand Afghani. He is a good friend."

Looking at the VSSA Anaconda commander, Hayes said, "Have Hernandez in Tarin Kowt work with Anaconda to do more projects."

Samad continued. "I have to live every day and I need the government to help me every day. I tell my people these things. We have received no projects yet. I get real support from the Coalition Forces and the district government. I'm responsible if you are attacked. I will stop it if it happens. We need your support. The Taliban commanders are from this valley. I can bring them to the government if we get real support."

"I will sit with the Taliban and tell them we will not target them," Hayes said.

Samad then talked about his connections to the Taliban in his area. "Mullah Zarqawi [Taliban commander] will come down from the mountains if we help. It is very easy to convince them but they have to see something. We have not had any salaries for four months."

"The money doesn't make it back to the people," Hayes said. "The U.S. gives millions of dollars to the government but it never reaches the people."

Samad continued his pitch to the group. "I am already talking to Mullah Zarqawi. He can't fight the Taliban and support his family. We must convince the Taliban. I will not leave the area. All we get are promises. We are 99 percent with the government if we get support. If we see projects, we will support the government of Afghanistan."

The conversation continued for a while, but the art of negotiation was clearly one of Samad's strengths. He needed and wanted our support and was quite willing to encourage other Taliban to join the government, but he wanted tangible proof that the government of Afghanistan was serious.

We wanted more Taliban to give up fighting and join our side, which Samad knew, and he dangled the prospect of more Taliban fighters giving up if we dealt with him honorably and gave him evidence that cooperation was rewarded. One reason the reintegration program was slow was the anticorruption rules in place to make sure the money was not misspent. Additionally, being a national program, it was not as responsive as it needed to be to fluid local situations, and many of the staff members of the program were not well-trained. We finally reached an understanding that more projects would be coming to his village through our base in Khas Uruzgan and we would continue to pressure the reintegration committee to undertake its work. I was hopeful this would be the case since we had a Navy commander working on it full-time. We also agreed to look into whether Samad and his men could formally join the Village Stability Operations program and become Afghan Local Police. We also figured it would be good to bring Police Chief Matullah to Samad's house as well. As we waited for the helicopters to pick us up, we socialized with Samad's men. They asked us about our gear, commented on the sophistication of our rifles, and kindly offered us fresh fruit. Many of their AK-47s had been "jingled out," decorated with brightly colored tape. We finally departed in the late afternoon realizing that some enemies could become friends.

✧

One of my jobs was to meet with Afghan leaders and to get their perspective on local politics, tribal relations, and how we could do our jobs better. I had been working closely with Major Bradley, our Provincial Augmentation Team lead, and he and I had systematically met with all sorts of Uruzgan officials, including local directors of central government ministries, members of Parliament, civil servants in the provincial government, and tribal, village, and religious leaders. One of the major tribal leaders I had long wanted to meet was Haji Khoshal, ostensibly in charge of the Barakzai tribe and one of the sons of the Barakzai tribal leader Rozi Khan, who had been killed in 2008. I've recounted the sordid tribal conflict between the Barakzai and Populzai tribes in chapter 3, but part of our role at the SOTF was to use all our influence to bring stability to the province, no matter what it took. If we could bring some sort of peace or at least a grudging understanding between the two tribes, we would have increased security in the province. Because there was really no local democracy in Uruzgan and no real way for the disaffected to hold local officials accountable, resorting to the Taliban became the norm for alienated tribes. Thus, the Barakzai tribe provided a safe haven for the Taliban as a way of checking Matullah's power, even as it participated in local politics. Matullah, however, was not without his own tools to exercise influence.

The chief problem facing Khoshal was that he was young. I think he was in his early twenties and did not have the full respect of the Barakzai tribe. His father had been a highly respected mujahedeen commander and was the undisputed leader of the Barakzai tribe. However tragic his death, his first-born son, Mohammed Daoud Khan, had been up to the challenge of leading the tribe and did quite well. He assumed not only his father's position as head of the tribe but his position of district chief of Chora until he was removed by the central government in 2010 due to Populzai political influence. He was eventually assassinated in 2011 by unknown assailants widely thought to be aligned with the Populzai tribe. Matullah and the Populzai quickly took advantage of the tumult within the Barakzai tribe. When Matullah became provincial chief of police in 2011, all the Barakzai tribal members were fired or, depending on your point of view, left of their own accord. Matullah then supported the election to Parliament of Barakzai tribal member Obaidullah, who had once been district chief of Chora, in a bid to split the tribe. Most glaringly, he then gave a job in the police department to Rozi Khan's brother, which was a direct slap to Rozi Khan's family and a clear effort to sow discord between different family lines. Matullah also supported other Barakzai tribal members who craved power, and many others were in the wings, ready to serve. To his great credit, the new provincial governor Akunzada, had hosted both Matullah and Khoshal to seek some sort of understanding between both men, but to no avail. President Karzai himself called Akunzada and told him to waive off, which prevented a peace deal between the men. The politics between just these two powerful tribes was complicated enough, but these kinds of struggles for power and influence took place through-

out each and every village and valley of Afghanistan. This is not to say
that working with the tribes was impossible or that some level of stability couldn't be brought to Afghanistan, but that a deep knowledge of
the people, their concerns, and history along with a willingness to do
something about it were key to success. To paraphrase General David
Petraeus, "Hard is not hopeless."

I had known Khoshal in 2005 when he had attended the Tarin Kowt
high school, and it was touching to meet with him again. Our meeting
had been arranged by my former interpreter Mohib, who had connections to nearly everyone it seemed, including Matullah, and he joined us
for our get-together. One of the thoughts that had occurred to me was
that Khoshal was looking for a way to increase his influence within the
Barakzai tribe, sideline his opponents, and improve his standing against
Matullah. His tribe had sheltered Taliban commanders in the past and still
did so to some degree, which served as sort of an insurance policy against
any of Matullah's efforts to kill him, to kill members of his tribe, or to take
his property. I figured we could expand the Village Stability Operations
program in the district of Chora, where a lot of Barakzai tribal members
lived, while also getting Khoshal to turn in Taliban commanders to us or
to at least get them to reintegrate. Unfortunately, the VSO program was
not allowed in the provincial capital, since it was viewed as a rural stability program, but Khoshal could give us the names of his tribal members
who could join VSO in other parts of Uruzgan Province. My sense was
that this effort could really balance Khoshal's self-interest with our own to
achieve the public interest of greater security in the province.

In mid-September, my colleagues and I met with Khoshal to discuss
these and other issues and to get to know him better. I met Mohib
and Khoshal at the main gate of our base and welcomed both of them
back to the base; Khoshal had also been meeting with the Provincial
Reconstruction Team in the past. He was well-dressed and had an air of
authority about him, and he wore the same black turban his father had
always worn. As he shook my hand I noticed his left hand holding prayer
beads. His black beard was neatly trimmed and he wore a dark gray vest
along with a darkly colored *salwar kameez*. He looked like a spitting image

of his father. We finally sat down in a meeting room on base and caught up. I gave him several pictures of his late father I had taken in 2005, and he appreciated them deeply. He told me and my colleagues that roughly one hundred members of his tribe quit the Uruzgan police force in 2011 when Matullah became police chief and that they now worked in Myeshin District in Kandahar Province, where they reported to provincial chief of police Abdul Razziq, a member of the Achikzai tribe. The Barakzai and Achikzai tribes often aligned with each other against the Populzai not just in Uruzgan but in Kandahar as well. It was one of the Darwinian rules of tribal politics to join with others when you were weak to balance against those who were strong.

He also told us that he was in in frequent contact with Taliban commanders in Uruzgan and often discussed with them the merits of reintegrating with the government of Afghanistan. He said, however, they were distrustful of the Afghan government, in particular Matullah Khan, but were willing to explore the possibility if they could speak directly to U.S. personnel. We told him about our reintegration officer and he pledged to continue the conversation with him. We then told him about our idea to consult with him on and to include more Barakzai tribal members in the Afghan Local Police in Chora, and he lit up at the prospect. He welcomed the opportunity to suggest names to us and invited us to his home to discuss the idea further. This was an encouraging sign to say the least! He also told us that the wall the Chora team had built across the Chora valley had significantly improved security in the area and that he rarely heard security complaints from the people now. This was a wonderful acknowledgment of the effectiveness of the strategy Village Stability Platform Chora had been implementing in the area. Our meeting eventually finished and we pledged to meet again and to continue the conversation. Once again, having an understanding of local politics and using the good reputation of the United States sometimes did more to fight the enemy than any number of combat operations.

——◆◆◆——

SIXTEEN

Plugging a Ratline

> Only someone who had been in the field would know how
> things really were, not how they should work. But the people
> in the field were never consulted before a policy change; they
> were only informed after the change had taken place.
>
> —JOHN L. COOK, *The Advisor*

The Village Stability Operations approach had significantly improved the security situation in Uruzgan Province, but I was always aware that the province had long had an enduring relationship with U.S. forces and a population very much inclined to support the government of the Islamic Republic of Afghanistan. What I was intrigued with was how an area with a much lower U.S. presence, where in many places U.S. troops had either never been or had been withdrawn at some point, would receive the VSO approach and a Village Stability Platform. Zabul Province was the third and final part of Special Operations Task Force–South East's area of responsibility, and the general feeling of the command was that we could improve the situation there but since we didn't have enough troops we could never really pacify it. As we transitioned the bases in Uruzgan to Afghan control or simply closed others, our strategy was to divest ourselves of that province and invest our resources in Zabul. A complicating factor was that since Zabul bordered Pakistan it always served as a natural entry point for insurgents into Afghanistan. Since this made it easier for the Taliban to quickly replenish their forces, the task of pacification was that much harder. The most important aspect of Zabul from the perspective of decisions makers in Kabul were the three districts (Shah Joy, Qalat, and Tarnak Wa Jaldak), which the Ring Road, the main highway that connected Kabul to most of the country's provinces, passed through. In late summer of 2012 it was decided that a new VSP would have to be placed in the northeastern section of Arghandab District, just north of the Ring Road, to help blunt foreign fighter flows and to expand population security. The Taliban had long used a ratline on the eastern edge of the province to enter Afghanistan and would then either split to the left, going down the Arghandab River Valley, or continue north, where they eventually either went to Uruzgan Province to the west or to Ghazni Province to the east. The general strategy was that a well-placed VSP could interdict this ratline while also standing up a local police force to thicken out our presence. To that end, I joined Hayes as well as some of our other leadership on a trip to Arghandab District and to our Village Stability Platform there called Bagh.

When one thinks of Afghanistan, a number of images come to mind, including desolate mountains, primal mountain streams, barren escarpments, a primitive but proud people, and the sense of total and absolute isolation. As our helicopters journeyed southeast from Tarin Kowt toward Zabul Province, the reality of Afghanistan's great empty expanses became all the more evident to me. Uruzgan had a familiar, even homey feel to me after all the time I had spent there, and its modest size had really allowed me to get to know the people and their challenges. Zabul Province was an enormous and untamed land from my perspective, and several of its districts either had no Coalition Forces or such modestly sized forces that the jagged mountains of the Hindu Kush simply swallowed them up. The tribes of the area were predominantly Ghilzai, which meant they were less well-off than their Durrani colleagues, had weaker tribal structures, and were still nomadic. As we journeyed to VSP Bagh, I noticed that village clusters were much smaller and less frequent and that the mountainous terrain thoroughly dominated the region, unlike Uruzgan, where it mostly became a reality in its northernmost reaches. The province had once had more U.S. troops, and each district had had a forward operating base at some point, but many of them had been closed in the previous years.

I suspected that the local population was not as inclined to support us after seeing our forces arrive and then depart in just a few years. From their local perspective, we weren't really a reliable partner. Additionally, Zabul always had to contend with Pakistan, which made local stabilization efforts even more difficult. Any local uprising to repel the Taliban could easily be squashed by Taliban reinforcements sent across the border or even delivered via the Ring Road. I was looking forward to visiting Arghandab District to gain a better understanding of its challenges and how our team at VSP Bagh saw the situation. Interestingly, the base and the Advanced Operations Base in charge of the province were run by SEALs from Team Two, so I was especially interested in seeing how they had adapted to the problem set of the area.

Our helicopters made a quick pass of the site as a member of VSP Bagh tossed a smoke canister into a dry river bed near the small base, signaling the pilots where to land. I glanced out of the Blackhawk's windows to catch a swift glance as we descended. The base was set on a small knoll overlooking the Arghandab River to its south and was at the nexus of two barren valleys. The local bazaar stood three hundred yards away from the base across a dry river bed. A reinforced combat observation post had been erected on a nearby hill overlooking the valleys and the VSP, which was a mix of Alaskan tents, temporary wooden buildings, and a few harder structures made of concrete. A collection of gray parachutes and boxes from our airdrops were lined up just outside the main wall along with a series of MRAPs and MATV trucks, which were parked in neat rows. As our helicopter touched down I also noticed a number of men standing watch on each of the corners of the small base manning crew-served weapons. Several Razors were driven down into the dry river bed to pick us up as we exited the helicopters. The Razors were a sort of tactically modified golf cart with rugged tires, a souped-up engine, and gun mounts, and they were painted tan and black. They allowed the SEALs to be more nimble and to go off-road where the much large MRAPs and MATVs couldn't venture. We drove up the embankment through the outer Hesco and concertina wire perimeter and came to a stop in front of the tactical operations center.

The team at Village Stability Platform Bagh was led by a SEAL lieutenant who led a group of fourteen SEALs, ten Army infantry soldiers, two
explosive ordnance disposal sailors, two civil affairs soldiers, two military
information support operations soldiers, two communicators, one Navy
Seabee, one intelligence sailor, and one cook. Like most of our sites, it also
had a sizable Civil Mine Reduction Group force of twenty-eight Afghans.
The team was a balanced mix of capabilities, backgrounds, and mission sets
that worked well in the fluid environment of Village Stability Operations.
The team had enough combat power to operate on their own, enough force
protection capability to protect themselves, and the ability to not only
understand the Afghan human terrain but to also shape and influence it.
As the team visited villages after they had cleared them of Taliban, the civil
affairs team would conduct needs assessments and engage local leaders.
The information officers would assess the Taliban's messaging strategy and
also build on the work of the civil affairs soldiers by stressing the positive
messages of the government. The explosive ordnance disposal sailors would
eliminate any threats from munitions. The intelligence officer would chat
with the locals, try to establish some sources, and see how the village fit
into the Taliban's local strategy. Additionally, a team of medical personnel
could also be brought out from Tarin Kowt to conduct a medical outreach
effort to treat local Afghans. The goals of the totality of these efforts were
to defeat the Taliban militarily, engage the community holistically, and
build rapport so that the villagers felt comfortable volunteering their sons
for the Afghan Local Police program. The challenge for the team at VSP
Bagh was that their local Afghan partners were either not in the district
or were unable or unwilling to engage local communities with the team;
some of the officials were also corrupt.

The initial team at Bagh had been inserted in late 2011 but, for all
of its efforts, had only been able to recruit twenty-eight Afghan Local
Police. When we visited the new VSP, the team was in the midst of
training around twenty more. It caused no small amount of frustration
for the team since, being SEALs, they were extremely motivated, and
even though they constantly engaged local villagers were unable to get
them to commit. They used their time well, however, even in this isolated

section of Afghanistan, and they aggressively went after the Taliban to create a sense of safety for the villagers. Unfortunately, the initial team at Bagh from the prior rotation had lost one of its SEALs to a land mine that had been buried along a mountain footpath. To commemorate his loss, the team had constructed a small cross and erected it at the top of a nearby mountain they could see from their small base. They had also electrified it with solar panels so that the small lights they had put on it faintly glowed at night. The team at the base this day had had a few scraps with the enemy as well. The assistant officer in charge had been shot through the thigh and had been returned home for recovery (he returned later after healing). Additionally, an explosive ordnance disposal sailor had stepped onto a land mine as he descended the back of an MRAP that had struck its own land mine. The back of his calf had been blown off, but he had survived. The team itself was aggressively patrolling, often going out at night, and would frequently bring the U.S. Army soldiers to build out their force. The team at VSP Bagh represented an amazing evolution in thinking about the war and was a powerful capability in the Arghandab River Valley.

After we arrived we grounded our gear and received a quick tour of the modest base. All sorts of communications gear lined the roof of the tactical operations center and a makeshift gym had been erected using an old Alaskan tent. The men were engaged in a competition called "feats of strength" to see who could lift the most, do the most push-ups, sit-ups, and so on. One of the more interesting aspects of the base, which had been designed to repel an assault as well as serve as a platform for engagements, was an automatic mortar tube designed by an Israeli firm. All you had to do was punch in the predetermined location and it would adjust its elevation accordingly. You then had to drop the mortar in the tube and everything else was handled for you. The men at Bagh would often fire off illumination rounds at the ALP's checkpoints so the Afghans would feel safe at night and to keep the Taliban off balance. It was an amazing combination of technology and traditional war fighting. The men would take guard duty in shifts, with "green" (Army) on duty for twelve hours and "blue" (SEALs, Navy) for the other twelve. After the quick tour we put our gear back on and took the Razors up the hill to the combat observation post.

As we trudged up the hill in the Razors, the logic of the terrain became more apparent. The observation post dominated the area and provided a clear view of all of VSP Bagh. A contingent of Afghan guards from the VSP protected the two-story building surrounded by Hescos. From this vantage point the VSP commander gave us an overview of his area of operations. He handed out some printed slides of the terrain that looked like gummy worms meeting at VSP Bagh. Each valley had been color-coded based on its permissiveness, with "red" being enemy country, "yellow" being contested, and "green" being permissive. He explained how the team was pushing out from Bagh and constructing checkpoints along the valley to control the terrain, interdict Taliban movements, and protect the local population. At one point he and his men were conducting a nighttime operation against the Taliban and had intercepted the enemy's radio traffic. Instead of calling in air cover from Kandahar Air Field, he and his men continued to pursue the Taliban, because once the aircraft had gone aloft, the Taliban either through informants or through other means of early warning would turn off their radios, making it harder to find them. Additionally, the Taliban had been seeding the surrounding roads with bits of metal to confuse our metal detectors and would then conceal mines among the debris. They were also messaging the villagers by telling them our men were leaving and that the Taliban would be there forever, which frankly wasn't entirely wrong, but it had a chilling effect on our ALP recruitment drives. Another example of how ingenious the enemy could be was that further into the district, the government of Afghanistan had built a clinic that served several villages. Once it had been completed, the Taliban seized it and scared away the workers, which prompted the government to stop funding it. The Taliban claimed to the local population that the government had tried to close down the *Taliban-*constructed clinic but that the Taliban had reopened it. Thus an Afghan man from the northern part of the country had moved to the area to stock and man the clinic. Even though he knew the Taliban controlled it, he worked for them because he made money off of them. The Taliban had skillfully used the government's ineptitude for its own advantage.

The VSP Bagh commander expressed his frustration with recruiting ALP in the area. While he and his men were adroit at fighting the Taliban, the conditions he operated in made his mission that much more difficult. Clearly, this part of Zabul was difficult human and physical terrain to work with, which helped to further frame my thinking about why some VSPs worked while others struggled to achieve their goals. One of the more interesting tidbits to come from the trip was that even though the number of ALP recruits was still quite low, the few they had brought on had already achieved some positive results. The team had constructed two ALP checkpoints at the local bazaar, one at the end and the other in the middle since the other side was overseen from the VSP, and the number of local businesses had increased significantly. Stores that had been shuttered for a long time had now been opened, and there were plans to construct even more. This example stood in contrast to our VSP in western Uruzgan called Tagaw, where the Taliban had ringed the bazaar with land mines, turning them off during the day to allow commercial traffic and then switching them on at night. Most of the stores were closed and the few that remained open were pretty barren. These two examples summed up the different approaches of the Coalition and the Taliban. We protected the population and allowed the Afghans to be Afghans, whereas the Taliban controlled the population with the resulting effects.

Further up the Arghandab River stood the brand-new Village Stability Platform of Sayagez, which was in the old capital of the district. Some feuding had gone on between the residents of Sayagez and Bagh over who should have the capital since Bagh was closer to the provincial capital to its south. Additionally, a large, unbroken mountain chain formed the southern border of Arghandab District, and the river flowed southwesterly from the Hindu Kush Mountains to the north. Any resident of Sayagez had to travel all the way around the mountain in order to visit the Zabul provincial capital of Qalat. The Sayagez area had several other advantages that Bagh did not, and it seemed to benefit from them. The local tribe was led by a dominant figure that past reporting had indicated had been supportive of Coalition Forces. Further, we had once had a conventional forces base there at some point and so the local experience with Americans was positive, although, like other parts of Zabul, villagers were a bit skeptical of our ability to stay in the area for the long term. While the river valley was the dominant feature in the area, smaller side valleys also dotted the landscape, and the mountain ranges funneled the population down the river valley. The team at VSP Sayagez was also led by a Navy SEAL lieutenant who had run another VSP in Uruzgan earlier in the tour before it had been handed over to Afghan forces.

The commanding officer of Sayagez was Lt. Magnus Norton, a solidly built Naval Academy graduate who sported a thick brown and reddish beard. A former member of the Academy's wrestling team, his approach to confronting the Taliban reflected his muscular yet deft demeanor. He was thoughtful about how to engage the Afghans and showed a special kindness to them in his engagements. His team had originally been in the Uruzgan district of Chora but had been sent to Arghandab to bolster our presence in Zabul Province. He led a team of fourteen SEALs, eight infantry soldiers, two civil affairs soldiers, and seven Afghans with the Civil Mine Reduction Group. His team had been inserted into Sayagez after a deliberate clearing operation by Afghan commandos advised by embedded SEAL mentors. As part of his preparation to take over the area, Norton had read past intelligence reports on the area and found that it had once had a U.S. forward operating base that had written up a number of engagements with the local population. The reports indicated a positive relationship with the area's tribal leaders and their desire to have the district government return to their area. This clearly was an incentive for them to collaborate with the team.

While some SEALs were not particularly enthusiastic about the VSO/ALP mission, Lieutenant Norton took to it immediately. The valley they were located in became "his" valley and the people who lived there became "his" people. It was not uncommon for him, for example, to shake hands with every villager he met on a foot patrol. A positive leader, he inspired his men by the great joy he exhibited in his work, and he happily shared their burdens as they lived in some of the most austere circumstances imaginable. He was an innovative thinker and once planned to take a mule train up the Arghandab River Valley to check out a village for a potential Village Stability Platform site, a trip that would have taken several weeks. He so thoroughly loved his job and the challenge of command in war that his men were motivated and determined even though they hadn't had a shower in weeks. He was an articulate advocate for his position and he brought all of his team together to brainstorm a problem, another example of a strong and confident leader, which was common in the SOF community.

Norton and his men convened regular shuras with the area's tribal leaders, and the earlier intelligence reports on their abilities and intentions turned out to be correct. Within a month of being embedded in Sayagez in the summer of 2012, the VSP had already recruited, trained, outfitted, and deployed twenty-seven Afghan Local Police. They had twenty-eight in the training pipeline and more on the way. The villagers were also keen to work on development projects, so Norton and his men worked with the locals and built a wooden bridge reinforced by Hesco bastions across the Arghandab River. This not only allowed the team to cross the river to conduct combat operations, but it made it much easier for the locals to traverse this difficult terrain feature. Once the snow melted off the Hindu Kush, the river would become a frothing torrent, so the villagers were very happy with the bridge. In fact, about sixty of them stood on the bridge and posed for a photo with their fists raised high in a sign of celebration. It was an amazing moment for the team and a remarkable accomplishment for a SEAL team in particular since it was so contrary to their military culture. One of the real keys to the team's success, though, was that they had a fourteen-man Afghan commando team embedded with them that was led by a Pashtun. His ability to engage with the local communities was amazing, and the people really responded to his leadership and example. The combination of strong tribal leadership, favorable terrain, an enthusiastic VSP team, a community that had had a positive experience with Coalition Forces previously, and an Afghan commando team led by a Pashtun made for a powerful combination the Taliban could not defeat.

SEVENTEEN

Enlisting the Population in Its Own Defense

I know body count, you know—it has something about it, but it's really a l-o-o-n-g way from what's involved in this war. Yeah, you have to do that, I know that, but the mistake is to think that that's the central issue.

—GEN. CREIGHTON ABRAMS, U.S. ARMY. Quoted in Lewis Sorley, *A Better War: The Unexamined Victories and Final Tragedy of America's Last Years in Vietnam*

To a great part of the world the desert means fear, exhaustion or at best discomfort. For ten years, it replaced for me the relaxation, the happiness and the affection of home.

—JOHN BAGOT GLUBB, *The Story of the Arab Legion*

Over the course of my tour I visited fifteen of our eighteen Village Stability Platform sites in SOTF–SE culminating in thirty-five different trips. The teams were focused on defeating the Taliban, both militarily and politically, principally by mobilizing the communities they were embedded in and, through village empowerment, enabling development to take place. The complexity of their various operations was measured in different ways, but the pre-eminent measurement was how many Afghan Local Police forces they had recruited. The more Afghans who stood up against the Taliban the better. A number of other factors were also looked into by higher headquarters, such as the effect the team's insertion had on violence levels and other aspects, but the number of ALP was the key variable. Every week a slide would be prepared detailing how each and every VSP site had done at recruiting Afghan Local Police. Trends were calculated each week, months were compared against past months, and so on. Thus, while other effects the team might have achieved were nice, such as how empowered tribal shuras could now solve community problems, the incentivizing measurement was the number of ALP a team recruited. Some of the traditional measures such as how many enemy a team killed, how many IEDs they found, and how many missions they went on, etc. were still important and, frankly, probably the only things that truly mattered to a young officer. But higher headquarters were still mostly focused on ALP numbers. In fact, a common expression at the time was that SOF was so focused on Afghan Local Police numbers that it sometimes felt like we were working at a "puppy mill." A number of RAND Corporation social scientists were involved in developing all sorts of metrics to determine the effectiveness of the ALP program and there were even some operations research system analysts, uniformed military personnel who pore over the data to study how systems operate. Most of this analysis was looking into how long it took for a VSP site to get to 300 ALP for their district and what effects the team had on security in their area. However, the number 300 was a curious thing with an unusual history.

A great deal of effort was being made to recruit 30,000 Afghan Local Police all over the country of Afghanistan. The thinking was that every district in Afghanistan had about ten villages with 100 residents each and that if you managed to recruit thirty people from each village you would end up with 300 ALP for that district. Added together, you would then be able to cover 100 Afghan districts each with 300 ALP in a country with roughly 400 districts. This would have a noticeable impact on the war. The challenge with this rough breakdown of ALP was that each district was different, with some requiring fewer ALP and others needing more. Some accommodations had already been made to reflect these varying local conditions (e.g., Uruzgan's district of Shahid-e-Hasas had four VSP sites), but these were rare. If a team was unable to recruit 300 ALP or if a site went through a few rotations and the ALP numbers weren't strong, the general consensus was that either the team was no good and/or the Afghans weren't "ready" for the program. If a site didn't do well that meant all sorts of resources, and perhaps lives, had been wasted and some other part of Afghanistan had lost out on its opportunity to turn against the Taliban.

As I thought more about the problem, the analysis of VSPs seemed awfully limited in measuring success by just ALP numbers. The analysis didn't seem to understand why a VSP struggled to recruit more local police other than a fuzzy feeling that a team just didn't "get it." After visiting so many of our VSP sites in SOTF-SE, I noticed the successful ones seemed to share a few common characteristics: (1) favorable terrain, (2) long-term presence, (3) enablers (e.g., civil affairs, information operations), (4) capable Afghan partners, (5) strong leadership, (6) tribal homogeneity, (7) surrounding districts with a Coalition Forces presence, (8) a team that was embedded in the village, and (9) strong numbers of Afghan National Police and Afghan National Army soldiers. Other factors also seemed to play some role as well, such as (1) size of the district, (2) number of residents in the district, and (3) kilometers of district border shared with Pakistan. While my observations of SOTF-SE were interesting, absent an ability to compare all the ALP sites against each other, my insights were just that, interesting but not particularly helpful. Using my social scientist training, I ordered a statistical program I could use to compare the then 114 Village Stability Platform sites across Afghanistan to truly determine the characteristics of those that had successfully recruited Afghan Local Police.

While I waited for the statistical software to arrive and as I gathered data on the 114 VSP sites, I gave further thought to how useful the number 300 was as a measure of a team's success. Due to the huge variety of conditions in Afghanistan's districts, it seemed that the trick was in determining what was a district's "tipping point" wherein the desired security effects had been achieved and no more ALP were required. Some districts, for example, might have achieved sufficient security with 150 ALP and others might need fewer if the other factors listed above came into play. The challenge seemed to be finding other measures of effectiveness that really measured local sentiment and indicated how a community responded to the totality of a team's efforts. The number of ALP still mattered but measuring the community's other reactions might be more useful.

Going back to my earlier conversation with Mike, we needed to measure what *came from* a community and not what we did *to* it, because when an Afghan did something that proactively associated him with the Afghan government it was a significant moment. Every Afghan had a finely calibrated ability to measure the risks and rewards of a number of possible actions. If the totality of our efforts shifted their calculation in our favor, then we were defeating the Taliban. To this end, having a district chief or a district chief of police live in the district was an indicator of success, because they felt safe enough to do so. If local food prices started to go down because commerce was starting to flow again, that too was a positive indicator because it meant villages, farms, and roads had been secured and markets could now operate normally. If more bazaar shops opened, that was an indicator that Afghans felt that security had improved to the point that they could start a business and invest in inventory. If locals were sharing more information about the Taliban with Afghan forces, this was also an indication that they felt safe enough and that we were achieving some successes. The challenge was in designing a questionnaire that captured all these various dynamics and measured what was important to measure versus what was easy to measure. Additionally, knowing that units at VSPs were very busy, we had to determine what variables were easy for them to collect and the kinds of questions that seemed reasonable for them to answer.

As my thoughts came together on these important questions, I wanted to make sure that this work continued after I left Uruzgan and that the next SEAL team would be taken care of in terms of political advice and could also benefit from having someone on the staff with a different perspective. A friend of mine from the Navy reserves, Lt. (jg) Edward Crawford, had managed to secure a billet to Afghanistan, where he would be working on terrorist finance issues in Kabul. Unfortunately, his nine-month tour was abruptly cut to a month because of a decision to cut all headquarters staff in order to keep our troop numbers in the field as high as possible. Edward now faced the prospect of serving only one month in Afghanistan and then going home. It would most likely be his only opportunity to serve overseas due to family, business, and other personal commitments. Hearing about his predicament, I prevailed upon Mike to help him out, emphasizing how his background would help my work and also set the other team up for success. Edward had served more than two years in the Peace Corps in the Dominican Republic, where he had lived in a shack and helped build a local coffee cooperative. He was a banker at Goldman Sachs in Miami, spoke two languages, and had three master's degrees. If I could get him transferred to SOTF–SE, I would have two months to prepare him and he would then have six or seven months to work with the next team. It seemed like an ideal situation, and once I convinced Mike of its merits, we were able to bring Edward down to our base. Future events would indicate it had been a wise investment.

After his arrival on July 30, I gave Edward an advanced course on the tribes, politics, and personalities of Uruzgan, as well as on the principles of insurgency, of how to work with SEALs, and the U.S. military. He took it all in good stride and he went on several of our missions, quickly familiarizing himself with the terrain, people, and the job. We soon began to talk about the survey I was creating, and he gave me many great insights. Based upon his experiences in the Peace Corps and with the private sector, he suggested we come up with a basket of goods the Afghans typically purchased and figure out their prices. Each team could then collect the prices of the goods, such as cooking oil, tea, sugar, and fuel each month as a rough way to indicate how prices fluctuated. If security improved, prices went down. If the Taliban got stronger, the prices would go up. Another thought he had was determining how many projects went through the Community Development Councils (CDCs), which were local institutions expressly designed to focus on village development. If the CDCs had a lot of projects coming in, that indicated that not only were villagers working together, they were interacting with the Afghan state, which might have been a death sentence under Taliban rule. We also figured out that if the local government was hosting a large number of shuras, this was an indicator of villagers feeling safe enough to publicly associate with the Afghan government and to collectively work through their problems.

We continued to work on the survey and finally hammered out a "final" version (see appendix C), which we intended to distribute to our sites.

I finally received the statistical software I had been waiting for, and after gathering a large amount of data on Afghanistan's various districts, I got to work sorting out what really mattered for VSP success. I gathered data on 114 VSP sites and focused on the characteristics of the teams, the Afghan government presence, the human terrain of the area, and the geography of the district. Some of the variables included how many Afghans lived in the district, how many tribes there were, the number of square kilometers of the district, how many Afghan officials had been appointed to work there, what sorts of enablers the team had, how rugged the district was, how many other districts that bordered it had U.S. forces in them, how long had the team been there, how many kilometers of borderline the district shared with Pakistan, how many Afghan police and Afghan army soldiers were there, and so on. One of the real challenges was finding reliable data, and I scoured the Internet, reports from the United Nations, websites of nongovernmental organizations, and studies from the U.S. government. When they caught wind of my work, CJSOTF-A assigned me a RAND social scientist to help with the data, and she helped fill in a number of gaps. Using the hypotheses I had developed, I was looking at the factors a commander could use to shape his decision to place a VSP in a new district and how aggressively to pursue the relatively static three hundred ALP number. Using multiple regression analysis, which allows you to compare the relative importance of an independent variable on what you are measuring, I was able to roughly determine several variables that impacted how many Afghan Local Police there were at a Village Stability Platform. I say roughly because not all the data were as sound as I would have liked, but all in all they were "Afghan good enough."

The data I was able to collect included:

- *Village Stability Platform:* (1) phase number, (2) enablers (Civil Affairs, District Augmentation Team, Military Information Support Operations, Cultural Support Team), (3) size of VSP, and (4) presence of interagency in district

- *Geography:* (1) ruggedness of the area, (2) size of area, and (3) kilometers of district border shared with Pakistan
- *Population:* (1) size of population, (2) number of distinct tribes, (3) population density, and (4) literacy
- *Government of Afghanistan:* (1) number of Afghan National Police, (2) number of Afghan National Army, (3) number of ANA Special Operations Forces, and (4) number of Civil Servants in district
- *Other:* (1) kilometers of paved road and (2) cell phone coverage

I wanted to figure out why some Village Stability Platforms succeeded at recruiting Afghan Local Police while others struggled. Prior efforts had not been systematic, comprehensive, interactive, or empirical and often did not empower decision makers to make informed decisions about Village Stability Platform strategy, placement, and resourcing. My goal was to conduct a general statistical analysis using multiple regression of VSPs that would allow us to place VSPs more wisely and save time, resources, and lives while improving ALP recruitment. I collected data on 114 VSP sites in mid-2012, and while my analysis was useful, it had some limitations. Much of my data was at the district level and not the area of operations for the VSP, which meant there were some data quality challenges. What I found was that VSPs that bordered Pakistan had the hardest time recruiting local police; that the more rugged a district, the longer a VSP existed; the presence of U.S. Department of State and USAID advisors and greater numbers of Afghan National Police all made it easier to recruit ALP. I experimented with a number of other variables, but my resources were limited. I did show, however, that the analysis could be done and it could provide meaningful results about where to place VSPs. There was sufficient interest in my research that I was invited to brief the staff at the Special Operations Forces headquarters in Afghanistan and to give a summary of my findings at the Pentagon.

With more time and better data I could have figured out in greater detail why some VSPs were successful and others weren't, but by early 2013 the mission in Afghanistan had changed. We were no longer focused on perfecting the Village Stability Operations program and continuing its growth; we were now preoccupied with the drawdown. In February

2013, U.S. officials announced that the Afghan government had agreed to extend the VSO/ALP program another five years to 2020, which was a great indicator of the government's support, and to increase ALP numbers to 45,000 from 30,000. Within just a few months, however, all that changed. It was an odd thing to be told that we were "ending" the war in Afghanistan when the war continued on just fine; we were only really ending our participation and going home.

I left Uruzgan for the last time on October 6th on board a C-17, which took off from the soon-to-be-civilian-controlled airport at Multi-National Base Tarin Kowt. The great changes that had taken place in the province since our soldiers had first arrived there in 2001 were profound. The province had gone from a rural afterthought with no paved roads, no formal girls' schools, no mobile phone coverage, with little public infrastructure and less government activity to a significantly different and better place. Dozens of miles of paved roads had been built, similar numbers of schools had been constructed teaching both genders, cell phone coverage was ubiquitous, and the provincial government was much stronger and more established. The security situation had dramatically improved since the Taliban insurgency had come back in 2006 and while security concerns continued, the Afghans were quite able and willing to deal with the threats. Our efforts were increasingly in an "overwatch" position as the Afghans did what was necessary. We still played a useful role as facilitator, honest broker, and coordinator between the various government and security forces factions, which helped the Afghan system operate more smoothly. The revolution in how we thought about insurgency, stability, Afghan culture, and counterinsurgency was breathtaking. The adaptation to Afghan culture the Village Stability Operations approach embodied was profoundly significant and most likely never to be repeated on any other front of this continuing war on terror.

Within a month of my departure, the Village Stability Platform sites in Khod, Tagaw, and Sayagez were closed. Within two months the VSPs in Saraw and Nawbahar (Zabul) were transitioned to the Afghan National Army, and within six months the bases at Cobra, Anaconda, Tycz, and

Chora were transitioned to the Afghan Auxiliary Police, which were aligned with Matullah. The SOTF's attention was now focused on Zabul and Ghazni Provinces as Uruzgan was given back to the Afghans. Within a year of my departure the Tarin Kowt Provincial Reconstruction Team formally closed, ending its nine-year run. Six months after I left Uruzgan, Taliban leader Mullah Omar died in Pakistan on April 23, 2013, which ended his murderous sway. Uruzgan governor Akunzada was removed from office on March 10, 2014, only to become governor of another province. On April 4, 2014, the Afghans held their presidential election and Hamid Karzai formally ended his ten-year rule as the elected president of the country. This particular moment was especially significant since his rise to power had begun in Uruzgan Province. Provincial chief of police General Matullah Khan was assassinated by a suicide vest attack and small arms fire in Kabul on March 18, 2015, ending his violent life. It had always been a matter of time before someone killed him, and he had finally met his fate.

My colleague Edward Crawford worked out quite well with SEAL Team Four after it had formally taken over from SEAL Team Two on September 29, 2012. The new team seemed focused on fighting the Taliban, which they appeared to interpret as combat versus a holistic combination of hard and soft power, like growing the Afghan Local Police. Their enthusiasm for the Village Stability Operations approach was lackluster and they only grudgingly supported it. Their commanding officer, Job Price, definitely understood the initiative but he had to juggle a war that was quickly focusing on drawdown and a shifting mission set. Crawford became the tribal and political advisor I had hoped he would become and was soon put in charge of all the major engagements for the command. The SEAL team really embraced him and pretty soon he was organizing his own key leader engagements and trying to actively shape the human terrain of Uruzgan. Edward was able to finally arrange a meeting with Mohammed Nabi Khan Torkhi, one of the two prisoners Hamid Karzai had requested the Taliban release in 2001. He was a member of the Ghilzai tribe and had long been hounded by Jan Mohammed Khan and his nephew Matullah. As Edward later related to me, he and his small engagement cell had flown out to the compound where Nabi Khan lived to finally meet the great man and to discuss the province's situation. As soon as they arrived they noticed his home was surrounded by security guards, and the estate itself was not only well-apportioned but also quite grand.

After exchanging pleasantries with Nabi Khan, Edward asked him about his situation and what he thought about the province's state of affairs. Nabi Khan thanked Edward for visiting, lamenting that he had not met with many Americans since the war had begun, and shared his views. In response from a question from Edward asking him about the security guards around his compound, Nabi Khan said that President Karzai paid for the guards himself as well as gave a monthly stipend to him for his other costs. Nabi Khan then said that he and Matullah did not get along and that the police in the province never ventured to his tribal area because they knew they would get attacked. It was a most interesting conversation since President Karzai was essentially balancing the power of his own Populzai tribesman with the leader of another tribe that historically had not had good relations with the Populzai. It was a classic example of divide and rule and balancing power blocks against each other. Nabi Khan was interested in the Village Stability Operations initiative, but he knew that since his tribal rival was in charge of it in the province, it would most likely never happen. Another significant development upon my departure was Edward's work in attempting to resolve the ethnic conflict between the Pashtuns and Hazarans in Uruzgan's eastern district of Khas Uruzgan. Using the relationships we had developed with the Hazaran community, Edward was able to convince the provincial and national governments to establish a separate district for the Hazarans, bringing Uruzgan's final total to seven districts. Absent the political will and structural incentives to work together, it seemed reasonable to divide the district in this manner. In many respects it mirrored the division of the province into two separate entities in 2004. Another benefit of this reform was that it made it much more difficult for the Taliban to play the different ethnic communities off one another, and it de-escalated the political and other rivalries of the communities. It was a marvelous achievement and wise solution for a seemingly intractable problem.

EIGHTEEN

"Last Reflections on a War"

These tribesmen did, however, make one important contri-
bution to the war effort, though possibly without realizing
that they had done so. They taught Lawrence desert strategy
and tactics. He applied the lessons and by so doing earned
praise, as a natural military genius, from some members of
the higher command in Cairo. Perhaps it was a touch of
genius on his part to recognize that advice from his followers might be of more practical value than the dogma of staff
college graduates.

—ALEC KIRKBRIDE, *An Awakening: The Arab
Campaign 1917–1918*

You've got to have the statistics, there's no question about
that, absolutely no doubt about it. It's the way you get things
pointed, and the way you commit assets and that sort of
thing. But we've got to fight all the time to look past those,
and bear in mind what the real purpose is, and then face the
real results in a realistic way. And it's tough.

—GEN. CREIGHTON ABRAMS, U.S. Army
Chief of Staff

As I prepared to leave Afghanistan for what was likely the last time
(how often had I said that?), I reflected on the great challenges of
the U.S. experience in the country and in Uruzgan specifically.
We had begun our journey as a country in this part of the world after being
attacked by al-Qaeda. It was a war that was honorable and moral, and so

223

many people devoted their lives to its execution. Although I have served three tours in Afghanistan, one as a civilian and two as a military officer, my two years in country pale in comparison to many who have devoted upwards of eight years to the conflict. What compels a man to undertake such an endeavor, to sacrifice so much, to repeatedly leave one's family or even defer the creation of one to serve one's country? When people back home complain about how long the war has been and how tired they have become of it, I often think of how long it has been for a select few whose names are largely unknown. Why then did it take so long and how did Uruzgan change for the better? It is often said that if only President Bush had sent more troops to Afghanistan or if President Obama had not established a deadline for the pullout of the U.S. presence, among many, many other arguments, things would have gone better. These more partisan views are perhaps true in part but they miss the broader sets of issues central to an understanding of why things took so long and were so difficult. As someone who has worked on Afghanistan policy in Washington, D.C., completed three tours in country, written extensively about the conflict, and seen the war from the field, from Kabul and from the military and civilian sides, and then had two comparison tours to Iraq, I have some observations that may shed some light on our nation's difficulties in this country and more broadly when it comes to winning small wars.

Nation-States and Big Wars

The challenge for the United States when it comes to dealing with small wars almost begins at their inception, because when a region of the world that had heretofore not been on the radar screen of U.S. policy makers is suddenly thrust upon them, it is often due to a violent attack. This frequently forces the U.S. government to respond quickly, often in an uninformed and unwise way, and because little is known about the challenges there, the national security bureaucracies of the United States initially view the problem through the prisms of their own institutional lens. Thus, an attack from afar is viewed as requiring a military solution that is viewed from a conventional warfare perspective, with the political roots of the conflict often largely unknown. What this means in practice is that "victory" is often declared upon the conventional defeat of the enemy, when defeat should be measured along very different, which is to say irregular, warfare lines. Too often, Special Operations Forces are misused and are seen as either unconventional warfare forces or as a direct-action capability. Most SOF forces are used to train and mentor an indigenous government's Special Operations Forces units and do not train that same government's conventional forces, which the U.S. Army's Special Forces were expressly designed to do. Additionally, initial planning for military operations takes place in a civil-military structural environment that privileges the views of civilians, many of whom have had little experience in war and are most susceptible to public opinion, and in an environment of constrained military advice due to a truncated chain of command (see the civil-military divide section below). Thus, initial claims of "victory" are frequently understood as "conventional warfare" victory when true victory has not yet been realized. As the war continues and the insurgent movement reconstitutes itself, a crisis point is usually reached where the declarations of victory are incompatible with the reality of a newly resurgent enemy. When this point is reached and the U.S. government realizes it must try a different approach, new ideas, concepts, and ways of organizing usually come from units and leaders with substantial experience in the war but at a lower level. These leaders have had to deal with the war unfettered from limited notions of the conflict or politically understood ideas of "victory." The challenge for the campaign at this point is that public support for the conflict has waned at just the moment when wisdom has been reached about it by the U.S. military. At this stage, the U.S. military then has to hurriedly implement its now wiser plans against a political timetable that is not favorable to victory.

At its heart, the government of the United States is organized to fight conventional wars, conduct conventional diplomacy with nation-states, collect intelligence on national-level institutions, individuals, and trends, and implement development efforts through national governments. Additionally, our main focus has typically been on strategic concerns, and so "nonstrategic" parts of the world, such as Afghanistan before 9/11, frequently get little attention and are often completely misunderstood. The practical effect of this lack of wisdom about a country or region is that a conventional focus reverberates throughout the bureaucracy and an ambitious military officer, bureaucrat, civil servant, or diplomat recognizes that certain kinds of assignments, work products, and methods of thinking will be rewarded with a move up their respective career ladder. What this usually means in practice is that the metrics by which a successful government employee are evaluated are often tied to conventional world views. Thus, a military officer's success is determined by a whole slew of nation-state war measurements such as enemy killed, territory seized, bombs dropped, and improvised explosive devices found. An intelligence officer is typically focused on national-level personalities and issues and/or on finding the enemy and threats to the force. A diplomat is also focused on national-level interactions in countries where sovereignty is largely established. Their success is often measured by the number of reporting cables they draft, how well they achieve U.S. policy goals at the national level, and their ability to leverage influence with indigenous national governments. Development officials are often considered successful if they can produce a long list of projects they've completed. Many of these institutional priorities are also rooted in budgetary and congressional election cycles, which focus on meeting short-terms objectives and tend to accelerate the need to produce "results." Too often, success is measured by what the U.S. does to an indigenous population versus what comes from that population, which is the fundamental determinant of the success of the totality of our efforts. Additionally, frequent rotations of personnel throughout the bureaucracy diminish the development of expertise and wisdom, and separate bureaucratic approaches prevent a unified conceptualization of the problem as well as a synchronized strategy to contend with it. Careerism also incentivizes a low tolerance for risk, which is particularly acute when small wars challenge conventional thinking. Finally, the problems of small wars are often viewed from the perspective of the nation's capital instead of from the field, which further incentivizes an incomplete understanding of the totality of the problem.

The Civil-Military Divide

Several factors have contributed to the inability of military bureaucracies to deal with small wars in a comprehensive and thoughtful manner. In addition to the usual challenges of frequent rotations, a strategic focus, and certain career-incentivized behavior, the uniformed military has also seen its ability to formulate coherent plans fractured and its information and leadership feedback loops broken. The removal of the Joint Chiefs of Staff from the chain of command by the U.S. Defense Department Reorganization Act of 1958 eliminated a crucial link between the fielded force to uniformed leadership in Washington, D.C., and it also removed the Joint Chiefs of Staff as a corporate body able to review war plans. Through the struggle over roles and missions between the services on the Joint Chiefs and their separate perspectives on how to conduct war, the initial draft of a war plan can be greatly improved, a process that would have helped the initial Iraq and Afghanistan war strategies immensely. Another benefit of having the Joint Chiefs of Staff in the chain of command is that it not only protects the military from the political machinations of an administration, but it protects the administration as well by providing it with the political cover of professional military advice it would need to transition a war plan mid-conflict. Past efforts to increase civilian control of the U.S. military have had the unintended effects of weakening the ability of the U.S. military to present coherent and interservice agreed-upon war plans as well as undermining an effective chain of command. Additionally, because the U.S. military has become weakened and civilian control is much stronger, inexperienced civilians have replaced uniformed decision makers, leading to far less well-conceived defense policies and more frequent use of military power overseas. In many respects, the institutions that bear the responsibility and costs of implementing a war plan have seen their ability to shape decisions to intervene weakened, and this has led to (1) more overseas interventions, (2) poorly conceived military plans, (3) less accountability, and (4) much longer wars.

A second contributing factor to the difficulties military bureaucracies have in adapting to small wars was the shift to an all-volunteer force. While the benefit of trading unmotivated soldiers for motivated soldiers was quite positive, it also removed the systematic exposure of the U.S. military to unconventional thinkers who brought with them an array of civilian perspectives and skills when they served. This is not to say volunteers can't think creatively or that all draftees possess some greater wisdom about war, but it did diminish the ability of the bureaucracy to take advantage of the unique capabilities of a broader swath of the American people in addressing unconventional problems. Furthermore, by relying primarily on active-duty forces that are not draftees during small wars, the broader American public is not as frequently exposed to the dynamics of the conflict to which a more regular rotation of draftees would have exposed them. This diminished understanding brings with it less pressure from the American people on the U.S. military to adjust to the challenges of the small war. The robust careerism that came into existence in the U.S. military following World War II also created what used to be referred to derisively as "lifers," military personnel more focused on advancing their careers than on accomplishing missions. This tendency became particularly acute as the need to develop "balanced" officers who had rotated through a variety of career milestones supplanted a determined force to win the nation's small wars. For an ambitious officer keen to make a career in the U.S. military, it is more prudent to adopt conservative conventional notions of combat than to challenge accepted ways of thinking to adapt to the unique requirements of small wars.

Complex Narratives of Victory

The next challenge to fighting small wars is that narratives of victory are complex and the U.S. government struggles to describe victory, not just to the American people but to others who shape public opinion. Too frequently, "victory" is described in conventional terms, such as the number of Taliban killed and compounds destroyed. when actual "victory" has more to do with the ability of the indigenous government to handle its own internal security threats in the long term. Small wars don't often deliver to a commander a decisive battle he can win to achieve total victory, which means that a constant drumbeat of daily death begins to sap the will of the "invader" and confuse the narrative of victory at home. As time goes on, the initial goals of the campaign tend to broaden to include other objectives linked to the defeat of the enemy but hard to communicate to the home front as the attention of the American public recedes. Because reports of violence are often viewed through the prism of conventional war, it is hard for the home front to both support the narrative of victory when the facts of it are not that strong (again from a conventional military perspective) and are being undermined. Additionally, "victory" against the insurgent might take years beyond the term of the administration that had initially begun the conflict, further complicating the ability of that government to project a departure date from the war.

Small Wars and Electoral Politics

Unlike conventional wars, irregular wars often struggle to garner the sustained support of national elected officials. This is not to say that members of Congress and others do not support the goals of our soldiers involved in small wars, but that protracted conflicts that often pose moral and political quandaries make it difficult to sustain long-term political support. Additionally, because small wars almost, by definition, only involve a fraction of the armed forces, the broader American public as well as elected members rarely participate in them firsthand. This makes direct knowledge of the conflict difficult to gain and complicates sustained backing. While small wars often use the tools of big wars, such as fighter jets, tanks, and armored personnel carriers, they don't frequently use large-scale weapons platforms that have electoral constituencies linked to them. In a sense, small wars borrow the weapons platforms of big wars, but the dedicated tools of small wars often lack broad congressional political support. Small wars are largely infantry wars, which is a constituency that lacks political cachet with many members of Congress. Furthermore, because initial claims of "victory" in small wars must inevitably be revised as the protracted nature of the conflict emerges, political opposition groups within the United States find it difficult to resist opposing an administration that had claimed success at the outset. It is also customary for many American lawmakers to view small wars through the ideological lens of great power struggles, which tends to diminish the localized causes of the conflict as well as regional solutions to the conflagration.

Mis-Remembering War[1]

A central challenge to fighting small wars is that the broader American public's understanding of them tends to come from incomplete representations of them in movies and books. As a general rule, the book publishing business principally publishes conventional-warfare-oriented books in which combat and "action" get the most attention. Additionally, due to the large number of participants in conventional wars, these books tend to sell well. Most books about small wars from firsthand participants tend to cover the beginnings of wars, where conflict is often the most conventional, and then cover kinetic activities like shaping and clearing operations. These books are frequently published by junior officers on their first combat tours, and they often lack a long-term perspective on an area, indigenous narratives of the conflict, or any discussion of the "hold, build, and transition" phases of the "shape, clear, hold, build, and transition" construct that is often used in counterinsurgency campaigns. Additionally, because small wars are frequently controversial and have a variety of moral complexities to them, movies tend to (1) be antiwar political screeds (e.g., *Green Zone*), (2) highlight combat narratives (e.g., *The Hurt Locker*), (3) focus on the lives of soldiers (e.g., *Taking Chance*) and (4) depict high-profile combat missions (e.g., the hunt for Osama bin Laden). They tend to privilege visually appealing missions, focus on the actions of U.S. military personnel and U.S. leaders, and have a short time frame. They also tend to adopt popular cultural "understandings" of small wars, which inevitably are either incomplete or inaccurate (e.g., long-range patrols in the jungles of Vietnam). The cumulative effect of these representations of small wars contributes to a profound misunderstanding of the roots of these types of conflicts and the solutions that are required to prevail.

Small Wars Redux

The United States will continue to be bedeviled by the complexities of small wars unless it does a better job of organizing itself for the types of conflict that exist between peace and conventional war. While small wars will always have some conventional aspects to them, they are, at their heart, direct challenges to the status quo in how our country wages war, conducts diplomacy, uses intelligence, and promotes development. Hidden within each bureaucracy are individuals, offices, capabilities, and ways of thinking that understand how to wage and win small wars, but they are not incentivized or organized to do so and are often bureaucratically weak. The United States should treat unstable countries and regions as special cases that require a tailored strategy rather than the usual approaches our bureaucracies typically adopt.

Persistent Presence. The constant rotation of personnel throughout the bureaucracy inhibits the development of wisdom about a region, relationships with indigenous leaders, and long-term solutions to complex problems. In unstable areas where conflict occurs, personnel should be incentivized to remain in a region well beyond the normal rotations. They should be allowed to take their families and be rewarded for their service through other career incentives.

State Building. Small wars begin because the indigenous governments of nation-states are too weak, too strong, or are not considered legitimate, capable, and efficacious by the local population. One of the core tasks of personnel dedicated to winning and preventing small wars is the methodical building up of the indigenous government in a manner that promotes long-term stability.

Bottom-up Strategy. While logistical, security, and political factors can inhibit a determined focus on bottom-up stability, it must be factored into any effort to win small wars and promote long-term stability. A bottom-up focus combined with a top-down strategy will confront all aspects of the conflict in a more holistic manner.

Regional Expertise. While a long-term focus on a region will facilitate the development of expertise, the U.S. government should foster dedicated research on those areas of the world that tend to be academic blind spots for universities, think tanks, and U.S. intelligence services.

Synchronized and Blended Approach. Too often, strategies for fighting small wars take place using bureaucratic approaches that are not synchronized or integrated, and personnel often lack knowledge of and expertise in all the disciplines in which they must be conversant. Dedicated personnel who focus on the problems of small wars must be cross-trained in and gain access to the resources that are part of the military, intelligence, diplomatic, and development communities.

APPENDIX A

Key Lessons from SOTF-SE's Deployment

- The insurgent is principally focused on how HE influences and maneuvers the population away from the government and toward the insurgency, with the goal of frustrating the counterinsurgent to the point of giving up.
- If the population is unwilling or unable to join the government due to insurgent actions, this raises the costs for the counterinsurgents since they will have to continually clear areas of insurgents.
- When a local villager joins with the government, it is a conscious choice on his part to reject the insurgency both because he wants to and because he can.
- What we need to measure is not what is done to a local community but what comes from it.
- The Afghan Local Police (ALP) program aims to defeat the Taliban, as much a fighting force as a political movement, by organizing itself along similar lines: village-based, long-term, decentralized, blending civil-military approaches seamlessly while enlisting the population in its own defense.
- The ALP program provides a bottom-up approach to stability in Afghanistan by hiring local villagers and organizing them into defensively oriented forces to protect their own communities from Taliban intimidation.

- By serving as an outside catalyst and honest broker between village factions, Village Stability Operations (VSO) prevent the Taliban from leveraging community grievances to its advantage and channels them instead into a positive alternative supportive of GIRoA and its policies.
- Security effects across Afghanistan indicate that a comprehensive VSO approach focused on outcomes will allow for a reshaping of ALP *tashkeils* that will foster a strategy tailored to local conditions rather than a rigid, formulaic approach to determining the requirements of security.
- While the Taliban will impose their will on villagers if they have to, and they have often done so violently, they also have a positive agenda that seeks to entice supporters to their banner.
- Because the Afghan people are largely unable to hold corrupt or ineffective provincial officials accountable, outside of utilizing contacts in Kabul that most communities lack, they often turn to the Taliban to address injustices or to "right the imbalance" of accountability at the local level.
- What is required is a new and complementary approach to foreign internal defense called foreign internal governance that seeks to use an integrated influence initiative to prompt GIRoA to defeat the insurgency's political arm more effectively.
- As much as the Afghan Local Police (ALP) program removes the freedom of movement for insurgent fighters through constructing and manning a network of checkpoints, it also enlists the population in its own defense, robbing the insurgency of a ready-made recruiting pool of poor and unemployed military-age males.
- The creation of the Afghan Local Police program in the last few years provides a possible way forward for an Afghan war strategy that defeats the Taliban *and* is financially sustainable.
- An Afghan war strategy for the future should drastically expand the Afghan Local Police program as part of a light, lean, and long-term military presence in Afghanistan.

- The Afghan Local Police program not only provides local security but also serves as a tribal rehabilitation program to empower local leaders to resist the insurgency.

- Special Operations Forces partnered with local police forces provide the necessary support to GIRoA to reassure the community that the Taliban will not return.

- Physically shaping the terrain of a village can also have positive effects on the disposition of a community, reassuring its members that security is not a temporary condition but an enduring one.

- Taliban propaganda efforts can sometimes be as effective as Taliban offensive operations and need to be as relentlessly countered.

- Village Stability Operations must enlist nonkinetic enablers to defeat the Taliban's political program, of which propaganda is a part.

- Strike first, strike fast, and strike often to defeat the enemy propaganda machine.

- Personable and professional working relationships with GIRoA at all levels creates an environment of open dialogue and access.

- The Afghan population generally supports the government, but without an adequate way to protect itself, it will succumb to Taliban intimidation.

- A powerful village elder will significantly increase the success rate of Afghan Local Police recruitment.

- An embedded Afghan National Army Special Forces team that is Pashtun can significantly improve Afghan Local Police recruitment.

- Small projects establishing good will with Afghan communities and a respectful attitude to the population can dramatically improve a Village Stability Platform's success.

- Village Stability Platform sites are well placed to take advantage of local dynamics that split the insurgency.

- Splitting the insurgency by pitting local against foreign Taliban provides a means of joining with the community against the insurgency by stressing themes of justice and community cohesion.

- As the community enlists with the Afghan Local Police program, low-level and part-time Taliban face greater incentives to break off from the insurgency and rejoin their villages.
- Reintegration opportunities increase as the Village Stability Platform is seen as a steady ally against the insurgency and as an even-handed partner in tribal disputes.

APPENDIX B

Characteristics of Successful Village Stability Operations

- Develop the ability to have a sympathetic understanding of the concerns, fears, and hopes of villagers as well as seeing things from their perspective.
- Harness community leaders (e.g., tribes, religious, business, civil) to create a network to expand your white space and resist Taliban intimidation.
- Enlist the community in its own defense.
- Build stability through regular meetings between the Afghan National Army, the Afghan National Police, and Afghan Local Police leaders.
- Think unconventionally; the enemy does and so must you.
- Move beyond your comfort zone.
- Build institutions and processes and think about how things will function after you depart.
- Multitribal situations require robust tribal engagement so no group feels left out.
- Fight the insurgency's soft-power strategy and use your enablers.
- Live embedded mentoring (working and living alongside your indigenous allies) and actively partner with your Afghan colleagues.
- The Afghan Local Police are your first layer of defense; treat them as such.
- Do what is required, not what's comfortable.

- Sometimes the greatest action is inaction.
- It's about what the population does, not what we do.
- It's about moving Afghans from a culture of "learned helplessness" to one of "educated empowerment."
- Think indirect action, not direct action.
- We protect the Afghans, the Taliban control them.
- Let the Afghans be themselves, be humble about how much and how quickly we can change them.
- Treat others with respect and dignity; this is their country, not ours.
- Relentlessly pressure the enemy on all fronts.

APPENDIX C

Village Stability Survey

DISTRICT_____

VILLAGE_____

Governance

1) Which of these officials live in the district where your VSP is located? Rate them 1=bad .10=great.

◯ DGOV   ◯ Deputy DGOV   ◯ DCOP   ◯ NDS Representative   ◯ Chief Judge

| 1   5   10 | 1   5   10 | 1   5   10 | 1   5   10 | 1   5   10 |
| 0000000000 | 0000000000 | 0000000000 | 0000000000 | 0000000000 |

2) Number of Shuras held both inside and outside the district center   Inside _____Outside _____

3) Number of projects submitted by Community Development Councils- village level to District Development Assembly and through district government. _____

Comments_____

Security

1) Number of ALP (Current/Training/Taskil) _____/_____/_____

3) Approximate population in white space, amber space vs total population.
   White _____ Amber _____ Red_____ Total_____

4) How frequently do Afghans inform GIRoA/ANSF on Insurgents/IEDs? How many (CCIRs- Commander Critical Information Reports)?_____

5) Do you think GIROA can support your ALP after you leave?_____

6) How many ALP are paid by ASFF funds? _____

Comments_____

Development

1) CPI Consumer Price Inflation -Basket of goods (Cooking Oil, Tea, Sugar,) (Fuel)

Cooking Oil_____($1L)   Tea_____($1K)   Sugar_____($1K)   Fuel _____($1L)

2) Is there a public call center? What percentage of people have access and use cell phones.

   ◯ <25%   ◯ 25%   ◯ 50%   ◯ 75%   ◯ 100%

4) How many bazaar shops do you have? How many are regularly open?_____

COMMENTS:_____
_____
_____
_____
_____
_____
_____

NOTES

Chapter 2. The Village War

Epigraph: Sean Naylor, "Program Has Afghans as First Line of Defense," *Army Times*, July 20, 2010.

1. Rusty Bradley and Kevin Maurer, *Lions of Kandahar: The Story of a Fight Against All Odds* (New York: Bantam Press, 2011), 1–280.

2. Daniel R. Green, *The Valley's Edge: A Year with the Pashtuns in the Heartland of the Taliban* (Dulles, Va.: Potomac Books, 2011), 1–246.

3. An earlier version of this chapter was published by the University of Chicago Press in 2017 as "Organizing Like the Enemy: Special Operations Forces, Afghan Culture, and Village Stability Operation," in the book *Our Latest Longest War: The US Military in Afghanistan*, edited by Aaron B. O'Connell.

4. Daniel R. Green, "Defeating the Taliban's Political Program," *Armed Forces Journal*, November 2009, 18–21, 36–37.

5. Pashtunwali means "the way of the Pashtuns" and is a tribal honor code that has governed the Pashtun way of life for centuries. Center for Information Dominance: Center for Language, Regional Expertise and Culture, United States Department of the Navy.

6. Lutz Rzehak, "Doing Pashto: Pashtunwali as the Ideal of Honourable Behavior and Tribal Life among the Pashtuns," *Afghan Analysts Network*, March 2011, 1–22.

7. Brian Petit, "The Fight for the Village, Southern Afghanistan, 2010," *Military Review*, May–June 2011, 25–32.

8. William Doyle, *A Soldier's Dream: Captain Travis Patriquin and the Awakening of Iraq* (New York: NAL Caliber, 2011), 1–336.

9. Daniel R. Green, "The Fallujah Awakening: A Case Study in Counter-Insurgency," *Small Wars and Insurgencies* 21, no. 4 (2010): 591–609; Daniel R. Green, "Glubb's Guide to the Arab Tribes," Smallwarsjournal.com,

2007; Michael Eisenstadt, "Iraq: Tribal Engagement Lessons Learned," *Military Review*, September–October 2007, 16–31.

10. "Taliban 2009 Rules and Regulations Booklet," seized by Coalition Forces on July 15, 2009.

11. Linda Robinson, *One Hundred Victories: Special Ops and the Future of American Warfare* (New York: Public Affairs, 2013), 12.

12. Ibid.

13. Lisa Saum-Manning, "VSO/ALP: Comparing Past and Current Challenges to Afghan Local Defense," RAND Working Paper, December 2012, 3–4.

14. Ibid., 4.

15. Matthew Lefevre, "Local Defence in Afghanistan: A Review of Government-Backed Initiatives," *Afghanistan Analysts Network*, May 2010.

16. Lisa Saum-Manning, "VSO/ALP: Comparing Past and Current Challenges to Afghan Local Defense," RAND Working Paper, December 2012, 4.

17. Joseph A. L'Etoile, "Transforming the Conflict in Afghanistan," *PRISM* 2, no. 4: 3–16; Andrew Wilder, "Cops and Robbers? The Struggle to Reform the Afghan National Police," issue paper series, AREU, July 2007; "Afghanistan's New Militias Self Defence, a Victory of Hope over Experience?" *The Economist*, April 8, 2009.

18. Linda Robinson, *One Hundred Victories: Special Ops and the Future of American Warfare* (New York: Public Affairs, 2013), 14–16.

19. Ibid.

20. Ibid.

21. Ibid.

22. Ibid.

23. Ibid.

24. Ibid.

25. Ibid.

26. Dan Madden, "The Evolution of Precision Counterinsurgency: A History of Village Stability Operations & the Afghan Local Police," RAND Corporation, April 30, 2011.

27. Mathieu Lefevre, "Local Defence in Afghanistan: A Review of Government-Backed Initiatives," *Afghanistan Analysts Network*, May 2010, 1–23; Lisa Saum-Manning, "VSO/ALP: Comparing Past and Current Challenges to Afghan Local Defense," RAND Working Paper, December 2012, 6.

28. Lisa Saum-Manning, "VSO/ALP: Comparing Past and Current Challenges to Afghan Local Defense," RAND Working Paper, December 2012, 6.

29. Ibid., 6–7.

30. Ibid.

31. Linda Robinson, *One Hundred Victories: Special Ops and the Future of American Warfare* (New York: Public Affairs, 2013), 13.

32. Robert Hulsander and Jake Spivey, "Village Stability Operations and Afghan Local Police," *PRISM* 3, no. 3 (June 2012): 125–38.

33. Dan Madden, "The Evolution of Precision Counterinsurgency: A History of Village Stability Operations & the Afghan Local Police," RAND Corporation, April 30, 2011, 5.

34. Ibid.

35. Linda Robinson, *One Hundred Victories: Special Ops and the Future of American Warfare* (New York: Public Affairs, 2013), 25.

36. Daniel R. Green, "Defeating the Taliban's Shadow Government: Winning the Population through Synchronized Governance, Development and Security Efforts," *Australian Army Journal* VIII, no. 1 (2011): 9–21.

37. Linda Robinson, *One Hundred Victories: Special Ops and the Future of American Warfare* (New York: Public Affairs, 2013), 28.

38. Jonathan Goodhand and Aziz Hakimi, "Counterinsurgency, Local Militias, and Statebuilding in Afghanistan," United States Institute of Peace, 2014, 11.

39. Seth G. Jones and Arturo Munoz, "Afghanistan's Local War: Building Local Defense Forces," RAND Corporation, 2010.

40. Daniel R. Green, "It Takes a Village to Raze an Insurgency," www.foreignpolicy.com, May 29, 2013; Stephen N. Rust, "The Nuts and Bolts of Village Stability Operations," *Special Warfare*, July–September 2011, 28–31.

41. Joshua Thiel and Douglas A. Borer, "Withdraw and Win: Go for Victory in Afghanistan," smallwarsjournal.com, February 25, 2013.

42. Daniel R. Green, "It Takes a Village to Raze an Insurgency," www.foreignpolicy.com, May 29, 2013.

43. Robert M. Perito, "Afghanistan's Police: The Weak Link in Security Sector Reform," United States Institute of Peace, August 2009, 1–16.

Chapter 3. The Warlord's Shadow

1. Donald C. Bolduc, "Organizing Counterinsurgency Operations in Afghanistan," www.smallwarsjournal.com, 2009.

2. Ty Connett and Bob Cassidy, "VSO: More than Village Defense," *Special Warfare*, July–September 2011, 22–27.

Chapter 10. The Western Frontier

1. The term "vegetable emerald" is taken from *A Year on the Punjab Frontier in 1848–1849*, by Major Herbert B. Edwardes.
2. Daniel R. Green, "A Tale of Two Districts: Beating the Taliban at Their Own Game," *Military Review*, January–February 2014, 26–31.

Chapter 14. The Great Wall of Chora

1. Daniel R. Green, "Retaking a District Center: A Case Study in the Application of Village Stability Operations," *Military Review*, March–April 2015, 118–24.
2. Ibid.
3. Village Stability Platforms (VSP) are sites from which Special Operations Forces conduct Village Stability Operations.

Chapter 18. "Last Reflections on a War"

Note: The title of this chapter is taken from Dr. Bernard Fall's posthumously published book about the Vietnam War.

1. The idea of "mis-remembering war" is taken from Paul Fussell's seminal work on World War I titled *The Great War and Modern Memory*.

INDEX

Achikzai tribe, 30, 168, 174–75, 181, 183–85, 203

Afghan Hands, 31–32, 122, 155–56, 195

Afghan Highway Police, 26, 27, 52–53

Afghan Local Police (ALP): administrative responsibility for, 17; Bagh operations, 207–10; Barakzai members in, 203; checkpoint duties of to prevent insurgent intimidation, 19; Chora operations, 88, 177–78, 180, 184–89; command and control of forces, 19; creation of program, 17; Dai Kundi operations, 113–14; force strength of, 17; Gizab operations, 55, 162–64, 166–68; joining in Taliban insurgency by, 100; Khas Uruzgan operations, 139–40, 145–48; Khas Uruzgan sectarian violence role of, 150–51; LDI lessons and success of, 16; lessons learned and recommendations for, 233–36; protection of villages from Taliban intimidation by, 6, 34–35, 194, 209–10; recruitment and training of, ix, 18–19, 22–23, 53; recruitment in VSPs near Pakistan border, 219; recruitment of 300 for each district, 214–16; reintegrated

Taliban as, 194, 200; resignation threat from Kalach ALP, 178; role in holistic strategy to confront Taliban military and political strategy, 6, 22–23, 33–35, 194, 237–38; salary and support for, 19, 140; salary payment to, 55; Saraw operations, 117–20; Sayagez operations, 212; Shahid-e-Hasas operations, 42, 44–48, 56, 57–58, 93–100, 125–27, 184, 214; success of program, 168, 196; success of program, measurement of, 213–20

Afghan National Army (ANA): Chora operations of, 177–78, 182–83, 184–86; collusion of soldiers with Taliban, 62–63, 177–78, 179; Khas Uruzgan operations of, 144; local population, lack of connection to, 182–83; Shahid-e-Hasas operations, 118–19, 124–25; VSP/ALP program success and, 173

Afghan National Auxiliary Police, 14–15, 221

Afghan National Police (ANP): capabilities of, 57, 58; Chora operations of, 177–78, 182–83, 184–89; friction between ANAP and, 15; Gizab operations of, 165, 166–68; LDI assistance from, 16;

local population, lack of connection
to, 182–83; police and ALP
problems in Khas Uruzgan, 145–48;
Shahid-e-Hasas operations, 44, 123,
126; VSP/ALP program success
and, 173; as warlord forces, 14, 123
Afghanistan: abandonment fears of
people in, 2–3; adoption of culture
of by foreigners, 195; centralized
government and decentralization of
power, 70–71; civil servants in, 70,
145; conflict in and seeking revenge
or justice for past wrongs, 23;
cultural norms in, SOF adaptation
to, 18; education and training
of Afghans, 68, 70; elections in,
74–75, 82–83, 221; empowering
Afghans to help themselves, 56, 58,
170–73; ending the war, 220; future
of, 76, 153, 196; generational shift
in leadership and growing up under
US presence in, 30–31; government
responsibilities for justice, services,
and good governance, 169–70;
hospitality of Afghan people, 79,
151–53; instability in, sources of,
16–17, 18; leaders in, database of,
155; officials and leaders in, working
with to build good governance,
155–56; security conditions in
and resurgence of Taliban, 9–12;
security in, deterioration of, 14–15,
16–17; Soviet invasion of, 25;
strong and weak leaders in, goals
and ambitions of, x; understanding
of and knowledge about, x, 24–25,
114–15, 141, 225–26
Afghanistan War: Afghan responsibility
for, building capacity for, 34–35;
counterinsurgency approach to,
2–3; Enduring Freedom operation,
114–15; length of, 223–24; lessons
learned from, vii–xi; NATO forces
and mission, 114–15, 124; number

of units rotated through Uruzgan,
58; resources for, 2–3, 36; troop
levels for, 224; US personnel
for, rotation of, x, 62–63, 160;
US strategy and goals in, x, 2–3;
withdrawal of US forces, 2–3,
219–20, 224
Akunzada, Amir Mohammed, 85,
89–91, 101–5, 135, 136, 141–47,
168, 169, 201, 221
Anaconda Forward Operating Base,
43–44, 135, 137, 138–41, 152–53,
191, 194, 196, 220–21
Anaconda Village Stability Support
Area, 138
Arghandab District, 205, 206, 210,
211
assassinations, 88–89, 90
Australian forces, viii, 58, 114, 169,
178, 182

Bagh Village Stability Platform, 205–10
Barakzai tribe: alliance with Achikzai,
203; alliance with Taliban by, 201–
3; ALP program in tribal area of,
88; feud with Populzai, 28–30, 38,
87, 200–203; leadership of, 28–30,
87, 183, 200–203; power balance in
Chora, 86–88, 174–75, 181, 183–
85; power balance in Uruzgan, 30
bin Laden, Osama, 36–37, 107–8
Blehm, Eric, 24–25
Bradley, Scott: changes in Uruzgan,
opinion about, 36; character
and personality of, 31–32; Jan
assassination, meeting about, 84;
KAF trip with, 154, 160; political
and tribal-relations work of, 32,
34, 149–50, 156, 200; provincial
administration meeting attendance,
65, 68–69, 71

Chora District: Achikzai tribe
leadership of, 30; Barakzai

ABOUT THE AUTHOR

Daniel R. Green is a Defense Fellow at the Washington Institute for Near East Policy in Washington, D.C. He is a lieutenant commander in the U.S. Navy Reserve, has served in Iraq and Afghanistan, and received his PhD in political science from George Washington University in 2012.

The **Naval Institute Press** is the book-publishing arm of the U.S. Naval Institute, a private, nonprofit, membership society for sea service professionals and others who share an interest in naval and maritime affairs. Established in 1873 at the U.S. Naval Academy in Annapolis, Maryland, where its offices remain today, the Naval Institute has members worldwide.

Members of the Naval Institute support the education programs of the society and receive the influential monthly magazine *Proceedings* or the colorful bimonthly magazine *Naval History* and discounts on fine nautical prints and on ship and aircraft photos. They also have access to the transcripts of the Institute's Oral History Program and get discounted admission to any of the Institute-sponsored seminars offered around the country.

The Naval Institute's book-publishing program, begun in 1898 with basic guides to naval practices, has broadened its scope to include books of more general interest. Now the Naval Institute Press publishes about seventy titles each year, ranging from how-to books on boating and navigation to battle histories, biographies, ship and aircraft guides, and novels. Institute members receive significant discounts on the Press' more than eight hundred books in print.

Full-time students are eligible for special half-price membership rates. Life memberships are also available.

For a free catalog describing Naval Institute Press books currently available, and for further information about joining the U.S. Naval Institute, please write to:

Member Services
U.S. Naval Institute
291 Wood Road
Annapolis, MD 21402-5034
Telephone: (800) 233-8764
Fax: (410) 571-1703
Web address: www.usni.org